GENDER AND CHINESE HISTORY

GENDER & CHINESE HISTORY

TRANSFORMATIVE ENCOUNTERS

Edited by Beverly Bossler

UNIVERSITY OF WASHINGTON PRESS

Seattle and London

© 2015 by the University of Washington Press
Printed and bound in the United States of America
Design by Thomas Eykemans
Composed in Minion, typeface designed by Robert Slimbach
Display type set in Cinzel, designed by Natanael Gama
18 17 16 15   5 4 3 2 1

UNIVERSITY OF WASHINGTON PRESS
www.washington.edu/uwpress

LIBRARY OF CONGRESS CATALOGING-IN-PUBLICATION DATA
Gender and Chinese history : transformative encounters / edited by Beverly Bossler.
    ISBN 978-0-295-99470-3 (hardcover : alk. paper)
1. Women—China—Social conditions.   2. Women—China—History.
3. Sex role—China—History.   I. Bossler, Beverly Jo.
    HQ1767.G457 2015
    304.420951—dc23   2014047603

The paper used in this publication is acid-free and meets the minimum requirements of American National Standard for Information Sciences—Permanence of Paper for Printed Library Materials, ANSI Z39.48–1984. ∞

For Susan Mann

woman of talent, female exemplar

Contents

Acknowledgments

This volume began with papers presented at a research seminar titled "Moving Forward: Gender and Chinese History," held at University of California, Davis, on May 8, 2010. I am grateful to the University of California Humanities Research Institute, and to the Office of the Dean of Social Sciences at University of California, Davis, for their generous support of that seminar. The seminar brought together a number of scholars of gender in China to assess the state of the subfield. What had been accomplished? Where were the gaps in our knowledge? How had our studies of gender in China changed the way we thought about Chinese history and about gender itself? And most important, how could we take research on gender in China in new and exciting directions? Some of our answers to these questions can be found in this volume. Our seminar was also enhanced by the fascinating presentations of Cherie Barkey, Dorothy Ko, and Wang Zheng, and by the penetrating insights and incisive critiques by Joan Cadden and Catherine Kudlick (both European historians) and Margery Wolf (an anthropologist). I extend my heartfelt appreciation to all the participants, whose engaged and lively discussion contributed so much to the occasion and to this book.

It has been a special privilege to work with the authors whose research appears in these pages: collectively they represent some of the field's most accomplished scholars and some of its most promising young intellects. I thank all of them for their patience as I completed other projects before turning to this one. I am especially grateful to Ellen Widmer for offering assistance and encouraging me to persevere, and to Gail Hershatter for providing advice and humor on countless occasions. I thank the group as well for their exemplary adherence to deadlines and responsiveness to queries, which made the job of editor straightforward and rewarding.

Publication of this volume would not have been possible without the encouragement, support, and critical expertise of Lorri Hagman at the University of Washington Press, who shepherded us though the acceptance process and provided expert guidance on all matters editorial. Tim Zimmermann likewise patiently fielded endless questions about the illustrations, and Jacqueline Volin patiently oversaw the production process. I extend our thanks to each of them. The thoughtful comments of two anonymous readers were also instrumental in improving the individual papers and the coherence of the volume as a whole.

At so many different levels, by far the greatest debt of appreciation for the existence of this volume is owed to Susan Mann, whose contributions to the history of women and gender in China are legion. As a scholar and as a person, she sets a standard of integrity and generosity to which we all aspire. Directly or indirectly, she has served as a colleague, mentor, and friend to each of us. To her this volume is dedicated with respect, gratitude, and affection.

BJB

GENDER AND CHINESE HISTORY

INTRODUCTION

Beverly Bossler

W

HAT is gender in Chinese history? How has the study of gender changed the way we understand Chinese history? And conversely, how does the study of gender in China alter our understanding of what "gender" is? This volume considers these questions and explores how gendered analysis can be extended to new areas of historical inquiry.

On the surface, the meaning of "the history of gender in China" may seem self-evident, but closer inquiry reveals that all three of the central terms—especially in juxtaposition to one another—are subject to varying understandings. "History" in the European-American tradition once meant primarily the study of political events, the rise and fall of states and governing entities, or perhaps the study of ideas, as in the rise of the Renaissance and the Enlightenment. Likewise in the case of China, where a powerful and respected historical tradition was established more than two thousand years ago, "history" until well into the twentieth century focused especially on the rise and fall of dynasties or on developments in Confucian and Buddhist thought. In the mid-twentieth century, the introduction of the "new social history" expanded the purview of "history" to include the study of social groups, categories, and forces that had seemingly little connection to political or intellectual developments. In new historical studies of both the West and (somewhat later) China, one of the social groups that began to receive attention was women, and one of the social categories identified as important (along with class and ethnicity) was gender. As topics such as women and family became the focus of historical inquiry, the meaning of "history" itself began to change: it turned out that gender had a very close connection to political and intellectual developments and, indeed, was crucial to understanding them.

What we mean by "China" might seem more obvious and concrete, but in fact there were and are many "Chinas," especially if we consider change over time. Even today, "China" incorporates many ethnic populations, and whether certain geographical areas can be considered Chinese is a highly contested question. In the past, the situation was even more complicated: for centuries at a time, the area we now call China was divided into competing small states; during other periods, China was subsumed into larger empires ruled by foreign (non-Chinese) invaders, such as the Mongols and Manchus. In the face of this complexity, the term "China" becomes either so vague as to be almost meaningless or, more dangerously, a political assertion, an insistence on the presence and continuity of a unified nation-state well before one existed. We use "China," then, as shorthand, in full awareness that the term obscures important temporal and geographical variation.

What then of "gender"? Certainly "male" and "female" were and are among the fundamental (and fundamentally hierarchical) categories used by people in China (as elsewhere) to organize and comprehend human society, the animal world, and even physical phenomena. Yet some scholars have argued that "gender" operated differently in the Chinese past than in Europe or even in the Chinese present. According to this argument, in the European tradition "man" and "woman" were understood as among the most fundamental divisions in society, and maleness or femaleness was the quintessential basis of an individual's social identity. In China, by contrast, gender divisions of male and female were subsumed in other, more specific social categories based in family relations (such as "son," "daughter," "father," "mother," "husband," "wife").[1] Accordingly, in China before the twentieth century, individual identities were tied less to gender than to these familial roles. In part for this reason, the argument continues, gender identities in China were also less tied to bodily difference than in the European tradition: "What appear as 'gender' are yin/yang differentiated positions: not two anatomical 'sexes,' but a profusion of relational, bound, unequal dyads."[2]

Beverly Bossler

The historical implications of this analysis are admittedly still controversial, but the larger point here is that studying how gender hierarchies operated in China forces us to confront the limited and culturally bounded nature of concepts of gender—including those typically employed in Anglophone scholarship. In other words, we are challenged to rethink how we understand the idea of gender itself.

In short, by using the phrase "gender and Chinese history" in the title of this book, we do not mean to designate a concrete, bounded topic but rather to point to a field of scholarly inquiry, the terms of which are fluid, constantly shifting, and mutually constituting. To put it another way, we assume that the study of gender in Chinese history permits—or compels—us to develop new understandings of China, history, and gender.

Some sense of this process and its salutary effects can be illustrated first and foremost by reviewing how attention to gender has changed some of the standard narratives of Chinese history. A recent survey by Gail Hershatter has already extensively cataloged the contributions that the study of women and gender has made to the field of twentieth-century Chinese history; likewise, research on women, family, and gender has altered our understanding of the premodern, or imperial, period of Chinese history.[3]

One of the first and most fundamental contributions of the study of women and gender in imperial China was simply to demonstrate that the study of women in China's past was possible. As early as the 1970s, important anthropological work had begun to demonstrate the benefits of studies that focused on women, showing, for example, that Chinese kinship structures looked very different when they were viewed from the perspective of women.[4] But would-be historians of Chinese women, especially those interested in the imperial past, were frequently advised that relevant sources did not exist. Women in imperial China were largely illiterate and cloistered within their homes, so the received wisdom went, so they left no information about themselves. Moreover, since elite men's lives were devoted to the examination system and government service, from which women were barred, the sources they left us had nothing significant to say about women.

Intrepid researchers soon proved the speciousness of such warnings. Jennifer Holmgren showed that even the stylized official biographies of imperial women contained rich information for analysis of marriage customs, family power, and women's property rights; Priscilla Ching Chung demonstrated that the Song dynasty employed an extensive and highly specialized bureaucracy of female officials (many of whom were literate) to manage life within the imperial palace.[5] Patricia Ebrey mined funerary inscriptions, household handbooks, and anecdotal literature to elucidate the nature of family relations in the Song period.[6] Over the course of the 1980s, scholars also began to explore the significant roles women played in Buddhism and other Chinese religious traditions; documented the achievement and long-standing recognition of Chinese women painters; and showed how educated wives and daughters were central to literati family strategies in the late imperial period.[7] By the 1990s, no one could suggest that sources for the study of women in imperial China were lacking.

Over the course of the succeeding decades, research on women and gender began to reshape much of our basic understanding of Chinese history. Susan Mann's pathbreaking work on women and gender in the Qing dynasty demonstrated that, far from being irrelevant to the male world of politics and governance, women were a central focus of it. Emperors, bureaucrats, and philosophers alike saw the actions of women as critical to the overall peace and prosperity of the empire.[8] Individual families and the empire as a whole relied on the economic contributions of women, their production of cloth and other household goods.[9] Literati families relied as well on women's financial-management skills, for women managing the family budget allowed men to focus on their studies.[10] At court, women used their influence on emperors to shape and even control government policy.[11] And all families, at every level, relied on the reproductive capacities of women, making women's health an explicit topic of concern for both medical professionals and household heads.[12]

As this research progressed, it forced scholars to reassess the prevailing stereotype of Chinese women as hapless victims of an oppressively patriarchal society. Dorothy Ko brilliantly traced the evolution of this stereotype, showing how Chinese reformers (mostly male) in the late nineteenth and early twentieth centuries justified their calls for social change in part by erasing the long-standing tradition of female literacy. Ko argued to the contrary that literate women had helped fuel a dramatic expansion of printing in the late Ming dynasty, and she drew the attention of the Anglophone scholarly world to a surprisingly substantial body of surviving women's writings—mostly poetry but also essays, literary criticism, letters, and so forth—from the late imperial period.[13] Ko's scholarship in turn helped spawn a series of works devoted to the examination and publication of Chinese women's writings from the imperial period.[14] In combination with new recognition of women's power in the household, the exploration of women's own writings also permitted a new and more complex understanding of women's roles in the gender system in which they lived. While some writings by women indeed complained of the restrictions and limitations of the Chinese gender system, others detailed the satisfactions available to women in their varied roles as wives, mothers, and grandmothers. Even bound feet, generally regarded as the quintessential symbol of Chinese women's suffering and oppression, turned out to have had very different and frequently positive meanings in the eyes of women who possessed them. We learned that, as a sign of beauty, disciplined cultivation, and Chinese ethnicity, bound feet could be experienced as a source of pride rather than as a marker of subjugation. Scholars began to understand that the Chinese gender system (like those of America and elsewhere today) offered women rewards as well as injustices, and that its longevity rested in part on women's active participation and promotion.[15]

This awareness helped inspire and was reinforced by a reassessment of the figure of the faithful woman (*jie fu*) in Chinese culture. Like the bound foot, the faithful woman had figured prominently in reformist rhetoric of the early twentieth century as a symbol of Chinese society's unrelenting cruelty to women. In the late imperial period, two kinds of faithful women had been valorized. One category consisted of widows who refused to remarry after their husbands died. The other category included women who were martyrs to an ideal of bodily purity, who chose suicide rather than tolerate rape or other assaults—even strictly verbal ones—on their sexual integrity. In reformist rhetoric of the late nineteenth century and beyond, both types of women figured as pathetic victims of China's pathological gender system. Widowed women were portrayed as doomed to lead miserable and isolated lives: abused by relatives, stigmatized as unlucky, and shunned by society. Women who committed suicide for the sake of maintaining bodily purity came to be understood as benighted and misguided.

Over the past three decades, scholarship on what is often called the "fidelity cult" has challenged this picture on many fronts. This scholarship has shown the significant ways that demands for female fidelity evolved over time, while also tracing the cult's disparate institutional structures and social meanings. An early article by Mark Elvin traced the development of the cult in the late imperial period (roughly the fourteenth century to the nineteenth). Elvin explored the state's involvement, through the issuing of government awards, in the promotion of female fidelity (as well as other "Confucian" virtues), and the gradual easing over time of qualifications (age, years of chaste widowhood) necessary to receive awards.[16] Soon afterward, Susan Mann showed in even greater detail how and why the early Qing dynasty government attempted to redirect the fidelity cult away from martyrdom by providing incentives for maintaining faithful widows in the household.[17] A few years later, T'ien Ju-K'ang demonstrated that the cult of fidelity, and especially widow suicide, had expanded dramatically in the Ming dynasty, and argued that one important force behind the cult was the tendency of literati men to write about faithful women to assuage their own frustrations and anxieties about the competitive society in which they lived.[18] In the 1990s, Katharine Carlitz advanced our understanding of the cult with several articles that explored the popularity (and novelistic attraction) of texts extolling faithful female exemplars; she also detailed the usefulness, to local officials, of shrines to faithful widows and described how the cult was furthered by romantic interpretations that depicted suicide as an expression of female passion.[19] Mining legal archives, Matthew Sommer elucidated the ways that state and family concerns about loyalty and widows' property intersected in the cult during the Qing dynasty, while Janet Theiss demonstrated the complicated and often unexpected ways that the cult was used and abused to advance the varied interests of women, their families, and the state in that period.[20] The emotional, social, and political significance of the cult was further explored in Weijing Lu's 2008 study of one of its more extreme manifestations: "faithful maidens." These were women who pledged fidelity (through suicide or, more commonly, lifelong celibacy) to their deceased fiancés. All these scholars showed that the cult of fidelity in imperial China was a complex and contested phenomenon, shaped and used by women as well as men to further personal goals and create meaning in their lives.[21]

The topic of female fidelity in China is also closely related to women's property rights and their evolution over the course of the imperial period. Early articles by Jennifer Holmgren elucidated the gradual intensification of demands for widow fidelity and increasing restrictions on women's property rights over the course of the Song, Yuan, and Ming dynasties, showing that both developments tied women more closely to their marital families.[22] Holmgren's suggestions were further elaborated by Bettine Birge, who argued that women's property rights had expanded in the Song period, only to be reduced under the Mongol Yuan dynasty. Like Holmgren, Birge saw new Yuan laws restricting women's ability to take a deceased husband's property into a second marriage as partly a result of the imposition of Mongol ideas about property and widows on the Han Chinese populace, but she argued

Beverly Bossler

that success of such laws was also related to the efforts of neo-Confucian philosophers to impose a stricter standard of female morality on the populace.[23] Kathryn Bernhardt, conversely, asserted that laws established by the first Ming emperor created the most dramatic change in women's property rights, and suggested that, paradoxically, the fidelity cult helped to ameliorate the most stringent aspects of the new laws: worried that families could abuse the law to gain widows' property, judges tended to award faithful widows the right to appoint their own heirs and control property in trust for them.[24]

As T'ien, Carlitz, and others had shown, the fidelity cult was inextricably associated with men's writing about women, and critical evaluation of traditions of women's biography has also proven to be a fruitful window into historical change in the Chinese gender system. Lisa Raphals's 1998 monograph demonstrated that ideas about yin and yang became more hierarchical over the course of the classical period, and she showed how late imperial redactions of the Han dynasty work *Biographies of Exemplary Women* (Lie nü zhuan) were reorganized to downplay the importance of women's intellectual virtue.[25] My own recent work locates the rise of the fidelity cult in new trends in men's writing about women in the late Song and Yuan, trends that were shaped by disparate factors, including the precarious political situation of the Southern Song dynasty, a new craze for entertainment, and growing pressures of social competition. I suggest that many aspects of the fidelity cult were cyclical, with female loyalty taking on intensified salience at times of political or social instability.[26] The importance of biography as a source for the history of women and gender was also highlighted in a wide-ranging volume edited by Joan Judge and Hu Ying in 2011. The essays in that volume demonstrate the diversity and flexibility of the biographical tradition devoted to Chinese women while also highlighting its persistent themes.[27] In their own work, both Judge and Hu have demonstrated how the genre of biographies of exemplary women was expanded and reconfigured at the end of the imperial era, as male authors proposed new kinds of heroines as more appropriate models for women in a modern nation-state.[28]

As this discussion suggests, much research on the history of gender in imperial China has focused on women. By the 1990s, however, a number of historians had begun to consider how the Chinese gender system affected men. Several studies focused on male homosexual relations. One early monograph demonstrated that male homosexual bonds were widely accepted in imperial China, and argued that the repressive attitudes of the current government were a relatively recent phenomenon.[29] Later studies examined legal statutes governing homosexuality, suggesting that the government's concern was not male-male relationships per se but the maintenance of proper social hierarchies and the protection of young males from sexual exploitation.[30] Another scholar argued that Qing dynasty sources reveal multiple and varying understandings of male homosexuality, including some recognition of the possibility that male homosexual desire might be an innate characteristic of some men.[31] In 2000, a forum sponsored by the American Historical Association moved beyond the issue of sexuality to consider other types of male-male bonds in Chinese history, including friendship, sibling relations, and sworn brotherhoods.[32] The topic of male friendship was further explored in a special issue of the journal *Nan Nü*, which featured a group of articles devoted to the examination of male friendship in the Ming dynasty.[33] The issue of Chinese masculinity in the imperial period has also begun to attract the attention of scholars, though to date the topic of masculinity has been probed largely through literary texts. Although their specific findings differ, scholars have agreed that masculinity in imperial China was closely tied to social and perhaps political status, with different modes of masculinity operating in different social strata. They are also generally agreed that masculinity tended to be defined more in the context of hierarchical relations with other men than in reference to women, though at all social levels imperviousness to female sexuality was considered an admirable masculine trait.[34] The important contributions of these authors notwithstanding, much remains to be learned of how masculinity operated in various historical contexts, and how it changed over time. (Chapter 3, by Yulian Wu, addresses these issues.)

As this brief (and far from exhaustive) review of recent scholarship suggests, attention to gender has changed our understanding of imperial Chinese history in several important ways. It has revealed the imperial state's commitment to a gender order that it saw as both ordained by heaven and critical to the state's own survival, while also showing the flexible ways that the gender order could be deployed. It has demonstrated the inextricable links between the gender order, the Chinese family system, and wider social and political phenomena. Most importantly, it has shown the ways that women and men worked within and around the demands of a hierarchical gender system to pursue their own interests and agendas. Scholarship on the gender system of imperial history has also been important in increasing our understanding of the political and social history of twentieth-century

Beverly Bossler

China. As already noted, early-twentieth-century reformers helped justify their own policies and power by castigating the "backward" gender system of the imperial period. But as scholarship on the modern period has shown, many aspects of that system have continued to be salient in the twentieth century and beyond. To cite but one example: female fidelity and sexual purity were, ironically, key characteristics of the heroines that the Chinese Communist Party created to model their new socialist morality.[35]

The present volume builds on the rich legacy of the existing scholarship by taking the study of gender in China in a variety of new directions. Each of the chapters can be considered a case study of sorts, though the focus of the different chapters ranges widely, from images to individuals, from marriage to masculinity. Each chapter breaks new ground, thematically, methodologically, or both, while collectively the chapters trace a number of common themes across widely separated eras. Ann Waltner's chapter, which opens the volume, conspicuously probes the limits of historical sources and what we can know. The historiographical concerns she raises are taken up in later chapters by Yulian Wu, Ellen Widmer, Joan Judge, Emily Honig, and Gail Hershatter, all of whom turn to unconventional sources, or use conventional sources in unconventional ways, to consider how understandings of the past are created, transmitted, and put to use. The relationship between gender and government policies, central to Guotong Li's study in chapter 2, is also explored in the chapters by Judge, Honig, and Hershatter. These chapters reinforce the point that, in the twentieth century as in the eighteenth, those who ruled China saw proper gender relations as key to successful governance and a smoothly functioning society. At the same time, they demonstrate how radically ideals of female virtue could change over time.

Several of the chapters focus on women's talent, education, and writing. Guotong Li highlights the tensions between literate and nonliterate modes of women's education, and Judge describes a similar tension between the literary education of "women of talent" and twentieth-century efforts to extend education to more women. Weijing Lu, Widmer, Judge, and Yan Wang reveal the multiplicity of ways that women used writing—in poetry, political tracts, and family letters—to assert their identities and shape their interactions with the wider world. The chapters by Widmer, Judge, and Wang also show how differently women could experience and respond to the same historical circumstances.

All the chapters reveal how a focus on specific cases and intimate interactions can inform our understanding of larger social change. All expose the intricate connections between historical shifts in gender relations and other forms of social and historical change (economic growth, political change, new media). And all repeatedly remind us that the Chinese gender system was never static.

The chapters in this volume cluster in three key time periods: the eighteenth century, when imperial China was at the height of its power and prosperity (chapters 1 through 4); the late nineteenth and early twentieth centuries, when China was undergoing the wrenching transition between long-standing imperial traditions and new "modern," social formations (chapters 5 through 7); and the latter half of the twentieth century, which included both the radical social experiments of the Maoist period and the equally dramatic changes brought about by "socialist capitalism" under the Reform period (chapters 8 and 9). In the first two sets of chapters, the reader will encounter the term *late imperial*, which is commonly used in historical studies of China to designate the Ming and Qing dynasties.[36] A few authors, however, underscore China's connections with other parts of the globe by employing the term *early modern* to designate this period. This varied terminology already begins to show us how differing perspectives shape historical meanings.

In the opening chapter of the volume, Ann Waltner literally alters our perspective on China's eighteenth century by focusing on an illustration of a Chinese bridal procession that appeared in a French account of Chinese customs from that century. Waltner's juxtaposition of this European image with what we know about Chinese weddings from Chinese textual sources exposes transcultural similarities in gender regimes (for example, in both China and Europe, a proper wedding involved a procession and display of property), as well as important disjunctures (as the illustration blends what seem to be accurately rendered details of Chinese wedding rituals with European fantasies of exotic Chinese practices). Waltner's analysis also shows that gender relations are a touchstone for cultural interaction, and that the lens of gender transforms how we think about global and comparative history.

In chapter 2, Guotong Li continues the exploration of the intersection of gender and culture and adds the complicating factor of politics. Li takes as her subject the life and work of the moralist and local official Lan Dingyuan (1680–1733). A southern Fujianese whose own cultural heritage was mixed (his ancestors included both Han and minority She families), Lan was known for his commitment to Confucian moral transformation but also for his sympathetic and practical understanding of the realities of life on the empire's margins. Li elucidates the concrete measures by which Lan sought to promulgate Confucian "family values" at the local level, showing how his methods were influenced by his understanding of ethnic difference. She also notes the surprising resonances between Lan's views and those of modernizing reformers more than a century later: although those reformers explicitly rejected Lan's Confucian morality, they shared his assumption that women's behavior was crucial to the success of the state, as well as his conviction that women required the guidance and direction of men. Finally, Li's chapter highlights the close association in Lan's mind between female virtue and female labor: as we see in chapters 7, 8, and 9, the idea that women's virtue was tied to women's labor persisted well into the modern period.

Yulian Wu, in chapter 3, turns away from men's actions in relation to women to consider gender relations among men and, especially, the intersections of class and masculinity. From early imperial times, merchants had been disdained in Chinese society and were considered socially and morally inferior to scholars. Wu shows how gender played into this social equation, examining the ways that a wealthy eighteenth-century merchant, Wang Qishu (1728–98), actively positioned himself as masculine among his friends and acquaintances. In part by paying attention to material objects, Wu shows that, in the context of the eighteenth-century economic expansion, merchants like Wang were able to upend age-old moral codes and assert that the ability to accumulate wealth was itself a sign of masculine achievement.

In chapter 4, Weijing Lu returns to the topic of marriage by investigating the companionate relationship of one of the most famous scholarly couples of the Qing dynasty, Wang Zhaoyuan (1763–1851) and her husband, Hao Yixing (1757–1825). Lu traces the couple's emotional interactions as recorded in the poetry volume they jointly compiled. Lu shows that their writings not only illuminate their own romantic and intellectual intimacy but also reflect an eighteenth-century reconfiguration of the "cult of emotion [*qing*]," in which romance became less associated with tragic love affairs and understood more as a feature of ideal marital relations.

In the second part of the volume, chapters 5, 6, and 7 all focus on critical social transitions of the late nineteenth and early twentieth centuries, and all three are concerned with the question of how the "genteel ladies" (*guixiu*) or educated "talented women" (*cainü*) of the imperial period became the modern "New Women" of the early twentieth century.[37] In chapter 5, Ellen

Widmer argues that the changes began much earlier than we generally assume: she demonstrates that, already in the 1870s, educated upper-class women had begun to publish their poetry in the new media of newspapers and literary supplements. Widmer shows how the publication of women's writing in the new media represented both a continuity with traditional practices and an important departure from them. She concludes that the new media provided a venue for a new kind of public interaction among women, creating, she suggests, "the idea of a national forum for women."

In chapter 6, Joan Judge considers the ways that women's writing practices—as well as ideas about women's talent and the nature of women's education—changed in the late nineteenth and early twentieth centuries. Judge investigates the activities and experiences of three women from a single family, whose adult lives spanned a period from the 1870s to the 1960s. Extending the trajectory of women's learning explored by Widmer in chapter 5, Judge shows how, over the course of the early twentieth century, the poetry of classically educated "women of talent" evolved into expository (and often politically directed) prose. By analyzing photographs of her subjects, Judge also delineates an equally dramatic shift in the ways that the ideal female was visualized during this period. Judge's findings ultimately lead her to take issue with the widely held view that the 1911 Revolution was a "nonevent." Instead, she concludes, the Revolution was a significant turning point in terms of modes of civic engagement and social interaction, as manifested in the unprecedented opportunities in politics and public life available to women.

In the final chapter of this section, Yan Wang enriches our understanding of the late-nineteenth- and early-twentieth-century transition by detailing the transformation of a very different sort of "genteel lady." Wang's subject, Lady Zhuang (1866–1927), was modestly educated—literate, but not a literary talent like the women studied by Lu, Widmer, and Judge. Rather, Lady Zhuang's life is interesting (and documented) because she became the younger, successor wife of the powerful and wealthy modernizing official Sheng Xuanhuai. Making use of the hitherto untapped archive of Sheng Xuanhuai's family papers, Wang follows Zhuang's life as a "leisured lady of means" in the rapidly modernizing city of Shanghai. She demonstrates Zhuang's substantial role in managing not only the family's household budget but also many of her husband's business enterprises, handling large sums of money, investing in commodity markets, and relying on both her social networks and new technologies like the telegraph to obtain critical market information. Like the chapters by Widmer and Judge, Wang's study reveals

Beverly Bossler

how quickly and creatively erstwhile "genteel ladies" responded to the new opportunities of the twentieth century, as well as the variety of forms their responses could take.

The final two chapters of the volume bring us into recent times, with both Emily Honig and Gail Hershatter considering how events of the Maoist period have been understood and reinterpreted during the era of post-Mao reforms. Honig's innovative chapter explores the "life history" not of a person but of an iconic Maoist slogan: "The times have changed; men and women are the same. Anything male comrades can do, female comrades can do too." Honig's deft analysis reveals the surprising origins of the slogan and the very gradual process by which it became prevalent. Although the slogan is widely regarded as emblematic of Cultural Revolution attitudes, Honig also exposes the persistence throughout the period of a significant counterdiscourse to the slogan's emphasis on gender sameness. Her findings not only complicate standard interpretations of the Cultural Revolution but also suggest how profoundly our knowledge of the past is shaped by both inadvertent and deliberate misremembering.

The topic of memory and its relationship to history is taken up even more explicitly in Gail Hershatter's chapter. Hershatter probes the disjunction between rural women's attempts to convey their remembered lives to their daughters, and the daughters' understanding of their mothers' lives. In intensive interviews with an elderly mother and her middle-aged daughter, Hershatter uncovers the disparate ways they understand the past and each other. In the process, she also reveals the complex and convoluted manner in which the understanding of female virtue has changed over the last half century or so of Communist rule. Her conclusion reminds us that "bad transmissions" are useful to the historian, for in the "static" associated with such transmissions, we find clues to the ways that stories of the past are "heard and reencoded in contemporary terms, inflected by contemporary dilemmas." Together, these final two chapters expose both profound changes and deep continuities in China's gender regime and leave us with a heightened sense of the ways that visions of the past are shaped by contemporary concerns.

In bringing new approaches to the study of gender in Chinese history, the diverse chapters in this volume illuminate the multifarious ways that gender relations have influenced, and been influenced by, historical change in both the distant and more recent Chinese pasts. Individually and collectively, they encourage us to think differently about China, history, and gender itself.

NOTES

1 Barlow, "Theorizing Woman," 253–89. See also Rowe, "Women and the Family," 2–7.
2 Barlow, "Theorizing Woman," 259.
3 Hershatter, *Women in China's Long Twentieth Century*.
4 Wolf, *Women and the Family*; see also the various essays collected in Young, *Women in China* and in Wolf and Witke, *Women in Chinese Society*.
5 Holmgren, "Family, Marriage and Political Power"; "Observations on Marriage and Inheritance; "Imperial Marriage; Chung, *Palace Women*.
6 Ebrey, *Family and Property*; "The Early Stages"; "Concubines in Sung China."
7 Levering, "The Dragon Girl"; Cahill, "Performers and Female Taoist Adepts" (see also her *Transcendence and Divine Passion*), as well as Despeux and Kohn, *Women in Daoism*; Weidner, *Flowering in the Shadows*; Mann, "Widows."
8 Mann, *Precious Records*; Birge, "Chu Hsi and Women's Education"; Holmgren, "Imperial Marriage."
9 Mann, *Precious Records*, 143–77; Ebrey, *The Inner Quarters*, 131–51; Bray, *Technology and Gender*.
10 Birge, "Chu Hsi and Women's Education"; Mann, "Widows"; Ebrey, *The Inner Quarters*, 114–30; McDermott, "The Chinese Domestic Bursar."
11 Elliot, "Manchu Widows"; Chaffee, "The Rise and Regency of Empress Liu"; Bossler, "Gender and Entertainment at the Song Court"; Lee, *Empresses, Art, and Agency*; Ebrey, "Empress Xiang."
12 Furth, *A Flourishing*; Bray, *Technology and Gender*; Lee, "Gender and Medicine"; Wu, *Reproducing Women*.
13 Ko, *Teachers of the Inner Chambers*.
14 Chang, Saussy, and Kwong, *Women Writers*; Widmer and Chang, *Writing Women*; Idema and Grant, *The Red Brush*; Fong, *Herself an Author*.
15 Mann, *Precious Records*; *The Talented Women*; Ko, *Teachers of the Inner Chambers*; *Cinderella's Sisters*.
16 Elvin, "Female Virtue and the State."
17 Mann, *Precious Records*, 23–26.
18 T'ien, *Male Anxiety*.
19 Carlitz, "Desire, Danger, and the Body"; "The Daughter, the Singing-Girl"; "Shrines"; "The Social Uses."
20 Sommer, "The Uses of Chastity"; Theiss, *Disgraceful Matters*.
21 Lu, *True to Her Word*.
22 Holmgren, "The Economic Foundations of Virtue"; "Observations on Marriage and Inheritance."
23 Birge, *Women, Property, and Confucian Reaction*.
24 Bernhardt, "A Ming-Qing Transition?" See also her *Women and Property in China*.
25 Raphals, *Sharing the Light*.
26 Bossler, *Courtesans, Concubines, and the Cult of Female Fidelity*.
27 Judge and Hu, *Beyond Exemplar Tales*.
28 Judge, *The Precious Raft*; Hu, *Tales of Translation*.

29   Hinsch, *Passions of the Cut Sleeve.*

30   Sommer, "The Penetrated Male"; *Sex, Law, and Society*; "Dangerous Males."

31   Szonyi, "The Cult of Hu Tianbao."

32   Mann, "The Male Bond"; Kutcher, "The Fifth Relationship"; Davis, "Fraternity and Fratricide."

33   See the articles by Huang, Gerritsen, Lam, and Besio in *Nan Nü* 9 (2007).

34   Louie, *Theorising Chinese Masculinity*; Song, *The Fragile Scholar*; Huang, *Negotiating Masculinities.*

35   Hershatter, *The Gender of Memory*; Wang, "Call me 'Qingnian.' "

36   The term highlights the continuities in China's social, economic, and (to a certain extent) political systems through the Ming and Qing.

37   The question of what happened to the eighteenth-century "genteel woman" in the nineteenth century was raised, and elegantly answered, by Susan Mann in *The Talented Women*—see especially her summation of this issue in the epilogue, 195–200.

PART ONE

EARLY MODERN
EVOLUTIONS

CHAPTER ONE

LES NOCES CHINOISES

An Eighteenth-Century French Representation
of a Chinese Wedding Procession

Ann Waltner

Among the first details eighteenth-century Western travelers to distant lands noticed were the local marriage customs. Jesuit missionaries were no exception. Some aspects of Chinese family life made sense to missionaries; others were either incomprehensible or judged to be problematic. Images such as the one of a bridal procession included in a 1735 account of China by the Jesuit missionary Jean Baptiste du Halde (1679–1743; see figure 1.1) can be brought into conversation with multiple sources to illuminate the grounds of contact between China and Europe, placing marriage, family formation, and gender at the center. This excursion may not tell us anything new about Chinese marriage, but it tells us about how Chinese weddings served as a kind of touchstone in European thinking about China and gender, and it tells us in fairly precise ways how the imagination of the observer conditioned what was seen.

One of the most contentious issues in terms of how missionaries regarded Chinese families was what Westerners came to call ancestor worship, especially the honor shown to ancestral tablets. The Jesuits, by and large, had no great difficulty accepting ancestor worship, viewing it as an honor paid to one's forebears. But other religious orders, such as Dominicans and Franciscans, had differing opinions, and Pope Clement XI condemned Chinese rites (including but not limited to ancestral rites) in 1704. Mutual condemnations between the pope and the emperor of China followed. Du Halde's *Description of China* (Description de la Chine) was written in the decades after the Rites Controversy erupted; he acknowledged that the ceremonies attendant upon ancestors might have been excessive, but he stressed that beliefs that the souls of the deceased hovered over ancestral tablets, or that the spirits of the deceased consumed the food given them, were idolatry introduced to China by Buddhists.[1] Thus du Halde posited an original Chinese thought system that was pure and free of idolatry, one compatible with Christianity. Many Jesuits took this point of view, but in the end it proved unconvincing to the Vatican.

Another problematic area of Chinese family life from the standpoint of Western missionaries was concubinage, which, while not widespread among the population in general, was common among the elite, so much so that it affected how members of the elite imagined marriage. Concubinage was a serious issue: a number of would-be converts were denied baptism because they refused to send their concubines away. Other converts (Xu Guangqi and Yang Tingyun) did send their concubines away so that they might be baptized.[2] Chinese law and practice distinguished clearly between marriage with a principal wife and marriage to a concubine: most laws that dealt with concubinage were interested in keeping the distinctions clear and in particular stressed that a woman married as a concubine could not be made a wife, even if the principal wife were to die.[3]

But in other ways Chinese marriage (that is to say, marriage between a man and his principal wife) and Chinese weddings seemed to translate fairly well into the Jesuit universe. The image of a bridal procession under study here is a product of this Jesuit encounter with Chinese marriage practices, as well as of the history of such encounters. The illustration shows us ways in which Europeans saw Chinese marriage with a mixture of curiosity, comprehension, and misapprehension.

Du Halde's text is a fount of information on European views of China. Compiled from reports sent back to Paris by twenty-seven Jesuit missionaries, it followed on the heels of texts published in Amsterdam by Johan Nieuhoff (1618–92) and Olfert Dapper (c. 1635–89). The Nieuhoff text was

Ann Waltner

commissioned by the East India Company and was positioned very differ-ently from du Halde's in terms of function and ideology. Yet Nieuhoff used missionary texts as a source for his own, and du Halde made liberal use of both Nieuhoff and Dapper.[4]

Du Halde himself never went to China. His experience with China prior to compiling the *Description of China* was as editor of *Edifying and Curious Letters, Written at the Foreign Missions by some Missionaries of the Society of Jesus* (Lettres édifiantes et curieuses, écrites des Missions étrangères, par quelques missionnaires de la Compagnie de Jésus), an enterprise he took up in 1711. The editorial work gave him access to missionary accounts and pro-vided a foundation for his work. *Description of China* is richly illustrated, and the visual information contained in the illustrations is worthy of our attention.

China played an increasingly important role in the eighteenth-century European imagination. By the time du Halde published his book, numerous texts in European languages on China had been published. Nonetheless, the du Halde text made something of a splash. Voltaire wrote of du Halde: "Even though he never left Paris and knew no Chinese at all, based on the memoirs of his confreres, he has given us the broadest and best description of China that the world has ever known."[5] As with many books in its genre, du Halde's was a great success; it was published in the original French in Paris in 1735 and in La Haye in 1736 in what some scholars have called a "pirate edition." The first English edition followed in 1736, and a second English edition, by a different publisher, followed in 1741. (The formats of the two English edi-tions differ, and the translations are not identical.) German editions were published in 1747 and 1749 and a Russian edition in 1772.[6] While the phe-nomenon of the popularity of European books on China has been widely commented on, surprisingly little has been written on du Halde himself.[7]

In the preface to his book, du Halde takes pains to assure us of the accu-racy of the text: he tells us that the text was corrected by the Jesuit Cyr Con-tantin, who had spent thirty-two years in China followed by a year in Paris, where he had, in the words of the 1736 English edition, "sufficient leisure to alter, add, or retrench whatever he thought necessary for the Perfection of the design" of the text.[8] Du Halde writes in the preface: "I am convinced of the accuracy of everything I have presented here."[9]

The original French text was beautifully illustrated, and the accuracy that du Halde is at such pains to claim for the text extends to the illustra-tions. He tells us in the preface that all the illustrations were drawn (*invenit*)

FIGURE 1.1. *Les Noces chinoises*, a wedding procession from Jean Baptiste du Halde's *Description geographique, historique, chronologique, politique, et physique de l'empire de la Chine et de la Tartarie chinois*. Paris: P. G Le Mercier, 1735. Reprinted with permission of the James Ford Bell Library of the University of Minnesota.

by one A. Humblot (ca. 1700–1758),[10] who, he tells us, had completely entered into the style of paintings done by the Chinese themselves, which du Halde had provided him.[11] (Du Halde may have been responding to comments like those made by the German author and naturalist Engelbert Kaempfer about a book on Japan by Arnoldus Montanus: "Most of the plates, which are the chief ornamentation and are as it were the soul of transactions of this kind, depart a long way from the truth, and do not show things as they were but as the draughtsman imagined them to be.")[12]

Du Halde's preface offers further detail as evidence of the accuracy of the illustrations. He tells us that Humblot had access to Chinese illustrations

Ann Waltner

brought to Paris from China by M. de Velaër, who had lived for many years in Canton as a director of the East India Company. The de Velaër family had long been involved with the East India Company. It is tempting to think that the man who sent the pictures was Joseph Julien de Velaër (1709–85), but it may in fact have been his father, Joseph (1667–1747). We know that Joseph Julien spent much time in Canton, and that he married a Chinese woman, whose portrait still hangs in the family chateau in France at the Château de Lude.[13]

We know little about these source illustrations, but we can take seriously the assertion that there were source illustrations. We can, moreover, make some inferences. It is clear that Humblot had seen the *Assembled Illustrations of the Three Realms* (Sancai tuhui), an early-seventeenth-century illustrated encyclopedia. As Isabelle Landry-Deron has pointed out, two of his sericulture engravings are clearly related to texts in the *Assembled Illustrations of the Three Realms*, perhaps via Xu Guangqi's (1562–1633) *Comprehensive Treatise on Agricultural Administration* (Nongzheng quanshu), an illustrated agricultural handbook that was in the collection of the Bibliothèque National in Paris as early as 1716.[14] Landry-Deron has also identified a number of the illustrations in the 1735 text as being closely derived from previously published illustrated texts such as those by Athanasius Kircher and Nieuhoff.[15] But we have little information on the source illustrations that du Halde talks about in the preface, the pictures sent by M. de Velaër.

The actual engraving of the illustrations was done by a number of different engravers. That of the wedding procession was done by J. Haussard, who is probably Jean Baptiste Haussart (1679–1749, also spelled Haussard), the father of the well-known engravers Elisabeth and Catherine Haussard.

While du Halde may have believed Humblot's drawings to be imbued with the sense and style of the Chinese originals, it is hard for anyone who has seen Chinese illustrations to regard the wedding procession as being in the Chinese style. In fact one may be tempted to discount the story of source illustrations. But we should remember that Chinese artists in the eighteenth century were producing pieces for export, and that what constitutes a Chinese-style illustration in the eighteenth century is a complex matter. Although the earliest extant export watercolors date from the late eighteenth century, export porcelains with designs clearly catering to what Chinese imagined were Western tastes date from much earlier. Ming blue-and-white porcelain appears in Bellini's *Feast of the Gods* (1514), and Chinese porcelains regularly appeared in Dutch paintings by the mid-seventeenth century.[16] Tens of millions of pieces of Chinese porcelain were exported to the West, many of them with designs that clearly were made to please the Western consumer.[17] Beginning in 1734, at the very latest, the Dutch were ordering porcelains and specifying both the designs that were to appear on the pieces and the shapes of the objects themselves.[18] Thus the European market was full of objects produced in China but which were hybrid products.

There is substantial evidence that prints made expressly for a European market were exported prior to the date of the earliest extant exemplars. A character named Mrs. Furnish is satirized in *The Fine Lady's Airs*, a play by Thomas Baker (first performed in 1709), for having ordered "lots of fans, and China, and India pictures."[19] The earliest evidence of the export of "pictures" from China is an entry in the East India Company records of the ship *Prince Augustus* in 1727 specifying "Pictures, 4 Cases."[20] A company document dating from 1730 suggests that a single box of pictures might contain as many as four hundred sheets.[21] No evidence indicates that these pictures still exist, nor do we find pictures that might have been ordered by the likes of the fictional Mrs. Furnish. We do have extant wallpaper exported to Europe from China dating from the mid-eighteenth century. And in 1735, the same year that du Halde's book was published, Jean-Antoine Fraisse, who worked at the porcelain factory and textile factory at Chantilly, published his *Livre de Desseins Chinois* (Book of Chinese designs), one edition of which includes a foldout three meters long and thirty-three centimeters in height featuring a bridal procession through a Manchu village, which probably originated as wallpaper designed for the export market. The bridal procession was rendered by a Chinese painter but was "finished" by a Western painter.[22] The segments of the painting that I have seen look very different from the wedding procession in du Halde's book, but the beginnings of the processions are similar—each is led by lantern bearers and musicians. It is unlikely that Humblot saw the painting bound by Fraisse in his *Desseins*, but the existence of the Chantilly image demonstrates that "Chinese" paintings of wedding processions were in circulation in early-eighteenth-century Europe.

Du Halde's text itself provides another clue about the circulation of images. Within the text itself, we see evidence of pictures produced for export. The cartouche for the map of Guangdong, done by Dominique Sornique (1708–56), shows a Chinese merchant on a wharf selling paintings to men in Western dress, who are intently looking through his wares

FIGURE 1.2. Cartouche of a map of Guangdong, from Jean Baptiste du Halde's *Description geographique, historique, chronologique, politique, et physique de l'empire de la Chine et de la Tartarie chinois*. Paris: P. G Le Mercier, 1735. Reprinted with permission of the James Ford Bell Library of the University of Minnesota.

(figure 1.2). At the lower-right-hand corner of the cartouche are two paintings, which the merchant is offering his Western customers, clearly painted in the export style. This cartouche seems to suggest an awareness that the issue of entering into the style of paintings done by the Chinese themselves was already mediated by the export wares. Chinese art was marketed to Western taste; what was exported to Europeans to satisfy their desire to know the truth about China had been expressly manufactured to meet their taste. The cartouche suggests that both parties knew that that the transaction could be read on many levels.

What can we learn about cultural interactions, gender, and the study of history from looking at a portrayal of a Chinese wedding procession by a French artist? In both China and Europe in the eighteenth century, marriages were family affairs and were accompanied by property transfers. In both China and Europe, the dowry that accompanied a bride at her marriage was paraded through the streets: not only was property transferred but also the transfer of the property was public, and that public nature manifested the legitimacy of the marriage. In both cases, this transfer of property was more likely to involve moveable property than land, though it was not unheard of to provide daughters with land as dowry. There are, of course, crucial differences between marriage in China and France in the eighteenth century; there was no Chinese equivalent to the European Catholic Church, which exerted claims to authority over marriage that were sometimes seen as competing with those of the family or state. In the Catholic Church, marriage was a sacrament, and to be valid a sacrament must be willingly entered into: if a young woman or man told a priest that she or he was not entering into the marriage willingly, the priest was obliged to refuse to marry the couple. No one had the right to assert such authority over the marriage decisions of Chinese families. Another difference was the practice of concubinage in China.[23] But despite important differences, a European observer in China would recognize a wedding procession and see that it entailed the ritual transfer of a woman from one household to another. The observer would also recognize that property was being transferred and would understand the importance of the public display. In other words, a European observer would have recognized the ritual and its significance.

The illustration of the wedding procession, inserted in a section of the text that deals with a variety of customs, including marriage, is done with great care and precision. For example, the hairstyles of the men are rendered in enough detail that we can see they are sporting queues, the hairstyle mandated by the Manchu rulers of the Qing dynasty.

This procession is a large one: there are about seventy-four people in it. At the bottom right-hand corner, a woman welcomes the procession into the groom's house. Justus Doolittle, writing in the nineteenth century, suggests that the woman who welcomed the bride to the groom's house was selected for that role because she had borne many sons.[24] The procession is led by lantern bearers, followed by incense bearers, followed by decorated

Ann Waltner

boxes of goods. Next we see male musicians proceeding on foot. In the musical retinue are two kinds of horn, transverse flutes, panpipes, several kinds of stringed instruments, and drums. Next comes a man carrying a box that appears to hold two geese. Geese were an important wedding gift, though normally given by the family of the groom to the bride, so it is odd to see them in a bridal procession. Geese, thought to mate for life, were an auspicious wedding gift. Geese were also thought to lead in yang forces, balancing the yin of the bride. Hence they were an important component in the procession. These geese look oddly immobile, as if they are wooden. But rather than suggesting ignorance on the part of the painter, the wooden geese suggest knowledge. Indeed, Chinese ritual experts debated whether it was permissible to substitute wooden geese for living ones as wedding gifts.[25] M. Humblot may be showing us wooden geese because they were represented in Chinese drawings or prints that he had seen; or someone may have told him about the practice of giving wooden geese as wedding gifts. My point in underscoring this odd detail is to suggest that Humblot placed wooden geese in a wedding procession because he had concrete knowledge of Chinese wedding practices, although it may have been flawed knowledge. The procession is by no means simply the product of a European fantasy.

The man with the geese is followed by a man on horseback, who is clearly a person of some status: he is accompanied by people on foot who are carrying an umbrella to shield him. Indeed, he is likely the bridegroom, though as we shall see, the narrative that du Halde provides tells us otherwise. As we then turn the corner, there is a pause in the procession—the artist did not want to obscure any of the details of the procession behind the craggy rocks, suggesting once again that conveying information is a higher priority than a realistic rendition of a procession wending its way through a landscape.

We then see servants carrying dowry goods such as mats and bedding, which in fact would have been standard goods in Qing dowries. Just in front of the bridal palanquin itself are two women on horseback holding pennants. These women are probably entertainers.[26]

We have now reached the sedan chair itself; in writing about funeral processions Nicolas Standaert refers to the coffin as the "charisma at the center."[27] The bridal palanquin serves much the same role. Although we do not see the bride herself in the center of this procession, her sedan chair plays a central role in the visual representation of the procession. We know she is at the center of the story, even if the story of her marriage is in some ways not entirely about her: it is about the joining of two families and the continuation of the patriline.

Next to her are women carrying bedding. Chinese sources tell us that often a woman who understood the ritual would walk beside the sedan chair to prevent the bride from making errors. They are followed by men on horseback, who are in turn followed by men carrying placards with Chinese written (badly—some of it appears to be composed of genuine characters, but other writing seems to be made-up Chinese) on them. They are followed by people with lanterns, pennants, and small parcels. The procession is brought to a close by musicians, and here we again see female entertainers, this time female musicians on horseback.

The women all have an oddly (or perhaps not so oddly) European cast to them, and it is clear that none have bound feet. The women are probably not intended to be European—they resemble Chinese women as portrayed by Nieuhoff in a text that we can be reasonably certain du Halde had seen.[28] There are several possible interpretations of the feet. Perhaps M. Humblot did not know of bound feet, or if he did know, he could not imagine how to represent them. (Though the du Halde text does talk about bound feet, there's no reason to suppose that Humblot read the entirety of the text that he illustrated.)[29] But if we take the large feet seriously, they provide us with a clue to the sources of the image. The feet of Manchu women were not bound, and Manchu women did ride on horseback.[30] The Jesuits were well acquainted with the court in Beijing in the early Qing dynasty, and although du Halde tells us that the sources for the image are pictures sent from Canton, information in this one may have been gleaned from Jesuits in Beijing.

The odd rock arch resonates with forms that Craig Clunas says are common in eighteenth-century export watercolors (and wallpaper), to the point that they formed a stereotyped view in the British (and apparently also French) imagination of the Chinese countryside.[31]

The sources for the image, then, seem to be multiple and are probably both visual and textual. They come from the merchant community in Canton and the Jesuit community in Beijing. These images may have been conflated in the imagination of du Halde's illustrator, resulting in a triangular connection between Canton, Beijing, and Paris. Amsterdam, too, might be added to this constellation, because of the ways that illustrations published there influenced the du Halde text.

Ann Waltner

We know quite a bit about Qing dowry processions from the work of Susan Mann, Mao Liping, and others.[32] Mao argues that dowry was essential to Chinese marriages, and that having an insufficient dowry kept some women from marrying as principal wives. Such women generally became concubines. Indeed, some of the intensity of discussions of dowry in Qing China comes from the fact that a dowry is one detail that distinguishes marriage as a principal wife from marriage as a concubine. The multiple forms of marriage in China (as wife, as concubine, as little daughter-in-law), each of which had a different meaning and legal status, meant that drawing lines between them mattered.[33] For a woman in China, marriage was not simply one thing; dowry was a marker of class and respectability. This complexity sharpened the procession: it made clear to everyone that the bride was marrying as a principal wife and showing off the material possessions of the family.

But excess dowries and extravagant weddings were deplored by eighteenth-century commentators.[34] Chen Hongmou, for example, wrote,

> When it comes to marriage, people only care about keeping up with the times. They spend extravagantly on material things. When they present betrothal gifts or make up a dowry, the embroidered silks and satins and the gold and pearls are matched one for one. Utensils and articles for the home and business are the finest and the most expensive, and they must be beautifully made as well. The decorated pavilion to welcome the bride and her elegant sedan chair, the banquet where two families meet and exchange gifts, all require the most fantastic outlays of cash. One sees the worst of this among poorer people, who will borrow heavily to give the appearance of having property, all for the sake of a single public display, ignoring the needs of the "eight mouths" at home. Families with daughters are most burdened; the families with sons can procrastinate and put off [marriage plans].[35]

Note that the issue Chen is articulating here is not simply his concern with the amount of spending but also the public display. Chen suggests that the financial burden is great on both families (he speaks of the need for the goods provided by each family to "match" the other's contributions). In fact, he also argued that it made more sense to give daughters land as dowry, as a way of cutting down on lavish waste. Observers in many parts of China felt that wedding expenses were too lavish, and that the expenses of marriage fell disproportionately on the family of the bride, to the point of causing families to kill baby girls rather than raise them. (While the nature of Chinese demographic data makes it hard to find concrete figures on female infanticide, it is clear that contemporaries linked the practice with high-priced dowries.)[36]

In the Humblot picture, we see that the bride herself is being conveyed to her new home. She is in a liminal position as she moves from the family of her birth to the family of her marriage. Christian de Pee has expressed the contexts of that liminality well: "On the wedding day the bride becomes the epitome of yin, at once vulnerable to evil forces and dangerous to the groom's family and its deities. Suspended between households, between adolescence and womanhood, between virginity and defloration, the bride is carried through openings in time that are auspicious days and hours, and through the openings in space that are the safe gates and doorways, veiled and swathed both to shield her body from baleful penetration and to protect her new household and its benevolent gods from her harmful emanations."[37]

With this in mind, let us turn to what du Halde writes about the wedding procession:

> When the day for the wedding arrives, the bride is locked in a magnificently decorated sedan chair. The entire dowry which she brings with her accompanies her. Among commoners, the dowry consists of the wedding clothes, contained in boxes, and some other clothing, and furniture, bestowed on the bride by her father. A procession of people hired for the occasion accompanies her with torches and lanterns, even in full daylight. Her chair is preceded by pipes, hautes-bois, and drums, and is followed by her relatives and special friends of her family. A trusted servant keeps the keys to the door which lock the sedan chair so that [the bride] will be given only to her husband, who awaits the wife who has been selected for him at his door, magnificently clad.
>
> As soon as she arrives, he receives the key which the servant gives him and opens the chair with excitement. It is then that he sees her for the first time and can decide whether his fortune is good or bad.[38]

If the bridal procession should somehow get waylaid, the bride herself would be locked in the sedan chair. Being locked in the chair does not make her safe—she might drown or starve to death, but her locked body would not be subject to violation by the eyes or hands of others. Du Halde is articulating anxiety about chastity and liminality at a moment of transition, an

Ann Waltner

anxiety that can be resolved (perhaps only in his imagination) by lock and key. The moment at which the groom unlocks the chair is richly suggestive: he unlocks the sedan and brings the bride out of the chair, a moment that precedes (though not by much) the consummation of the marriage, when he unlocks her body. The metaphor of the lock and key suggests, of course, the Western image of the medieval chastity belt, a topic of lively interest in eighteenth-century Europe.[39]

There are several problems with the du Halde description (and hence with my reading of it). The first is that sedan chairs were rarely secured with lock and key; they were more typically curtained.[40] Locks were, of course, not unknown in eighteenth-century China; we know from the novel *Dream of the Red Chamber* that things of value were commonly kept under lock and key. Wang Xifeng, the clever and ruthless daughter-in-law who manages the Jia family estate, is frequently seen with a set of keys. It is possible that du Halde took a regional variant to be a description of a practice common throughout China.

In conducting this research, I asked a number of Chinese colleagues if they were familiar with a practice of locking a bride in a sedan chair. One colleague responded that while she knew nothing of locked sedan chairs, she did know from talking to her grandmother that it was essential for the bride, once she had entered the sedan chair, not to leave it for any reason. Thus it was customary for brides to deprive themselves of food and water for twenty-four hours before the ceremonial procession so as to prevent excretion, but also to carry a chamber pot in the sedan.[41] Not leaving the chair voluntarily is quite different from being locked in it, though perhaps it does express some of the same liminality—the bride is on a dangerous journey; once she begins, she may not leave the chair. The chair is the site of her in-between-ness. The fast (which I have not read about in eighteenth-century sources but heard of from other sources) would also serve as a kind of purification before marriage. Doing away with the need for elimination would render her body closed and hence radically intact.

We have limited evidence about the experiences of brides in the eighteenth-century sedan chair. Gan Lirou (1743–1819), who married in 1763, wrote poems about her wedding, including this one, "Hastening the Bride's Toilette":

Pearl headdress and patterned robe suddenly put on my body,
In marrying, I take leave of my family and take leave of those I love.

> The way of the daughter comes to an end; the way of the wife begins.
> But there is no mother to tie my sash with her hands.[42]

In the first line, note her passivity—the headdress and robe are put on her body (*ji jia shen*), and in the last line note her loneliness—her mother had already died when Gan Lirou married. But the two lines of most interest here are the middle two, which clearly express Gan's consciousness of her own liminality—she has left the way of the daughter (*nü dao*) and is about to begin the way of the wife (*fu dao*). Grace Fong, who translates and discusses this poem in *Herself an Author*, tells us that a bride writing her own leave-taking poem was somewhat unusual; more frequently such poems were written by friends.

Gan wrote a second poem, called "Mounting the Sedan Chair," and provided commentary for it.

> About to set out, freshly bathed, I ascend the platform.
> Who carried me to the sedan and forced me to leave?
>> According to local custom a bride when getting on the sedan should not
>> step on the ground. A prosperous elder carries her into it.
>
> Sitting alone, I close the door and swallow my tears in secret.
> How is it that drums and music carry me along?
>> I had read in the *Li jing* (Classic of Rites) that music should not be used
>> in marriage rituals. Now we too follow custom and proceed with pipes
>> and drums.

Gan Lirou is the author of a poetic autobiography, compiled when she was seventy-six *sui*, but the poems in it are presented as having been written at the time of the events they describe.[43] Thus Gan presents these texts as a young bride's own reflection. She knows what the classics prescribe; she knows what the local system is. The pipes and drums Gan describes appear in du Halde's illustration. Note that in this illustration, the bride is locked in the sedan chair, while in Gan Lirou's poem she herself closes the door (*an shan*, perhaps more accurately rendered as "draws the shutters" than as "locks the door"). No doubt she closes the door because women did that, but the next phrase, "swallow my tears in secret," suggests that she takes advantage of the privacy to conceal her tears. Tears were conventional (as well as heartfelt) when a young woman left her natal home, but still, one would not

Ann Waltner

want to make one's own weeping body the center of the spectacle. Gan Lirou was spunkier than the average bride, but we should not let the image of the bride who herself closed the door go away as we think about these transactions.

There are other inaccuracies (or at least surprising observations) in du Halde's description. The man who appears to be a personage of some significance in the procession is in all likelihood the groom, who would in most cases have gone to fetch the bride from her house and escort her to his own. The text says that the groom is waiting for the bride at his house. Here the image permits a reading different from the one given by the text, which may suggest the existence of a now vanished visual source.

What have we learned from this excursion? The art historian Dawn Odell, working on Chinese porcelain exported to the Netherlands, has shown the complicated ways in which European images of China were produced and received. Export porcelains were a commodity made with European customers in mind, and in this way European views of China were shaped by Chinese mercantile interests. Odell is interested in the interplay between printed images and images on the surface of porcelain; her work focuses on Dutch texts produced in Amsterdam. Nonetheless, the visual moment she has identified—where text and image intertwine to present European viewers with what they accepted as realistic views of China—is one in which the du Halde text participates as well. It is a moment of ethnographic contact. Like Johan Nieuhoff (some of whose illustrations are copied in the du Halde book), du Halde noted the rituals performed in other societies and represented them in words and images. Du Halde did not go to China; he was an impresario of the fashionable interest in China and an advocate for Jesuits. He began circulating an advertisement for the book (with a fairly complete table of contents) two years in advance of its publication in order to obtain subscriptions that would finance the book. He was responding to and taking advantage of a market with a lively interest in China.

We can infer from the way Humblot constructed his visual images that he had consulted illustrated Chinese texts (such as encyclopedias and agricultural manuals) brought back to France by missionaries; the books presumably were cataloged in the French royal library by Arcade Huang.[44] These texts were not manufactured particularly for Western eyes. They circulated in China for Chinese purposes—to show an industrious and peaceful people or to disseminate information about textile or agricultural technology. While these illustrations did not arrive in France by chance (Xu Guangqi, the author of *Comprehensive*

Treatise on Agricultural Administration, was a Christian convert and had close relations with Jesuits), they were not made for the French. Some of Humblot's illustrations are clearly modeled on these texts.

A second source for Humblot's visual imagination is much less accidental: export prints or watercolors. Humblot's ethnographic eye was informed by what Chinese export artists wanted him, as a Westerner, to see. Another twist to the story of Humblot's visual imagination is geographical. Du Halde tells us that the "pictures" Humblot had access to were from Canton. We should not overstate the significance of the fact that the prints came from Canton, which would have been one of the main points of transit for the transmission of objects from anywhere in China to Europe. There are no geographical indicators as to where this wedding procession takes place. Much of du Halde's text is located very specifically in place, but the sections on customs are not place-specific—they describe customs in a spatially vague and abstract "China." But we have seen visual clues—the women with unbound feet on horseback—that some of the details may come from Manchu sources. And it should be noted that the wallpaper from Chantilly, published by Fraisse, features a Manchu procession. It may be that what Humblot has drawn uses a mélange of textual sources, a possible Cantonese print or two, descriptions of Manchu customs (perhaps verbal, perhaps visual), filtered through a French imagination.

Thus this picture is in multiple ways the product of an early modern moment, influenced by contact, curiosity (mainly European), and the market (both Chinese and European). There are a plethora of images in the du Halde text: I have focused on this one because it is of particular interest to me as a historian of the family and of gender. It serves as a kind of palimpsest, in which things are both seen and not seen. The image is mediated by the market illustrated in the cartouche on the map of Guangdong showing Chinese merchants selling to Westerners, and by the market shown in the circular advertising du Halde's text. In the illustration of the wedding procession, we see the interactions of worldviews mediated by markets and gender ideology, which is what makes this an early modern image.

NOTES

1   Du Halde, *Description geographique, historique, chronologique, politique, et physique de l'empire de la Chine et de la Tartarie chinois* (hereafter *Description de la Chine*), 2:154.

2   On Xu Guangqi, see, among others, Catherine Jami et al., *Statecraft and Intellectual Renewal*. On Yang Tingyun, see Standaert, *Yang Tingyun*, 87.

3   See Waltner, "Breaking the Law."

4   On Nieuhoff, see Laura Hostetler, "Mapping Dutch Travels." On Dutch travel writings (and illustrations more generally), see Odell, "The Soul of Transactions." On the ways in which the illustrations in du Halde referred to earlier texts, see Landry-Deron, *La Preuve par la Chine*, 153. Note that Nieuhoff's name has a number of variant spellings.

5   Quoted on the back cover of Landry-Deron, *La Preuve par la Chine*. The citation is from the entry on du Halde in Voltaire's catalog of writers of the century of Louis XIV: "Quoiqu'il ne soit point sorti de Paris, et qu'il n'ait su point le chinois, a donné sur les memoires de ses confreres la plus ample et la meillure description de l'empire de la Chine qu'on ait dans le monde." All translations are my own unless otherwise noted.

6   Du Halde, *Ausführliche Beschreibung des chineseischen*.

7   In addition to the work by Isabelle Landry-Deron cited earlier, see Foss, "A Jesuit Encyclopedia for China."

8   Quoted from the 1736 English edition, preface, unpaginated. The 1735 French edition puts it this way: "Il eut tout le loisir de lire plus d'une fois cet Ouvrage, & de l'examiner, comme je le souhaittois, avec l'attention la plus sérieuse, & avec la plus sévere critique" (1:ix).

9   From the preface to the 1735 edition, 1:ix. "Je me suis assuré de l'entiere exactitude de tout ce que j'avance." The same precise phrase appears in an advertisement for the book published in 1733. Landry-Deron, *La Preuve par la Chine*, 368.

10 Dates are from Reed and Demattè, *China on Paper*, 154.

11 Noted in the 1735 edition, 1:xlix: "Qui est parfaitment entré dans le goût des Peintures faites par les Chinois memes."

12 Cited in Odell, "The Soul of Transactions," 225.

13 A description of the painting is in Carné, *Revue historique de l'ouest*, 625–26. I visited Le Lude in 2010 and saw the picture.

14 Landry-Deron, *La Preuve par la Chine*, 155.

15 Ibid., 153.

16 Mungello, *The Great Encounter*, 108, says that by 1700, large numbers of folding screens, hand-printed wallpapers, and pictures on paper were circulating in France.

17 Ibid., 107.

18 Volker, *The Japanese Porcelain Trade*, 78–79. I have found Dawn Odell's work to be particularly useful in thinking about the interactions between Dutch and Chinese visual culture.

19 Cited in Le Corbeiller, *China Trade Porcelain*, 3. "India pictures" seems to mean wallpaper with Chinese scenes on it. The name *India pictures* probably comes from the fact that the objects were transported by the East India Company. See Leath, "After the Chinese Taste," 54.

20 See Clunas, *Chinese Export Watercolors*, 10.

21 Ibid., 12.

22 Miller, "Jean-Antoine Fraisse at Chantilly," 94–96. The text exists in a number of editions, which Miller details, and one of the editions was republished in 2011 (n.p., Fraisse, *Livre de desseins*, 2011). The painting of the wedding procession is Chinese. Miller argues that a Western painter has added to the painting. She reproduces segments but not the entire painting. I have not yet had the opportunity to see the painting.

23 See Maynes and Waltner, "Women's Life-Cycle Transitions," for a fuller comparison of marriage in China and Europe.

24 Doolittle, *Social Life of the Chinese*, 83.

25 See discussion in de Pee, *The Writing of Weddings*, 32.

26 On entertainers at Qing weddings, see Hansson, *Chinese Outcasts*, 42, 101.

27 Standaert, *The Interweaving of Rituals*, 68.

28 See for example the peasant women in Nieuhoff, *Der Gesandschaft der Ost-Indischer Geselshaft in den Vereingten Niederlanden an der Tartarsichen Cham und nunmehr auch sinischen Jaiser*, 291. Landry-Deron asserts that du Halde had likely seen Nieuhoff and other sources (*La Preuve par la Chine*, 153).

29 This refers to the 1735 edition, 80–81.

30 See Elliott, *The Manchu Way*, 246–47.

31 For an exemplar, see *Monkey Picking Herbs*, c. 1780–90, reproduced in Clunas, *Chinese Export Watercolors*, 27. See also Arnoldus Montanus, *Landscape with Pagoda 1671*, which is a European representation of a Chinese scene and has distinctive craggy rocks. Reproduced in Odell, "Porcelain, Print Culture, and Mercantile Aesthetics," 144.

32 Mann, "Grooming a Daughter for Marriage." Mao, *Qingdai jiazhuang yanjiu*.

33 "Little daughters-in-law" were young girls, or even infants, who were adopted into their future husbands' families to be reared by their future in-laws. This custom spared the family the expense of obtaining a grown woman as a bride.

34 Mann, "Grooming a Daughter for Marriage" is the key text here. But marriage is also a key issue in Mann's *Precious Records, The Talented Women of the Zhang Family,* and "Dowry Wealth and Wifely Virtue."

35 Cited in Mann, "Grooming a Daughter for Marriage," 205. The source is a reprint of *Huangchao jingshi wenbian*, 68, no. 4 (Taipei: Guofeng, 1963).

36 See Waltner, "Infanticide and Dowry in Ming China."

37 De Pee, *The Writing of Weddings in Middle-Period China*, 168.

38 *Description de la Chine*, 2:121. "Lorsque le jour des nôces est venu, on enferme la fiancée dans une chaise magnifiquement orné: tout la dot qu'elle port, l'acompagne & la fuit. Parmi le menu people, elle consiste en des habits de nôces, enfermés dans des coffres, en quelques nippes, & en d'autres meubles, que le pere donne. Un cortége des gens qui se loüent, l'accompage avec des torches & des flambeaux, meme en plein midi. Sa chaise est precedee de fifres, de hautes-bois, & de tambours, & suivie de ses parens, & des amis particuliers de la famille. Un domestique affidé garde la clef de la porte qui ferme la chaise, pour ne la donner qu'au mari; celui-ci magnifiquement vêtu attend à sa porte l'épouse qu'on lui a choisie. Aussi-tôt qu'elle est arirvée, il reçoit la clef qui lui remet le domestique, & il ouvre avec empressement

la chaise. C'est alors que s'il la voit pour la première fois, il juge de sa bonne ou de sa mauvaise fortune."

39 See for example the discussion of the eighteenth-century fascination with the chastity belt in Classen, *The Medieval Chastity Belt.*

40 Judicious asking around, as well as a post on H-Asia, revealed that I am not alone in my perplexity here. I did locate several examples of sedan chairs with locks and keys, but they are few and far between.

41 Wu Yanhong, personal communication, about April 5, 2009.

42 Gan Lirou, *Yongxuelou gao,* I.35a (both poems). Translations by Fong, *Herself an Author,* 23. As Fong notes, the reference to the mother tying the sash comes from the *Shi jing,* the *Classic of Poetry.* Gan Lirou's mother died before Gan married. The poem is number 156, "Dong shan," and the lines (as translated by Arthur Waley) are: "A girl is going to be married / . . . Her mother ties the strings of her girdle." Gan Lirou was from Fengxin county in Jiangxi, and the man she married, Xu Yuelü, was from the same county. Xu died in 1774.

43 See the discussion in Fong, *Herself an Author,* chap. 1.

44 Arcade Huang was born in 1679 in Fujian to a Catholic family. His parents had four daughters; they promised their next child to God if it were male. It was; they gave Arcade to the Society of Foreign Missions of Paris. He was brought to Paris in 1702. He did not take holy orders, but rather became assistant to the king's librarian and cataloged Chinese books in the French royal library. In 1713, he married a woman named Marie-Claude Regnier with the approval of her parents and in spite of the disapproval of some churchmen. Shortly after, she died in childbirth. Huang died in 1716, and his daughter (also Marie-Claude) died several months later. For a discussion of Huang, see Hsia, "The Question of Who?"

CHAPTER TWO

THE CONTROL OF
FEMALE ENERGIES

Gender and Ethnicity on China's Southeast Coast

Guotong Li

THE first advice book for women published during the Qing dynasty was *Women's Learning* (Nüxue) by Lan Dingyuan (1680–1733), who served as a magistrate in Puning and Chaoyang counties in Guangdong.[1] Lan was a southern Fujianese of mixed heritage: his ancestors included both Han and minority She families. His work is unusual both for its dedication to women's learning and for his attention to gender issues in the migrant society of Taiwan. By focusing on the history of this locale, we can see how state policies such as "family values" were articulated and implemented at the local level and how local administrators used the umbrella of the dynasty's "civilizing project" (*jiao hua*, the effort to transform borderland peoples into "civilized" Chinese subjects) to lobby the court in support of their own local causes. And by examining the empire from its margin, rather than from the heartland of the Lower Yangzi region (which has been the focus of most research on eighteenth-century China), we are able to place existing findings for the Lower Yangzi region in a broader context.

Recent scholarship on the Qing has demonstrated how paying attention to gender and ethnicity enriches our understanding of Qing government and society. Some time ago, Susan Mann pointed out that the history of gender relations in the Qing is distinctive from that of the late Ming, pushing us to reconsider the importance of Manchu identity and Manchu values in the making of Qing society.[2] Mann and others have stressed the difference in adjustment made by men and women to Manchu bodily practices. Han Chinese men accepted the Manchu hairstyle of a shaved forehead and a long braid as a sign of submission. Han women kept their bound feet as an ethnic marker, whereas Manchu women were distinguished by their natural feet.[3] Scholars have also shown that ethnicity played a central role the Qing government's attitude toward widows. The implementation of the chaste-widow campaign was integral to the Manchu civilizing project, and the state encouraged chastity among Han and other borderland peoples, often erecting commemorative arches to honor chaste widows who brought glory and financial benefit to their deceased husbands' families.[4] Yet where Manchu women were concerned, the Qing ruling house emphasized fertility rather than chastity. Manchu widows were encouraged to remarry and produce more children.[5]

Finally, scholars have highlighted the diverse ways that women participated in the Qing civilizing project, observing that women, acting as indispensable transmitters of proper behavior, played a key role among borderland peoples.[6] The poet Wanyan Yun Zhu, a Han woman who married into an elite Manchu family, compiled a huge collection of women's poetry—the *Correct Beginnings*—during the heyday of the Qing. Although her interest in celebrating the imperial civilizing project may have resulted from her Manchu marital ties, Han women also used poetry to convey political messages.[7] Such efforts on the part of genteel women continued into the Republican era.[8]

Lan Dingyuan advocated women's education in the context of this larger Manchu civilizing project and contributed to the literati debate on women's education in the early modern period of Chinese history.[9] Parallel to the female political tradition among educated women was a male elite consensus on the need for men to direct or "rectify" (*zheng*) control of female energies. This consensus persisted from the Ming and Qing into the early twentieth century: while Ming-Qing scholars like Lan sought to direct women in order to consolidate the state-family structure of the early modern period, early-twentieth-century reformers blamed women for the "backwardness" of the country and sought to drag them into nation-building efforts during China's transition from empire to nation. Gender and ethnic hierarchies coalesced in the writings of both Lan Dingyuan and later reformers like Liang Qichao (1873–1929), such that the "male gaze" and the "colonial gaze" overlapped. Thus, by linking Lan's fear of aboriginal energies to his desire to regulate female energies, we can better understand male elites' anxieties about unregulated female power and their embrace of the civilizing project to solve local administrative problems. This, in turn, will contribute to the larger cross-cultural discussion of women and the colonial gaze.[10]

UNDER THE MALE GAZE: LAN DINGYUAN AND HIS *WOMEN'S LEARNING*

Biographies of Lan Dingyuan suggest that he was a man of action more than a thinker. He never passed the prefectural-level *juren* examinations, but owing to his participation in a military campaign against rebels in Taiwan, he received the title of tribute student (*gongsheng*) and was recommended to the emperor in 1724. The Yongzheng emperor recognized Lan's talents and immediately appointed him to the position of county magistrate in eastern Guangdong. Before this time, however, in 1712, Lan Dingyuan had already compiled the six-chapter *Women's Learning*.[11] He divided his text into four sections (*pian*): women's virtue, women's speech, women's appearance, and women's work, following the framework of the text *Fuxue* (Women's learning), which was part of the ancient classic *The Rites of Zhou* (Zhouli). Each of Lan's sections contains a collection of extracts from Confucian classics, literature, and historical works to illustrate proper female behavior, using role models from the past to educate contemporary women.[12]

Previous scholarship on Lan's *Women's Learning* has primarily focused on its content.[13] But if we examine the circulation of Lan's work and his motivations for writing it, we find that Lan went beyond merely compiling and put his thoughts into action. He presented his book to other county magistrates and wrote eulogies for exemplary women, aiming to convert people to his teachings in *Women's Learning*.

Lao Zunsan, a native of Hanyang in Hubei, was a friend of Lan Dingyuan. Lao was appointed to serve as a county magistrate of Zhaowen in Jiangsu, in the center of the Chinese heartland. Anxious to see his ideas circulated in central places, Lan presented his book to Lao along with the following advice:

> A magistrate should be like the father and mother of people. Parents are responsible for feeding their children, educating them, and caring about their troubles. Magistrates should care for everything, not only squeeze people for taxes. . . . Magistrates should visit rural areas and talk with senior farmers about the weather and their everyday lives. They should promote agriculture; establish schools in order to recruit talent for the state; found academies to civilize people; limit monks and nuns to reduce the number of unmarried persons; reward the filial and righteous; take care of orphans and widows; and fight against bullies. . . .
>
> To teach people how to manage their households, you should start by civilizing women. The usual custom of women burning incense in the temple and taking pleasure trips to the suburbs should be changed. Now I present you with a copy of *Women's Learning*. Please spread the ideas for me and put them into action.[14]

In this preface, Lan Dingyuan went beyond describing the routine duties of a local magistrate to emphasize women's role in the civilizing process. He explicitly stated, "To teach people how to manage their households, you should start by civilizing women." And like other magistrates, he drew particular attention to ways that women's religious practices outside the household threatened the social order.[15] Lan understood that not all women could afford to exhibit the ideal proper behavior of staying in their homes, as elite women did. On the southeast coast where Lan lived, ordinary women had to work on the coast or in the fields "with bare feet and loose hair" to earn a living. They overstepped the boundaries between inner and outer and between women and men every day. Nonetheless, Lan concluded that, with proper role models, even poor women of the coastal regions could gradually learn what their proper behavior should be.[16] He was even more eager to see the behavior of women in the heartland rectified, and so he presented his *Women's Learning* to Magistrate Lao.

Further evidence of Lan's active interest in regulating women's behavior lies in another of his writings, a colophon to a poem mourning a faithful widow. This piece is really an argument for the usefulness of women's education in the civilizing process.

After reading the commemoration of Madam Zheng, née Lin, I felt very sad for her. But then, it was a great relief to learn that she found her fortune in the end. When women are faithful [widows], it is different from being a martyr. To be a martyr, a woman just needs to pluck up a little courage in the face of death. Her faithfulness is immediately evident, and she will become famous. But the bitter loneliness of a faithful widow lasts her entire life. She cannot enjoy any fame until she becomes old, with gray hair and loose teeth, and close to death. Some women are especially unfortunate, for no filial descendants or contemporary gentry will commemorate their faithfulness, so that it fades in the uncultivated mountains and remote valleys.

Madam Zheng maintained faithfulness for thirty years. Fortunately, she had a filial son. After her death, her son, Yangfeng, wrote a memorial for her and cried for his faithful mother. The gentlemen in our community sympathized with her and composed poetry to eulogize her enduring-frost faithfulness and the long-lasting fragrance after her death.[17]

Madam Zheng's experience is fortunate. "Fame" [*ming*] and "teaching" [*jiao*] are two words that women cherish as much as men do. Since I felt unsatisfied that there was no classic especially dedicated to women's education, I compiled the six-chapter *Women's Learning*, a collection excerpted from the classics and ancient instructions. I boldly dared to use it as a bridge to civilization [*feng hua*]. Now I learn that Madam Zheng benefited from the *Book of Filial Piety*, the *Inner Principles* [Neize], and the *Biographies of Exemplary Women* [Lienü zhuan]. As a result, I now believe even more that the function of learning is great and that civilizing people and transforming custom must start with learning. How could this be true only for men? Accordingly, I compose these few words to celebrate Madam Zheng's glorification of the moral teachings [*mingjiao*].[18]

Lan clearly indicated that Madam Zheng benefited from advice books for women, since she had preserved her faithfulness for thirty years. He used her as evidence to illustrate the function of women's learning and further testify to his agenda: promoting women's learning for the purpose of civilizing people and transforming custom.

Lan Dingyuan continued to promote his agenda in other biographies he wrote for women. In these, he paid particular attention to women's early education in their natal families. As he had pointed out in *Women's Learning*, women's education is different from men's: men can devote their entire lives to study, whereas women can study for only a decade or so before they marry. Not surprisingly, Lan depicts most of the subjects of his biographical sketches as reading advice books for women and obeying the instructions strictly. The Exemplary Martyr Lin read Ban Zhao's *Precepts for My Daughters* (Nüjie) with a woman teacher while she was living with her natal family, and her father teased her, saying that she was a female erudite (*nüboshi*). She committed suicide after she had received a rejection of her request to attend her deceased fiancé's funeral and to adopt a male heir for him. Lan wrote in her eulogy, "Although her nature was good, she benefited from Ban Zhao's *Precepts for My Daughters*. Nowadays people are inclined not to teach girls to read. What a big mistake!"[19]

In addition to admiring the martyr's conduct, Lan Dingyuan placed a high value on the contributions that educated women could make to their husbands' careers and their sons' educations. He described in great detail the support that Madam Wang, the mother of Fujian governor Gioro Manbao, devoted to her three sons' education. After she was widowed, she first sold her apparel to hire a noted teacher for her sons; and when she was no longer able to afford a private tutor at home, she sent her sons to school. Finally, as the household economy worsened, Madam Wang herself served as a teacher for her sons. Although they could not afford a house and had rented empty land on which they simply built a hut to live in, Madam Wang still continued supervising her sons' studies day and night. Eventually, the sons passed their examinations; two received the prestigious metropolitan-level *jinshi* degree and the other passed the provincial-level *juren* examination.[20] Lan celebrated Madam Wang's great success as a teaching mother. These women's biographies further validated his effort in compiling *Women's Learning*.

The expected audience for *Women's Learning* was local magistrates and literate women. Lan hoped magistrates would use his text to help fulfill their duties to regulate women's conduct and direct them to the civilizing process. He hoped literate women would read it and follow the role models portrayed in it, thereby maintaining Confucian order in the family, where the civilizing process began. Though little is known about the book's actual readers, Lan's work circulated widely. *Women's Learning* was reprinted several times—in 1865, 1879, and 1882—and was included in Lan's collected works and the series *Jinhe guangrentang keshu* (A collection for children's or beginners' education). When circulation of the text within a series became inconvenient, more than seventy officials in Beijing sponsored the reprinting of *Women's Learning* in a special edition in 1897. The text of this edition espouses the hope that "every family" could have a copy of *Women's Learning* to regulate family order.[21]

But while some scholars at the dawn of the 1898 reforms thus felt that Lan's advice was still relevant in their own day, others no longer accepted his premises. One modern reformer, Zheng Guanying (1842–1922), in his work titled *Women's Teaching* (Nüjiao), commented neutrally, "Among people of our dynasty, Lan Luzhou [Dingyuan] collected and edited excerpts from the classics, history, and anthologies into a collection of exemplars for women. It is titled *Women's Learning*. It has been regarded as a meticulous work."[22] Reformers like Zheng appreciated Lan's interest in women's education but not always his morality-centered theories. Lan had argued that women's behavior should "center on morality" (*fu yi de wei zhu*) and thus depicted women's virtue in extensive detail.[23] His book was concerned with governing the state through regulation of the family more than it was with promoting women's literacy per se. Radical reformers rejected this focus on morality, even charging that overemphasis on women's virtue (especially the canonical "three obediences and four virtues")[24] had wasted women's talents and, in the end, made the country backward.[25] However, the very foundation of Lan's Confucian vision—the family-as-microcosm-of-the-state paradigm—itself was carried into the twentieth century.

In promoting their own agenda, early-twentieth-century reformers ignored or deliberately marginalized the work of Lan and other Qing scholars who, like him, had promoted women's education and literacy. Recent scholarship has begun to uncover the contributions of other men, like Lü Kun (1536–1618), who advocated women's education. Likewise, Chen Hongmou (1696–1771) promoted women's literacy as part of a larger reform campaign against prostitution and trafficking in kidnapped women and girls. Yuan Mei (1716–96) encouraged women to write poems and recruited fifty female students, half of whom wrote collections of poetry or poems that were anthologized by later editors.[26] In contrast to the widespread image of female illiteracy as a reason for China's failure to modernize at the turn of the twentieth century, these revisionist studies point to what Mann has called an early-modern program promoting the education of girls and women in China, at least among the elite.

To be sure, as William Rowe has noted, this early-modern program promoting women's literacy can be seen as "in effect defending traditional notions rather than introducing 'progressive' ones."[27] With a few exceptions (such as Yuan Mei), scholars like Lan, Chen Hongmou, and others stressed the limits and "proper" purpose of women's education and were not interested in women's talent for its own sake. They ignored women's interests in the wider polity.[28] They saw women as crucial to the governance of the state, but only when they acted as moral managers confined to the home. As Susan Mann has suggested, women's talent was dangerous unless it was tempered by Confucian morality.[29] It was not that officials such as Lan and Chen failed to recognize the diversity of roles women played in their local communities, but that they directed women's potentially dangerous talents toward the civilizing project.

Ironically, although twentieth-century reformers rejected the approach of the early-modern promoters of women's education, they shared many similar assumptions. The legacy of the early-modern program is evident in the reform proposals (i.e., the 1898 reforms and the 1907 New Policies), which advocated "wise mothers" for the home and "industrious workers" for the factories as the new goals in the education of China's daughters. As Joan Judge argues, "Only in China did history remain so integral to newly politicized visions of the mother's role."[30] Reformers drew on the historical legacy to promote their nationalist views of motherhood. Most important, like their predecessors, these reformers assumed that only when women's behavior was "rectified" by men could the state be properly governed.

UNDER THE COLONIAL GAZE: LAN DINGYUAN'S SOLUTIONS TO PACIFYING A MIGRANT SOCIETY

In the 1720s, Lan Dingyuan encountered new opportunities to apply his theories on women's learning. As a middle-aged man with political ambitions, he saw his chance to take action in 1721, when Zhu Yigui, a Fujianese migrant, led a revolt in Taiwan.[31] Lan wrote to his cousin Lan Tingzhen (1664–1729) to suggest that the latter go to Taiwan to help suppress the revolt, and offered to go along to assist: "It is [your] time to set out on the right path. Among the generals in Zhejiang and Fujian, you are the most suitable to lead this battle [against the rebels]. . . . Although [I] am not talented, [I] would like to sail with you as your assistant."[32] Once in Taiwan, Lan served his cousin as a policy advisor, ultimately earning imperial recognition and establishing his name in Taiwanese affairs. His devotion to Taiwan is evident in his writings, including two books and several policy proposals. Both the Yongzheng and Qianlong emperors recognized his statesmanship.

Lan's concerns in Taiwan centered on two issues: the constant revolts among migrants from Fujian, and disturbances caused by the "uncivilized" aborigines. Here again, Lan saw women as the key to civilization. Between 1724 and 1727, Lan recommended a series of gendered solutions to pacify the constant rebellions among the migrants. He had found that the migrants were all single men with no wives and children, which made the frontier settlement almost a bachelor society.[33] He observed that hundreds or thousands of migrants might live in a single settlement, none with a wife or family (*wuqi wushi*), and that within four or five hundred *li* there might be only a few hundred native women. In a memorial to the Yongzheng emperor, Lan suggested that this abnormal gender ratio had led to constant chaos in Taiwan migrant society. He recommended that to solve the problem, family migration be encouraged instead of migration by single males, so that men would be concerned about supporting their families instead of making trouble.[34] According to his theory, once men had settled down in households, they would not easily take risks at the cost of losing their families. Similarly, Lan criticized Taiwan's marriage customs, which required such a high brideprice that the marriage of women was often delayed even into their thirties. Moreover, expensive dowries, too, caused delayed marriages among middle- and upper-class families. According to Lan, "Such delayed marriage hurts the harmony of heaven and earth and sooner or later may cause flood and drought. Urgently, women older than twenty-four or -five *sui* must get married within three months. Should anyone disobey, her father and brothers should be punished."[35]

Lan's preoccupation with gender as a solution to Taiwan's crises is even more striking when his memorial is compared to the Taiwan policy proposal of one of his contemporaries. Shen Qiyuan (1675–1763), a native of Jiangsu, while serving as a prefect in Fujian, wrote a memorial on Taiwanese affairs to the emperor in 1727. In his memorial, Shen focused on the easy access to the coasts of Taiwan and the difficulty of regulating immigration from the mainland. He recommended that the government open a legal gateway for law-abiding subjects, which would allow a magistrate to distinguish them from outlaw smugglers. "Anyone who is caught trying to cross secretly will be punished harshly. In this way, the innocent will be distinguished from the guilty, and good subjects will be able to enjoy honest occupations."[36] In Shen's memorial, only one sentence mentioned that "settling down with family members" might help build a peaceful society, but he did not discuss how and why this might be accomplished.

In 1732, family migration to Taiwan was sanctioned for the first time, as part of the major procolonization policies of the late Yongzheng era.[37]

The change in the imperial migration policy may have been influenced by broader concerns about the dangers of single men ("bare sticks") to Confucian family order, for such men had become a threat even in the more developed Lower Yangzi region.[38] In any case, Lan Dingyuan's effort to change the unbalanced sex ratio and calm the turbulence in Taiwan ignored the Confucian ideal of women as cloistered ladies. Lan understood that many Fujian women were not cloistered but worked in the fields or on the coast and overstepped the inner-outer boundary every day. His family migration policy was thus an example of an elite male's compromise between the Confucian ideal of rectifying women's behavior and the practical need to manage the world (*jingshi*).

Yet Lan also sought ultimately to bring women in Taiwan closer to the Confucian ideal. Like ordinary women in Fujian, aboriginal women in Taiwan worked in the fields.[39] In order to transform Taiwanese customs, Lan strongly promoted the Confucian notion of proper women's work: weaving and spinning. According to Lan, mulberry and cotton had not been planted on the island. People were lazy, and women dressed in silk, adorned themselves with jewelry, and then hung around in their doorways, making a spectacle of themselves. Lan recommended that Taiwan be ordered to follow the examples of Zhangzhou and Quanzhou in Fujian and plant kapok (*mumian*), or to collect fiber-producing plants from inland areas and transplant them in Taiwan. "With plenty of hemp and ramie for cloth, women will be able to engage in weaving and spinning. Then diligence and frugality will transform the local customs in Taiwan."[40] In *Women's Learning*, Lan explained that "women's work" simply meant women's chores and family affairs and did not require special "merits" or "achievements." Women's tasks did not need to be complicated or highly skilled; they simply had to keep women hard at work. "Diligent work is important for women's self-cultivation and household management."[41]

With his exhaustive extracts from the Confucian classics, which illustrated to his readers the importance of women's textile production, Lan was in part pointing out the importance of women's contributions to the household economy. But as evidenced in the Lower Yangzi region, women's textile work not only played a significant role in the individual peasant's household economy but also reinforced the gendered labor roles central to Confucian ideals: men tilled and women wove.[42] Lan's efforts to borrow the inland model to spread Confucian economic ideals on the island was likewise intended to have both economic and social effects. By importing proper,

Guotong Li

controlled female role models from the mainland while also rectifying the unruly aborigines through the mainland model of women's work, Lan aimed to transform the island into a civilized society. As in Fujian, the transformation of aboriginal culture would begin with the rectification of women.

Lan also pursued additional strategies of cultural transformation. In addition to his gendered solutions to social instability, he promoted charity schools to attract ambitious young men who would study for the examinations. And since commoners in Taiwan were outsiders to culture (*jiaohua*), Lan recommended regular meetings led by the local gentry to spread imperial edicts and moral instructions among them.[43]

Perhaps sensitive about his own mixed ancestry and anxious to demonstrate his allegiance to Han ideals, Lan showed great concern about the need to assimilate Taiwan's aborigines, who constantly disturbed Han settlers (*min*). His depictions of aborigines presented them as brutal and dangerous beings. He adopted the standard categorizations of aboriginal peoples according to their relationship to Chinese authority, as "cooked" (*shu*, "civilized") or "raw" (*sheng*, "uncivilized").[44] Lan's basic program was to allow the Han settlers to till the lands of aborigines and to use the cooked aborigines to interact (*he*) with the raw, so that eventually the raw would be transformed into the cooked.

Before the Zhu Yigui rebellion in 1721, the general policy in Taiwan had been to control migration through quarantine. Chinese families had been barred from migrating to Taiwan. One of the unintended consequences of this policy was frequent rebellions by Han settlers who had migrated illegally. The government recruited a militia from loyal tribes of aborigines to fight against both aborigine revolts and Chinese rebels. In return, the land rights of loyal aborigines were protected by the government.[45]

Lan, however, believed the way to civilize aborigines was to start by ordering them to till their untilled lands, and he challenged both the quarantine policy and the government's protection of aboriginal land. In Zhanghua county in northern Taiwan, there was plenty of untilled land. Because the land rights belonged to aborigines, the local magistrate had prohibited migrant people from tilling the land. Lan argued that since the county seat had been established in Zhanghua, it was ridiculous to leave the land uncultivated. "If [we] care about aborigines' land rights, then why was the whole of Taiwan taken over from aborigines? If it needs to be restored, then we cannot afford it."[46] Lan urged the local magistrate to order aborigines to cultivate the lands into gardens and farms within one year. After that time, lands left uncultivated should be opened for settlers to till. The tillers would become owners of the land or pay a rent to the aborigines for the right to till that land.

The tilling of aboriginal lands significantly transformed the relationship between the Han settlers and the aborigines. On the one hand, the policy was promulgated under the authority of the imperial government, and state power penetrated the society of the island aborigines as never before. It was a showcase for the new occupying imperial authority to signal to the aborigines that their continued ignorance of or challenge to imperial authority might lead to the loss of their lands.

On the other hand, the policy of insisting that aboriginal lands be tilled also encouraged intermarriage between Han settlers and aboriginal women. John Robert Shepherd shows that there was a high demand for aborigine wives among Han frontiersmen.[47] This happened especially because, in an uxorilocal marriage, a Chinese son-in-law could "eventually gain control of the land inherited by his wife."[48] Although the Chinese men who married aboriginal women might have needed to adapt to some aboriginal customs, they still raised their sons in the Chinese style and transmitted their lands to their sons, not to a matrilineal heir as had been the aboriginal custom. Intermarriage between aboriginal daughters and Chinese men became an influential channel for transmitting aboriginal land to Chinese settlers, and Chinese culture to aboriginal communities.[49] Of course, it is also true that this provoked unhappy, devalued aboriginal males into revolt in some cases.

Lan's concern to assimilate tribal peoples is also evident in his recommendations for solving aboriginal problems in the southwest border provinces (bian sheng) of China. He divided the Miao aborigines by social status, into tribal chieftains (tusi) and tribal people (tumin). After describing how tribal chieftains bullied their people without mercy, he recommended a complex policy of "replacing native chieftains with rotating officials" (gaitu guiliu).[50] He suggested that tribal people, just like Han people, ought to be blessed by the emperor's benevolence; accordingly, should any tribal chieftain bully his people, he would be punished by loss of his lands and people. Lan concluded that tribal people who did not want to bear their masters' abuse should be allowed to change their registered status from aborigine to Han (gai tuji wei hanmin).[51] According to Lan, seizing their lands and people was critical to diminishing the influence of tribal chieftains. This recommendation was similar to his proposal on tilling the lands of aborigines in Taiwan, but it operated on a different pretext. Inspired by his social status analysis, the policy differed significantly by allowing tribal people to change their registered ethnic status, an idea that may have stemmed from Lan's own ethnic heritage.[52] Lan recommended that the emperor welcome tribal people's assimilation into "the culture of the dynasty."[53] The advantage to the government would be an increase in land and head tax revenue; and the advantage to tribal people would be that members from their next generation would be allowed to sit for the examinations (just as the Lan family had).

The two "civilizing" models in his aboriginal policies—top-down state assimilation and bottom-up aboriginal acculturation—showcase Lan's talents in statecraft. The state inserted imperial authority deeply into the frontier society or border provinces through the seizure of aboriginal land and power by local administrative offices. In addition, Lan's policies encouraged interaction among the aborigines (between cooked and raw) and Han Chinese and eventually led to intermarriages. The advantages of an advanced commercial economy and the benevolent governing of Han local officials would, in Lan's theory, encourage in aborigines a self-motivated embrace of "the culture of the dynasty." Significantly, Lan's unique view of the importance of gender relations in frontier society was the linchpin of his proposal.

REDEFINING WOMEN'S LEARNING

Lan Dingyuan advocated that women should work hard, as a critical aspect of their self-cultivation and household management. Governing the state came through ordering the household, and ordering the household began with regulating women. Lan's theory and his proposed policies were permeated by his recognition of the power of female behavior. His mixed heritage had prompted him to see the Han woman as the role model for transmitting culture in his family and the She woman as the breadwinner who maintained the household economy.[54] In contrast to the views of some Lower Yangzi literati, who appreciated women's talents in literary composition, Lan Dingyuan was concerned with how to harness female talent for the use of the civilizing project.[55]

Lan's views on women as a civilizing force were in many respects parallel with his views of aborigines in Taiwan. Just as he classified aborigines into "raw" and "cooked," Lan divided women into exemplary and unregulated. His writing stressed how to use exemplary women as role models to guide unregulated women. Similarly, in his policy proposals, Lan encouraged interaction between "raw" and "cooked" aborigines, expecting the "cooked" to lead the "raw" in the "civilizing process" (by cultivating their lands and paying taxes to the imperial government). Lan also promoted women's textile production among the natives (both aborigines and early Han settlers) in Taiwan. He believed that, just as "cooked" aborigines would lead the "raw," transformed women would lead uncivilized men into civilization. His enforcement of marriage for "aging" female natives and the reclamation of land rights among aborigines, within a certain time period, encouraged interaction and intermarriage between aborigines and Han settlers, all of which contributed to the dynasty's civilizing project.

Interestingly, Lan was not the only one who attempted to liken women to aborigines. Liang Qichao, a nineteenth-century reformer, also saw such a parallel. In his 1898 reform proclamation, Liang harshly criticized Chinese women as dependents relying on men for their livelihoods, saying that women were "idle like vagabonds and ignorant like tribal people."[56] Although the two men had different views of women's proper roles, this comment reveals that, like Lan, Liang believed women needed men to "rectify" their behavior.

Over the course of the nineteenth century, both Chinese reformers and Western observers of China had concluded that the behavior of women and the treatment accorded to women were measures of the level of civilization of a given society. As Chinese civilization encountered profound challenges by the Western powers, Chinese reformers came to adopt Western perspectives on the proper roles of women. From this new perspective, their predecessors' attempts to confine female energies to the home became an important target: the exemplary women praised by Lan became symbols of and scapegoats for the backwardness of the country.

Yet for all their critique of Lan, the reformers shared an important legacy with him. Although Lan's civilizing project was designed to keep women at home to reinforce Confucian ideals, and the modernization project was intended to break down the inner-outer boundary and direct female energies toward work outside the home, the assumption in both cases was that women's behavior was critical to the polity. Just as Lan wanted to make women work as part of the civilizing project of the dynasty, the later reformers wanted women to work as part of the nation-building project stimulated by the modernization process. Their common ground was to make women work. The nineteenth-century reformers ignored educated women's consciousness of the polity and continued a model of male leadership and hegemony over female behavior into modern times.[57]

Lan Dingyuan's *Nüxue*, and its entanglement of gender and ethnicity in the migrant society across the Taiwan Strait, modifies our understanding of women's roles and women's learning. It shows that women's work encompassed both the literary efforts of educated elite women and the efforts of lower-class women on the frontier. In the eighteenth century, virtuous women who worked for the Manchu civilizing project included not only those like the scholar-poet Wanyan Yun Zhu, who knowledgeably compiled a women's anthology, but also unnamed women who migrated with their families to settle in Taiwan. As they tied the "bare sticks" to the settlement, they established role models for aboriginal women to emulate. Without lauding either the success of Lan's procolonization policy or the emigration of Fujian women to the island, we can, by looking through the lenses of gender and ethnicity, celebrate the recuperation of women's stories from the narratives of elite men who sought to control them.

NOTES

1. According to the twentieth-century historian Chen Dongyuan, *Women's Learning* was the earliest advice book for women published in the Qing dynasty: *Zhongguo funü shenghuoshi*, 275. The text has prefaces dated 1712, 1717, and 1718.
2. Mann, *Precious Records*, 7.
3. Ibid.; Ko, "The Body as Attire."
4. Mann, *Precious Records*.
5. Elliott, "Manchu Widows and Ethnicity in Qing China"; Elliott, *The Manchu Way*.
6. Harrell, *Cultural Encounters on China's Ethnic Frontiers*.
7. Mann, *Precious Records*, 225; Mann, *The Talented Women of the Zhang Family*, 101–6.
8. Furth, review of Susan Mann's *The Talented Women of the Zhang Family*.
9. Rowe, *Saving the World*, 426; Ho, "The Cultivation of Female Talent."
10. The juncture between women as the "other" and the colonized as the "other" has recently drawn many scholars' attention. "Imperialism and gender were closely linked in a number of ways." Women were "alienated" as "uncivilized" under the male gaze, just as the colonized were alienated under the colonial gaze. See Hunt, introduction to Hunt and Lessard, *Women and the Colonial Gaze*, 1–5.
11. Hummel, *Eminent Chinese of the Ch'ing Period*, 441.
12. Lan, *Nüxue*.
13. Ho, "The Cultivation of Female Talent."
14. Lan, "Song Lao Zunsan ling Zhaowen xu," in *Luzhou chuji*, 6.11b–13b. All translations are mine.
15. Huang Liuhong (1633–93), the author of a popular handbook for magistrates, complained, "Women of prominent families go on outings as a pastime. Dressed in

finery and adorned with jewelry, they frequent temples and other places. On the pretext of worshiping Buddha and burning incense, they seek liaisons with dissipated youths in the secret passages of the monasteries." *A Complete Book Concerning Happiness*, 608.

16   Lan, "Chaozhou fengsu kao," in *Luzhou chuji*, 14.30b.

17   "Enduring frost" was a common way of characterizing the abstemious lives of faithful widows.

18   Lan, "Zhengmu wanshi ba," in *Luzhou chuji*, 16.14a–b.

19   Lan, "Lin lienü zhuan," in *Luzhou chuji*, 9.9b–11b.

20   Lan, "Zhenjie Wangtaijun zhuan," in *Luzhou chuji*, 9.11b–13b.

21   Ding, "Houji," unpaginated.

22   Zheng, "Nüjiao," 8.20b–22a.

23   Lan, preface (*xu*) to *Nüxue*, unpaginated.

24   This refers to a women's obedience to her father, husband, and son over the course of her life, and the four virtues were a woman's morality, speech, behavior, and work.

25   The Qing dynasty scholar Chen Hongmou once approvingly identified women's nature as obedient. In the early twentieth century, Chen Dongyuan satirized him, saying, "The home-grown chicken cannot fly; then would our Hongmou also recognize such as chicken's nature?" Chen, *Zhongguo funü shenghuoshi*, 277.

26   Handlin, *Action in Late Ming Thought*; Mann, *Precious Records*; and Rowe, *Saving the World*.

27   Rowe, *Saving the World*, 428.

28   I have discussed the interests of Fujian women in the wider social and political world in "Imagining History and the State" and "Reopening the Fujian Coast," chap. 6. See also Mann, "The Lady and the State."

29   Mann, *Precious Records*, 28–29.

30   Judge, *The Precious Raft of History*, 122.

31   Zhu Yigui, a Han settler from southern Fujian, led a rebellion against the Manchu government in 1721, aiming at recovering the Ming government in Taiwan.

32   Lan, "Yu Jingpu jiaxiong lun taibian shu," in *Luzhou chuji*, 2.12a–13a.

33   Lan, "Yu Wu guancha lun zhi Taiwan shiyishu," in *Luzhou chuji*, 2.18a–19a.

34   Lan, "Jingli Taiwan di'er," in *Luzhou zoushu*, 5a–10a.

35   Lan, "Yu Wu guancha lun zhi Taiwan shiyishu," in *Luzhou chuji*, 2.18a.

36   Shen, "Tiao chen Taiwan shi yi zhuang."

37   There is no evidence that the emperor was responding to Lan's suggestions. In any case, the change was short-lived: in 1740, Hao Yulin convinced the emperor to end the legal family migration to Taiwan, and the major procolonization policies of the late Yongzheng era were reversed. See Shepherd, *Statecraft and Political Economy*, 18.

38   Sommer, *Sex, Law, and Society*; Theiss, *Disgraceful Matters*.

39   Emma J. Teng's work shows the unique gendered labor roles of the aborigines: men hunting and women farming. See *Taiwan's Imagined Geography*, 180–81.

40   Lan, "Yu Wu guancha lun zhi Taiwan shiyishu," in *Luzhou chuji*, 2.22b–23a.

41   Lan, *Nüxue*, 6.24a–b.

42 Mann, *Precious Records*; Bray, *Technology and Gender.*

43 Lan, "Yu Wu guancha lun zhi Taiwan shiyishu," in *Luzhou chuji*, 2.19b–20b.

44 Teng, *Taiwan's Imagined Geography*, 122–40.

45 Shepherd, *Statecraft and Political Economy*, 15–16.

46 Lan, "Yu Wu guancha lun zhi Taiwan shiyishu," in *Luzhou chuji*, 2.24a–b.

47 Shepherd, *Statecraft and Political Economy*, 386.

48 Ibid., 387.

49 Ibid.

50 "Replacing native chieftains with rotating officials" means the central government appointed Han officials to govern the border areas where multiethnic groups lived together. This effectively prevented rebellion led by native chieftains and tied the border areas to the central government in late imperial times.

51 Lan, "Lun biansheng miaoman shiyishu," in *Luzhou chuji*, 1.23a–25b.

52 Some ancestral members of the Lan family had once changed their registration, from their original place of birth to other counties. See Li, "Reopening the Fujian Coast."

53 Here I use the term *assimilation* instead of *acculturation* because the tribal people changed not only their social customs but also their identity.

54 Li, "Reopening the Fujian Coast," chap. 3.

55 One might argue that these two views were related to class differences (literacy and morality for the upper classes, hard work for the lower classes). However, Lan also praised an illiterate peasant woman for seeking moral achievement, and hard work was one of the four virtues for every woman regardless of her social status.

56 Liang Qichao, "Bian fa tong yi lun nüxue," 38–39.

57 Both Joan Judge and Nanxiu Qian point out that the gendered nationalist agenda rejected "past expressions of feminine subjectivity" and dictated a cultural critique of women's matters. See Judge, "Reforming the Feminine," 178; Qian, "Revitalizing the *Xianyuan* (Worthy Ladies) Tradition," 440.

CHAPTER THREE

COLLECTING
MASCULINITY

Merchants and Gender Performance
in Eighteenth-Century China

Yulian Wu

I N the last three decades, gender studies, and especially women's studies, has been one of the most fruitful areas of Chinese history. Although
the field is flourishing, and the incorporation of gender perspectives into
analyses of male subjects is necessary to understanding gender relations,
only a few scholars of China have taken gender as a category of analysis
to explore the identity of men.[1] Over the past decade, the work of the few
scholars who have examined Chinese men through the perspective of gender studies has demonstrated the complicated processes of negotiating or
establishing masculinity within specific historical periods.[2] Beverly Bossler
locates a discussion of masculinity within the social transformation from
the Tang to the Yuan dynasties, showing how the model of the ideal literatus transformed from the *feng liu* (romantic) hero to "the serious bureaucrat
or the self-cultivated scholar."[3] Susan Mann's pioneering research on male

bonds in the Ming and Qing dynasties has demonstrated how Ming-Qing elites used early "Confucian" notions of friendship to "express their own ideas about manhood."[4] Mann stresses that male friendship improved men's intellectual lives and emotional connections and provided an important site for men to identify themselves as men and thus to construct their masculinity.[5] Conversely, though also focusing on late imperial China, Martin Huang discusses how male writers negotiated their male identity by using women as a defining "other" in cultural discourses.[6]

All these studies have been invaluable in demonstrating how educated literati, including both those who passed the examinations and those who failed, identified themselves as men within specific historical contexts.[7] Yet the gender identities of merchants, who were a significant presence in elite circles in late imperial China, have not received the scholarly attention they deserve. Of interest here is how manhood was constructed and negotiated in the eighteenth century by merchants who originally came from Huizhou but who lived in the urban centers of the Lower Yangzi area. Some of these Huizhou businessmen, as scholars have demonstrated, constituted one of the wealthiest merchant groups in eighteenth-century China. They were well educated and devoted to the cultural activities of the literati.[8]

The salt merchant Wang Qishu (1728–98) was famous as a collector of both carved stamps, or seals, and women's poetry. He constructed his gender identity through his collecting projects, which allowed him to display masculine qualities such as participation in broad social networks with other male elites, travel experience, and financial resources. A study of Wang Qishu's collecting projects provides useful insights into the gender identity of merchants and reveals broader shifts in male gender identities in late imperial China.

MASCULINITY AND THE STUDY OF MERCHANTS

What was masculinity in late imperial China? This question reveals an interesting but also frustrating phenomenon: there is no single word in Chinese that can accurately be translated as the word *masculinity*. The absence of terminology, of course, does not automatically imply the absence of the concept. In fact, sources from late imperial China, such as elites' writings, popular literature, and even genealogies, frequently talked about what a man—often referred to as *nanzi*, *dazhangfu* or *zhangfu*, *yingxiong* (heroic male), *haohan* (stalwart), or even *shi* (scholar)—should or should not do. The

Yulian Wu

idea of a fully realized man, in other words, was well discussed in varying contexts and was of critical concern to men.

This striking contrast—the nonexistence of the word *masculinity* and the ample discussions of men's masculine behaviors—also reveals that there is no singular definition of masculinity. Instead, masculinity is a complicated notion that contains many components and perspectives.[9] Previous scholarship that has explored the various meanings of the term in Chinese culture supports a complex definition of masculinity. Kam Louie, for instance, divides Chinese masculinity into two general categories: *wen* (the literary or civilized) and *wu* (the martial), traits commonly used to describe men's behavior in both the historical and contemporary periods.[10] Martin Huang's research highlights varying models of masculinity represented in late imperial cultural discourses, including sages, macho heroes, and romantic scholars.[11]

With all these models providing different traits through which a man could define his gender identity, male individuals, based on their own status, career, and age, would likely have had different conceptions of what an ideal man should or could be. In other words, when a broad spectrum of masculine traits and behaviors were available to men, a man could express his gender awareness by identifying himself with particular masculine qualities.

If male-identity construction was a process of presenting specific masculine traits, the audience for these displays was mainly other men. The connection between masculinity and men's interaction with other men was rooted in the strict segregation of sexes that characterized many aspects of China's late imperial society. In this society, women were supposed to stay inside the house, while men spent most of their social time with other men outside the domestic sphere.[12] In addition, discussion of ideal values for men most often appeared in writings that male elites composed for other men. In other words, the primary sources—written and read primarily by educated men—also reveal that late imperial elites discussed their masculinity with, and displayed it to, other men.[13]

While educated literati expressed their gender identity through writing, the wealthy merchants in late imperial China left much less textual evidence. Even the limited sources, however, still show that merchants were indeed aware of this issue of masculinity. Some of the Ming-Qing merchants' own statements—recorded in their biographies—clearly point to their desire to be successful *men* rather than successful people. For instance, Ni Mulin, a wealthy merchant from Huizhou, "studied Confucianism but failed to fulfill his ambition [to pass the examinations and become and official]." In the end, Ni gave up his studies and decided to be a merchant. He is quoted as asserting, "When a male child was born, people shot the rubus arrows off a bow of mulberry wood to heaven, earth, and the four cardinal points [*sang hu peng shi liu*; to symbolize that a male child should go far out into the world].[14] Therefore, [a man] should either obtain nobility or become wealthy [*bu gui ze fu*]. How can I be satisfied with only using a brush and staying in my hometown for the rest of my life?"[15] By explicitly using the term "a male child" (*nan zi*) and quoting the classical reference *sang hu peng shi liu* from the *Book of Rites*—which described the proper ambitions of males—Ni clearly stated his ideas about proper male behavior: he believed that a *man* should either obtain fame or wealth.[16]

At the same time, Ni's statement reveals an intertwining relationship between status performance and gender performance. Ni studied the Confucian classics in order to enhance his social status by passing the civil service examination. Later, owing to his unsuccessful experience with the examinations, he decided to become a merchant to pursue wealth as a way of achieving success as a man. His story reminds historians of a familiar theme in scholarship on late imperial China—namely, merchants' status negotiation. This scholarship often analyzes merchants from the perspective of social hierarchy, exploring how they employed different strategies to enhance their status. Ni's statement, however, shows that what has been overlooked in this analysis is the merchants' eagerness to assert a masculine identity. No matter what method he used to climb the social ladder, whether by obtaining nobility or becoming wealthy, Ni wanted to be a successful *man*. Since privileged social occupations were exclusively dominated by men in imperial China, a man's status performance was inextricable from his gender performance. In addition, because merchants had less-privileged status relative to scholarly elites, merchants may have been more motivated to project themselves as capable men by stressing their ability to demonstrate masculine traits.[17]

Ni Mulin was, of course, not the only merchant who sought to project a masculine identity. In fact in the late Ming, it was common for merchants to claim that they chose to do business because they wanted to become a *dazhangfu* or *zhangfu* (great man) or a *nanzi* (man).[18] The merchants' use of these specific words reveals the existence of a merchant masculine identity in late imperial China. It is in this context that Wang Qishu expressed his gender identity.

Wang was born to a successful salt merchant family from She county in Huizhou prefecture.[19] He prepared to take the civil service examinations but eventually chose to enter the salt business in Hangzhou because of "the burden of family responsibilities" (*ji yan jia lei*).[20] Wang came to be recognized as a merchant, poet, official, editor, and publisher.[21] He was most well known, however, for being a collector. Wang was primarily a collector of the carved stamps, or seals, that had been used for centuries to put official markings on documents. He collected thousands of seals and published more than twenty catalogs of imprints (*yin pu*) from his seal collections. Thanks to Wang's endeavors in seal collecting, even his contemporaries most often identified him as a seal collector.[22] Additionally, Wang was famous for selecting, editing, and publishing one of the largest anthologies of women's poems in the Qing dynasty, *Collected Fragrances* (Xie fang ji). This anthology included not

FIGURE 3.1. A portrait of Wang Qishu when he was twenty-one *sui*, from Wang Qishu, *Seal Impressions from the Flying Swan Studio* (Fei hong tang yin pu), published in the Qianlong period (1736–96). Courtesy of Harvard-Yenching Library at Harvard University.

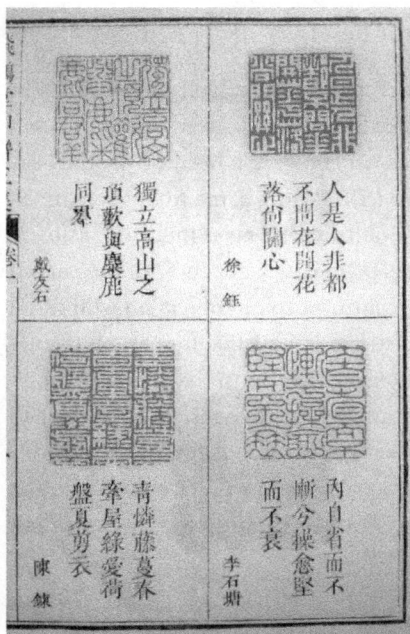

FIGURE 3.2. Seal impressions with explanations of inscribed characters. From Wang Qishu, *Seal Impressions from the Flying Swan Studio* (Fei hong tang yin pu), published in the Qianlong period (1736–96). Courtesy of Harvard-Yenching Library at Harvard University.

only women's poems but also the biographies of female poets. For our purposes, therefore, the concept of "collecting" includes the collection of physical objects (i.e., seals) as well as that of texts, such as poetry and biographies.[23]

Wang Qishu was one of the most famous merchant collectors in the high Qing, but he was by no means the only one. During the late Ming, when economic prosperity provoked an upsurge in the consumption of luxury items, the activity of collecting began to be widely practiced among wealthy people.[24] The wars of the Ming-Qing transition, although damaging to the economy, created an environment in which collecting culture reached its new peak, in the high Qing era.[25] After the conquest, the new Manchu rulers of the Qing dynasty immediately carried out policies to implement economic recovery. The improved economy and accumulated wealth provided an ideal environment for luxury consumption. In this context, various social groups, including the emperor, princes, scholars, merchants, and artisans, assembled collections through gift exchange, commerce, and patronage. Collecting thus became a popular activity in the eighteenth century. Huizhou salt merchants, who constituted one of the wealthiest merchant groups in this period, played an important role in high-Qing collecting culture. Wang Qishu was one of them.

Yulian Wu

There is no doubt that Wang's collecting project can be understood as a strategy of the sort that merchants often used to claim scholar/literati status. The practice of accumulating cultural objects, such as books, calligraphy, and paintings, had a long history in China and was considered elegant.[26] During the late Ming, possessing precious objects and the connoisseurship of them had become a mark of literati's privileged status.[27] It is clear that Wang's collecting project helped him acquire and display his *wen* (culture). Collecting seals and other scholarly objects, such as books and antiques, was a display of refined taste. Patronizing talented artisans such as seal carvers appeared to mimic what literati did. To a certain extent, then, Wang's cultivation of social networks with other famous literati can be seen as a classic status-negotiation strategy.

These activities, however, need not be interpreted merely as status performance. I argue that Wang's quest for *wen* was intertwined with his quest for masculinity. Wang's collecting projects embodied a variety of masculine traits and allowed to express his gender identity. Through his collecting projects, Wang asserted his own manhood and promoted new models of the ideal man.

DISPLAYING A BROAD SOCIAL NETWORK

In late imperial China, having many male friends was considered a sign of masculinity. As Susan Mann argues, Ming-Qing male intellectuals' writings stressed that "becoming a true gentleman cannot be a solitary project. Instead, a man becomes truly learned and morally developed, emotionally fulfilled and socially secure, in the process of interacting with and bonding with other men."[28] In other words, Ming-Qing scholarly elites believed that having male friends was an essential way for a man to become a true gentleman. Martin Huang also notes that "to have many male friends was often considered an important badge of masculinity," because the ability to obtain male friendship showed "a man's ability to travel and meet other men outside his family and beyond his hometown."[29]

Wang Qishu, like the men described in Mann and Huang's scholarship, was eager to construct a broad network with male literati. The main channel for Wang's social networking was his collection. Collecting seals and women's poems generated common interests among Wang and other male elites, allowing Wang to build up male friendships with men he called *tong-ren* (someone who shares my interests and hobbies), *tonghao* (someone who shares my interests), or *tongzhi* (someone who shares my ambitions). Constructing and displaying these male networks through his collecting projects facilitated Wang's effort to craft his male identity.

Constructing Networks through Seal Collection

In the late Ming, because seals represented aesthetic attainment, men of culture began to consider them to be valuable objects for artistic enjoyment.[30] During the high Qing era, the popularity of philological studies (*kaozheng*), a new intellectual movement that aimed to explore the original meanings of Confucius classics, further imbued seal collection with new intellectual value. The scholars of philological studies aimed to unlock the meaning of the ancient classics. To achieve this goal, they needed to correctly recognize and understand the meaning of ancient characters. To do so, these scholars employed "a set of epistemologically unified techniques," including paleography, the study of ancient characters written in seal style (*zhuan shu*) from before the Han dynasty.[31] Accordingly, seals became a valuable philological resource.

This increasing scholarly interest in seals helped Wang establish a broad network of relationships with male literati who appreciated the scholarly value of seals. In order to highlight the philological value of his seal collection, Wang always emphasized the connection between seals and epigraphical study. Since the scholars of philological studies believed that bronze and stone carvings provided reliable sources for understanding the ancient classics, Wang connected his love of seals to an appreciation of the study of bronze and stone.[32] He said, "The great writings by ancient people were always carved in bronze and stone and thus were able to be preserved forever. The [writings] that recorded official titles and names were preserved by carving them on seals. When Ouyang Xun saw the *Suo jing* stele, he stayed and gazed up at the stele for three days and could not leave. Regarding seal carving, I have the same obsession. I have searched for [these seals] using any and all means, preserved them in their bamboo cases, and made vermilion impressions of them."[33]

Here, Wang's statement first drew a parallel between the inscriptions carved on the bronze and stone and the official titles and names carved on seals in ancient times. In doing so, he skillfully implied a similar significance in seal carving for the study of philological research. Wang's ability to read ancient characters demonstrated his knowledge of philology. In comparing

Yulian Wu

FIGURE 3.3. Impression from a seal that the master carver Ding Jing carved for Wang Qishu. The inscription *(left)*, which was carved into the side of the seal, explains how Wang requested the seal from Ding. From Wang Jiading and Wang Qishu, *Surviving Traces for the Flying Swan* (Fei hong yi ji), likely published in 1937. Courtesy of the C. V. Starr East Asian Library, University of California, Berkeley.

his passion for seals to that of the famous Tang dynasty calligrapher Ouyang Xun (557–641), who obsessively studied steles, Wang demonstrated his own interest in and knowledge of the aesthetics of calligraphy.

Based on this shared passion for seals and philological study, Wang was able to construct relationships with male literati and to identify with them as "like-minded" friends.[34] As Wang stated in his editorial notes for his *Collection of Ancient Seal Impressions* (Ji gu yin cun), he frequently obtained old seals from the "precious collections of people who share my interests" (*de zhi tong hao zhen cang*).[35] In addition to collecting antique seals, Wang also requested seals from contemporary artists, which helped him to extend his connections to other elites. For instance, one of the most famous seal carvers of the day, Ding Jing (1695–1765), mentioned that Wang had always "sought seals" (*suo ke*) from him.[36] Through the process of requesting seals, Wang not only displayed his passion for seal carving to his elite fellows but also expanded his "like-minded" community.

Patronizing seal carvers—especially those in economic straits—also helped Wang to expand his networks. Many impoverished seal carvers became guests or retainers in Wang's house, where they could access seal impression books, appreciate Wang's seal collection, and carve new seals.[37] Wang also invited wealthier, more famous seal carvers to live in his house, where they not only carved seals for Wang but also helped him edit and publish his seal-impression books. They were given substantial compensation for this.[38]

Apart from expanding his "like-minded" community, Wang was also eager to display his male friendships to other literati. His intention to demonstrate his networks can best be seen in a collection of biographies of seal carvers that he wrote and compiled.[39] This biographical collection was designed to introduce the seal carvers whose seals Wang had selected and published in his *Seal Impressions from the Flying Swan Studio* (Fei hong tang yin pu). The title of the biographical collection, *Collection of Biographies of the Seal Carvers of Flying Swan Studio* (Fei hong tang yin ren zhuan), inherently implies that these male seal carvers were connected with Wang's Flying Swan studio. Moreover, each biography highlights Wang's personal relationships with the seal carvers. Wang not only recorded in detail how he patronized the seal carvers but also provided detailed information on how he met them on various occasions, such as at a friend's house, in his hometown of Huizhou, or even on the road. Although in many cases Wang had met with individual carvers only once, his narratives suggest that their common interest in seals had made them good friends. This biographical collection, therefore, masterfully paints a picture of Wang as surrounded by various talented seal carvers.[40]

Collecting Women's Poems as a Fashionable Activity

As with seals, Wang was able to use women's poems to facilitate his connections with other male elites. In the Ming and Qing dynasties, an increasing number of literati began to collect, edit, and publish women's poems as anthologies, for different reasons. Some of them tried to canonize women's writing and thus repeatedly associated women's anthologies with the classical canon. Some editors, such as Yuan Mei, aimed to promote women's literary innovations. Still other elites were most interested in extolling women poets' virtue.[41]

Yulian Wu

The increasing number of women's poetry anthologies points to the fact that by the eighteenth century, women's poems had become a valuable "objects" to be collected. Wang consciously participated in this fashion. In his editorial notes for *Collected Fragrances*, Wang articulated two major reasons for collecting women's poems. First, he intended to record and circulate talented women's poems because he appreciated women's literary innovations. In addition, he aimed to promote the moral function of female poets.[42]

As with collecting seals, Wang's efforts to compile women's anthologies allowed him to share his passions with other male literati, those who likewise appreciated women's talent or admired their morality.[43] This common interest, too, provided a foundation upon which Wang could construct broad networks with other men. In this case, Wang identified these connections as *tongzhi,* implying that he and his friends shared the same high purpose. He called on his friends and especially "men who share my high purpose" to send him women's poems they "saw or heard of" (*jian wen*).[44]

Since most talented women who could write poems came from scholarly families, collecting women's poems allowed Wang to connect with male literati who had talented mothers, wives, or sisters. For instance, Wang used a request for poetry by the mother of Jiang Shiquan (1725–85) to forge a connection with Jiang, one of the foremost literary figures of the Qianlong period and a recognized master of poetry and drama.[45]

That the willingness and even eagerness of male literati to publish women's poetry motivated them to connect with Wang is revealed in Wang's records. He tells numerous stories about how literati "asked me to select these poems for the anthology [*zhu xuan*]." Some men strove to publish their female relatives' poems in order to fulfill their filial piety and promote their family's reputation.[46] Others intended to publish women's poems to promote the reputation of the locality.[47] Finally, promoting women's morality was always an important reason for elites to preserve women's writing. Many elites, therefore, sent Wang poems written by chaste widows.[48]

Wang Qishu was also interested in recording and publicizing how he collected these poems from other male elites. All the stories just described were recorded in and ultimately circulated through Wang's own writings. Many descriptions of how Wang collected poems initially appeared in his anecdotal collection titled *The Leisure Records from a Water Transportation Official* (Shui cao qing xia lu).[49] Later, when he was compiling the biographies of female poets for *Collected Fragrances*, he constantly cited stories from this anecdotal collection. That he referred to his own book in a grander and more popular compilation certainly reveals Wang's intention to promote his own writings. At the same time, by circulating anecdotes about how he collected women's poems through other male literati, he also displayed his extensive social networks.

Wang's effort to depict himself as a man with many male friends was ultimately successful. Contemporary literati, including prominent scholars, acknowledged Wang's networking abilities. In a poem to commend Wang's effort to publish *Collected Fragrances*, the famous scholar Zhao Yi (1727–1814) noted that "Wang's social network is on par with people of former times, and his anthology also promotes [the names] of beauties."[50] Yuan Mei commented that Wang liked to "befriend famous scholarly gentlemen" (*ai jiao ming shi*).[51] Evidently, Wang's ability to collect many male friends was acknowledged and appreciated by other men.

BEING ACTIVE OUTSIDE THE DOMESTIC SPHERE

Traveling afar (*yuan you*) had always been an admirable activity for elite men, as is evident in the saying "A true man has a lofty ambition that reaches the four corners of the earth" (*zhangfu zhi zai sifang*).[52] The gender connotation associated with traveling also stems from the following excerpt from "familial principles" (*nei ze*) in the classic *Book of Rites*: "When a son and heir to the ruler of a state was born . . . the master of the archers then took a bow of mulberry wood, and six arrows of the wild rubus, and shot toward heaven, earth, and the four cardinal points."[53] This birth ceremony was held exclusively for male children. Shooting six arrows of wild rubus from a mulberry-wood bow in different directions symbolized that men should travel far to achieve accomplishment. This quotation thus provided the theoretical foundation for the masculine connotation of travel.[54] The connection between this gendered ideal of travel and the Confucian orthodoxy of the separation of "inner" and "outer" social realms was also obvious. According to the ideology of gender separation, men were responsible for the outer world and women belonged to the inner space. Traveling afar thus became an embodiment of masculinity.[55]

To be sure, this gendered meaning of traveling did not betoken an absolute division between the inner and the outer spheres. In reality, it was not unusual for Chinese women to cross this boundary: women did travel under certain circumstances.[56] The concern here, however, is ideological. Travel to pursue success was identified as an essentially male endeavor.[57] The connec-

Yulian Wu

tion between traveling and proper manly ambition made traveling part of the social conception of being a man.

One important part of collection ventures was taking trips. A collector had to go to various places to look for, evaluate, and obtain a large number of precious objects. Wang Qishu was no exception. As he stated, he often found old seals in the homes of other private collectors or in antique markets: "Either in the houses of collectors who were fond of ancient things, or in the antique markets, when I saw seals and confirmed that they were not forgeries, I was willing to spend ten pieces of gold or a string of pearls in exchange for them."[58] This statement, on the face of it, demonstrates Wang's love of antiques, an important value for cultured men. Yet it also implies that Wang, as a collector, was active outside of the domestic sphere.

Wang also traveled, and talked about how he traveled, to different places. Because of his contributions to the imperial treasury, he received an official position from the court and served in Beijing for several years.[59] Many times he traveled back to Huizhou to visit tombs or deal with family-related affairs. He also liked to travel in his leisure time, either to take vacations or to visit friends. His ability to conduct trips, short or long, allowed him to collect objects from various places.[60]

It was through his collecting projects that Wang was able to display his extensive travel experience to his male fellows and thereby win their admiration. His friend Shen Chu was impressed by Wang's collection of women's poems. In his preface to *Collected Fragrances*, Shen praised Wang for collecting, in the anthology, poems by more than two thousand female authors. When Shen asked how he was able to do this, Wang reportedly answered, "I was devoted to doing this. Wherever my feet landed, I collected stories from the past. Whenever there were good poems circulating, I always recorded and preserved them."[61] The words that Wang used in his answer, "wherever my feet landed" (*zu ji suo zhi*), depict a vivid image of Wang traveling on the road.

Shen Chu was by no means the only person who celebrated Wang's trips. In his preface for one of Wang's seal-impression compilations, Wang's friend Shao Daye explained that, owing to Wang's addiction to collecting seals, "wherever the wheel tracks took him, he always sought [them]."[62] Zhang Mei, who composed a preface for *Seal Impressions from the Flying Swan Studio*, also praised the fact that "wherever he traveled, [Wang] tried his best to collect [seals]." Because of this, according to Zhang, Wang was able to collect more than ten thousand seals made by contemporary seal carvers.[63]

All these authors, including Wang and his male friends, used the Chinese character *ji*—which refers to a footprint or wheel track—to describe Wang's collecting efforts. Through this word, Wang's collecting project was well situated in the context of travel. The fact that Wang's friends paid special attention to his trips in the limited space of their prefaces displays their admiration for his broad travels.

While the classical social norms of "inner" and "outer" separation applauded men's activities outside the domestic sphere, the rising influence of philological studies in eighteenth-century China also encouraged men to pursue their ambition to travel afar. As Benjamin Elman argues, "Qing literati stressed exacting research, rigorous analysis, and the collection of impartial evidence drawn from ancient artifacts and historical documents and texts."[64] This new scholarly movement to use evidence from ancient artifacts inspired elites' interests in newly discovered steles and bronzes. It also encouraged elites to go to faraway and unknown places to seek out these ancient artifacts themselves. Accordingly, a great number of elite antiquarians devoted themselves to traveling.[65] As the influence of philological study greatly expanded in the high Qing period, devotion to such study became another aspect of ideal manhood. Wang's display of his traveling experience expressed his desire to pattern himself on this new model of the ideal man.

WEALTH: A NEW STANDARD FOR MASCULINITY

The exploration of Wang's collecting enterprise brings us to the question of the connection between masculinity and wealth. The act of collecting itself implies affluence: the collector needed enough wealth for numerous purchases and enough space to store the commodities. Wang's extensive seal publications were, of course, a testament to the financial resources that allowed him to possess these objects. While male bonds and traveling afar had a long-established history as essential components of elite masculinity, wealth per se did not. It was even disdained by Confucian ideology, which scorned the act of pursuing profit. This situation, however, underwent a change in late imperial China.

The biographies of merchants, which had greatly increased in number since the late Ming, provide useful insights into shifts in male gender identities. The evidence reveals that in the context of the economic revolution of the Ming and Qing dynasties, the ability to accumulate wealth began to be admired to some extent. Being wealthy, in other words, became newly

Yulian Wu

valued as a trait for the ideal man. Moreover, merchants themselves were actively engaged in articulating this new ideal.

Xu Zhi, a late Ming merchant from She county of Huizhou, clearly stated that being wealthy made him a real man. First he explained his reasons for wanting to travel afar to conduct his own business: "A man [*zhang fu*] either is determined to study Classics and history or merges himself with nature. Each does what fulfills his ambition [*ge jiu suo zhi*] and hopes not to bring disgrace to his parents. As for people who have studied broadly and practiced moral deeds earnestly, and [who] have served parents filially, they can go to the central plain region, examine what is suitable for trade in this locality, and make a profit." Here, Xu discusses a man's responsibility. While he notes the conventional ideal pursuits of being a true man, such as studying classics and history, he particularly highlights the importance of a man having ambition (*zhi*) and not bringing disgrace to his family. By applying this logic, Xu states that pursuing profit, and thus being able to take care of his parents, was one way to achieve a man's ambition. His ambition to do business far away from his hometown, therefore, made him a successful man.

In the same text, Xu Zhi also argues that pursuing wealth was a masculine trait. After twenty years, when Xu had finally come back to his hometown as a successful merchant, he once again decided to expand his business, even in his old age. When he was asked why he would not stay at home and enjoy his retirement, he, too, alluded to the classic imagery: "When a boy was born, people shot the rubus arrows off the mulberry bow to the four cardinal points [*sang hu peng shi yi she si fang*]. [This activity] symbolizes a man's great ambition [*yuan zhi*]. Even though we are businessmen [*gu ren*], how can we not have the ambition to become like Duanmu Ci, who was able to compete on equal terms with kings wherever he went? How can I act like a farmer who only cares about his big hoe and knows how to differentiate beans and wheat?"[66]

Here, Xu legitimated the pursuit of wealth as an explicitly masculine trait by employing the familiar gendered metaphor from the *Book of Rites*. Shooting an arrow a great distance symbolizes a male child's future as a man with great ambition. Following the same logic as traveling afar, the pursuit of wealth was interpreted as proper male behavior in the framework of the inner/outer social order: a man who leaves his home to pursue wealth is also demonstrating great ambition. By emphasizing a man's ambition and quoting the classics, Xu differentiated himself from the negative image of merchants as pursuers of profit. Instead, he identified his business career as evidence of a proper masculine identity. As a merchant, he certainly felt that obtaining wealth helped him achieve a man's ambition, thereby making him superior to peasants who spent their whole lives at home.

Xu Zhi's texts were by no means the only instances of this sort of rhetoric in the late Ming. A statement by Ni Mulin, cited earlier, asserted his philosophy about being wealthy. In Ni's opinion, "[a man] should either obtain nobility or become wealthy [*bu gui ze fu*]." Ni's personal experience shows that even as a successful merchant, he still believed that the ideal man was an official who served the state. But when passing the examinations was no longer an option, Ni believed that being wealthy was an alternative model for masculine success. His account suggests that, at least in Huizhou, people began to interpret financial strength as a manly accomplishment.[67]

Ni Mulin's statement, however, was more aggressive than simple praise of wealth. Instead of being a poor scholar and studying in his hometown, Ni preferred to become a traveling merchant. In his view, "becoming wealthy" could bring honor to his family and, more important, make him a true man. Therefore, how could he "be satisfied with only using a brush and staying in my hometown for the rest of my life?"[68] He attacked the conventional notion that being a real man necessitated becoming a literatus. In his opinion, it was more masculine to become a wealthy businessman.

This revised attitude toward wealth and merchants was produced in the context of the economic expansion of the late Ming and high Qing. Historian Yu Yingshi has demonstrated that the commercial revolution in the sixteenth century made late Ming intellectuals reevaluate the meaning of business and wealth. The increasing influence of merchants in the society challenged the superior status of literati, who devoted themselves to pure learning and not practical matters.[69] This historical context helped provide the space for interpreting wealth as a masculine trait.

It was in this context that Wang Qishu's contemporaries praised his economic strength. The high Qing poet Zhou Xuanwu (fl. 1757?), in commenting on Wang's seal collection, compared Wang to the famous collectors Ni Zan (1301–74) and Gu Aying of the Yuan dynasty. Zhou remarked that Ni and Gu had been able to collect numerous precious works of art because they were wealthy. Zhou continued: "Wang's wealth was not less than that of these two people. Wang collected and accumulated ancient seals, thoroughly differentiated the genuine antiques from the forgeries, and finally compiled them into a book. His contributions matched these others' [Ni and Gu]. . . . Wang by nature was interested in ancient things, and his resources allowed

him to reach his goal [*li zu yi zhi zhi*]."⁷⁰ Here the word *li* (lit., power) emphasized Wang's economic ability to collect seals. Zhou was not the only person
who mentioned Wang's wealth. The poet and official Zhu Zhang (fl. 1771?)
once observed that Wang "was ready to spend substantial sums" (*bu xi zhong
pin*) to invite contemporary seal carvers to reside in his house.⁷¹ While praising Wang's generosity in patronizing seal carvers, Zhu's choice of the words
zhong pin also subtly points to Wang's financial strength.

Compared to Zhou Xuanwu's and Zhu Zhang's relatively implicit praise
for Wang's wealth, the comments of Wang's friend Sun Chendian were much
more direct. In the spring of 1747, Sun Chendian was invited to write a preface for Wang's ink collection. Sun openly commented that "Xiufeng [Wang
Qishu] owns a great fortune of wealth and is also devoted to ancient things
[*duo zi er hao gu*]," and he predicted that Wang's activities would inspire
prosperity for future generations (*qi fa hou ren*).⁷² In other words, in Sun's
opinion, Wang's masculine qualities—his financial capability and his love of
ancient things—should be treated as a model for later generations to follow.

It is important to note that, although many moralists in this period criticized merchants for their luxurious lifestyles, they did not criticize wealth
per se. It was only when the merchants wasted their money on useless things
that their activities were considered contrary to Confucian moral principles.
In other words, being wealthy in itself was legitimate. It was on the basis of
this standard that Zhou Xuanwu, Zhu Zhang, and Sun Chendian praised
Wang. According to Zhou and Sun, Wang used his wealth to collect ancient
seals and thus satisfied his love for ancient things, a behavior befitting a man
of culture. Zhu's praise was built on the fact that Wang financially supported
other seal carvers and thus promoted the art of seal carving.

Although Wang Qishu himself rarely explicitly talked about his wealth,
one document hints at Wang's views. As noted earlier, Wang at one point
claimed that whenever he saw genuine ancient seals in antique markets, he
"was willing to spend ten pieces of gold or a string of pearls in exchange for
them."⁷³ Wang's main purpose here, obviously, was to highlight his passion
for ancient things, but his remarks implicitly showcased his ability to afford
expensive goods. To be sure, the lack of Wang's own statement on his financial situation reflects the still controversial attitude toward being wealthy.
However, his extensive and sometimes luxurious display of his impressive
collection itself intimated the financial resources behind these precious
objects. The ownership of a certain quantity of treasures—in Wang's case,
his seal collection—inherently defines an individual as wealthy. In this

sense, Wang's display of his precious objects was a way to display his success at creating wealth.

In sum, exhibiting wealth provided another way for Wang to assert his male identity. The concept of ownership—which clearly demonstrated Wang's financial power—defined another type of masculinity. When other male elites used the word *li* (power) to describe Wang's financial ability, they were showing their admiration for his masculine successes. His wealth and ownership of all kinds of valuable objects allowed him to demonstrate his masculinity.

CONCLUSION

Wang Qishu, a Huizhou salt merchant, performed his masculinity through his collection projects. Through his collections of seals and women's poems, he developed broad social networks with male literati who shared a common passion. Collecting also allowed him to display his traveling experience to other male elites. Finally, as the acquisition of wealth was reinterpreted as a manly accomplishment in eighteenth-century China, Wang's grand collection of precious seals represented his financial strength.

Although the evidence here is largely limited to the specific case study of Wang Qishu, it is suggestive for our understanding of late imperial masculinity on a broader scale. Wang's case first provides new insight into merchants' devotion to collecting culture in the eighteenth century. On the face of it, collecting culture has seemed like a way for merchants to use wealth to mimic the behavior of men of letters. Yet an examination through the lens of gender performance offers an alternate interpretation. Among merchants, collecting not only represented the elegant lifestyle of men of culture but also provided a channel for the expression of male gender identity. Moreover, by deploying alternative models of ideal masculinities, merchants were able to carve out their own unique cultural niche. Here it is significant that Wang did not emphasize the ideal of moral strength, which remained an important literati trait in the eighteenth century. Rather, Wang displayed his gender identity by showing the masculine traits that could be best deployed in his situation: his broad social network, extensive traveling experience, and solid financial position.

Wang Qishu's case also suggests the important role that wealthy merchants played in asserting new notions of ideal manhood in late imperial China. Early Chinese ideas and notions of the ideal man informed the concept of masculinity in later periods, but the way that men defined themselves and were defined by others always responded to historical change. The model of the ideal man that Wang identified with was shaped by the unique historical context of the eighteenth century. The commercial revolution in the late Ming and the high Qing changed social attitudes toward wealth. The dominant intellectual movement in the eighteenth century, philological study, renewed male elites' interest in traveling. Wang's case thus suggests a wider transformation and evolution of the ideals of manhood. Through the power of wealth, the activities of people like Wang gradually shifted the idea of what a proper man should be, eventually ushering in new ways of being masculine in late imperial China.

NOTES

1   The dearth of studies on men, as Susan Mann has argued, is first "an inevitable result of a backlash against the China field's obsession with problems of patriarchy and male dominance." Scholars of China have also been misled by the idea that "we know enough about Chinese men already." "The Male Bond in Chinese History," 1601.

2   Here, I list only scholarship that focuses on specific time periods. There are other important theoretical studies of Chinese masculinity, such as Kam Louie's discussion on *wen* (the literary or civilized) and *wu* (the martial). See *Theorising Chinese Masculinity*, especially 9–21.

3   Bossler, *Courtesans, Concubines*, 423.

4   Mann, "Women's History, Men's Studies," 83.

5   Ibid., 84–88. Gu Yanwu (1613–82), who represents the first type, believed that a true friend was a teacher who would correct your shortcomings or recognize your weaknesses. Mid-Qing scholar and essayist Hong Liangji (1746–1809) claimed that true friendship "was not a friend's intellectual qualities, but rather the emotional affinities that overrode differences of status, temperament, and learning." Mann, "Women's History, Men's Studies," 88.

6   Huang summarizes two strategies that male writers adopted—associating with or differentiating from the feminine—to establish their male identity. See Huang, *Negotiating Masculinities*, especially the introduction, 1–9.

7   Matthew Sommer, on the other hand, focuses on the commoners who were not highly educated and explores the meaning of masculinity through the perspective of legal history. Sommer argues that normative masculinity was "based on the sexual role of penetrator" and was also "harnessed to the roles of husband and father." "Dangerous Males, Vulnerable Males," 83.

8   Ho, "The Salt Merchants of Yang-Chou."

9   This idea was greatly inspired by my conversation with Johanna Ransmeier at the 2012 annual meeting of the Association for Asian Studies, and by email exchanges

with Johanna afterward. I am, of course, responsible for the argument here. Martin Huang has also argued that "different models of masculinity were proposed and negotiated in relation to the feminine" in late imperial China, and thus he was reluctant to offer "an overarching definition of Chinese masculinity." See Huang, *Negotiating Masculinities*, 9.

10   Louie, *Theorising Chinese Masculinity*.

11   Huang, *Negotiating Masculinities*, 89–182.

12   Susan Mann argues, "Any historian of China whose subject lies outside the domestic sphere—in the bureaucracy, in trade and commerce, in secret societies or rebellions, in scholarly academies or the civil service examination—will find himself or herself studying almost exclusively men and their relationships with each other." See "The Male Bond in Chinese History," 1602.

13   Martin Huang argues, "In a patriarchal society such as that of late imperial China, masculinity was most likely a homosocial enactment since what mattered to a man most were the judgments and scrutiny of other men." See *Negotiating Masculinities*, 4. Paul Rouzer also shows how male competition was a defining characteristic of literati society in early China. He argues, "The interactions of literati (their treatment of each other, their speech, their evaluations of their activities) give a strong impression of the importance placed on the male social community." *Articulated Ladies*, 86.

14   Ni is alluding to an important passage from the *Book of Rites* about how a man should behave. I discuss the significance of this passage later in the chapter; the point here is that Ni saw his decision to become a merchant as an expression of his identity as a man.

15   Ni's biography is found in *The Genealogy of the Ni Clan* from Yinchuan in Qimen, part of which is collected in Zhang Haipeng and Wang Tingyuan, *Ming Qing hui shang zi liao xuan bian*, 150.

16   I explain the gender components of this quotation in the later sections.

17   Huang argues that "masculinity is a fluid concept, and paradoxically, a man becomes concerned with its articulation only when he feels discriminated against by other men." *Negotiating Masculinities*, 8.

18   For example, a businessman surnamed Jiang from She county once claimed that "a man [*zhangfu*] should observe social changes . . . and make up his mind to become wealthy." The quotation is cited in Zhang and Wang, *Ming Qing hui shang zi liao xuan bian*, 387 (here and elsewhere in the chapter, translations are mine unless otherwise noted). I demonstrate more evidence of this phenomenon later in the chapter.

19   Wang Qishu's grandfather and father had a salt business in the Lower Yangzi area and were quite successful. Like most of the salt merchant families, Wang's family invested in the education of their sons, with the expectation that they would pass the civil service examinations.

20   See Fang Yuejie's preface in Wang Qishu, *Fei hong tang chu gao*, 242.

21   In 1778, when Wang was fifty years old, he was appointed vice director of the Board of Revenue in charge of the Shandong office (Hu bu Shandong si yuan wai lang),

because he had contributed money to the imperial treasury to support the military campaigns in Sichuan. In 1781, Wang was promoted to director of the Bureau of Operations on the Board of War (Bing bu zhi fang si lang zhong). See *Qing dai guanyuan lüli dang' an quan bian*, vol. 21:54, 63, 353, and 356.

22 These compilations included some of the largest and most prominent seal-impression compilations in history, such as *Fei hong tang yin pu* (Seal impressions from the Flying Swan Studio), which contains forty volumes of contemporary seals. In the famous Qing-dynasty book of anecdotes *Qing bai lei chao*, Xu Ke (1869–1928) placed Wang Qishu in the category of connoisseur (*jian shang*) and depicted Wang as a person who was "addicted to ancient things" (*shi gu you qi pi*; 4240).

23 Sophie Volpp has argued that poems can be seen as one type of object because they are the material artifacts of the poet's state of mind. See "The Literary Circulation of Actors," 952.

24 Scholars have discussed collection and luxury consumption in the sixteenth and seventeenth centuries. Clunas, *Superfluous Things*; Li, "The Collector, the Connoisseur"; Wu, *Pin wei she hua*.

25 The wars of the Ming-Qing transition (c. 1640–80) deeply disturbed the social fabric and took a heavy toll on elite and commercial families. Many private collections owned by elite families flew into the market. Objects that had been preserved in private collections reentered the channels of exchange and became collectibles.

26 Patricia Ebrey discusses the collecting project of the imperial court in the Song dynasty in *Accumulating Culture*. She argues that collecting books was always considered a valuable elite activity. The increasing numbers of catalogues of private libraries after the Song dynasty show that private book collection was already a popular activity in that period. Similarly, Ronald Egan focuses on Northern Song elites' interests in collecting, demonstrating scholars' pursuit of "beauty" and aesthetic objects. See *The Problem of Beauty*.

27 See Clunas, *Superfluous Things*.

28 Mann, "Women's History, Men's Studies," 95. Mann identifies two major themes of male friendship: the intellectual interactions and the emotional affinities. While some literati believed that a true friend was a teacher who would correct your shortcomings, others emphasized the purely emotional connections among elites.

29 Huang, "Male Friendship in Ming China," 5–6.

30 In the Ming dynasty, the usage of soft stones for seal carving enhanced the cultural status of seals. From then on, elites' participation in seal carving steadily elevated the aesthetic value of seals. See Li and Watt, *The Chinese Scholar's Studio*.

31 Elman, *From Philosophy to Philology*, 26.

32 As Benjamin Elman has argued, scholars "were committed to the use of bronze and stone inscriptional evidence to verify the Dynastic Histories." Ibid., 71.

33 As quoted by the scholar and poet Lu Zengyu, in a preface he wrote for Wang's collection. See Wang Qishu, *Ji gu yin cun*, Lu *xu*, 2b–3a.

34 As Wang's friend Shao Daye stated, Wang always showed his new seal impression catalog to his *tongren*. See Shao Daye, preface to Wang Qishu, *Chun hui tang yin shi*, 1a–2b. Regarding the definition and usage of *tongren*, see *Hanyu da cidian*, 3:101.

35 Wang, "Editorial Principles," in his *Ji gu yin cun*, 2b.

36 Ding Jing's seal inscription in 1752, recorded in Qin, *Qi jia yin ba*, 139–40. Another famous scholar, Cheng Yaotian, stated in his biography that Wang once asked him to carve seals for inclusion in Wang's seal impression compilation (*suo yu ke zhang ru pu*). Cheng Yaotian, "A Biography of Seal Carving" (Ke zhang xiao zhuan), in Xu, *She shi xian tan*, 520.

37 For example, Zhou Fen, a son of an artisan, stayed in Wang's studio for several years. He learned how to carve seals by reading Wang's seal impression books. See Wang, *Fei hong tang yin ren zhuan* (Collection of Biographies of the Seal Carvers of Flying Swan Studio), 4.2a.

38 Ding Jing described this in one of the seal inscriptions. See Qin, *Qi jia yin ba*, 139–40.

39 Wang's largest seal impression compilation, *Fei hong tang yin pu* (Seal Impressions from the Flying Swan Studio), was also designed to display his broad network. This seal impression compilation includes only the seals that were carved by contemporary seal carvers. When Wang displayed his seal collections in this compilation, he simultaneously demonstrated his broad networks, because most of the seal carvers who contributed to this book were more or less connected with Wang.

40 *Fei hong tang yin ren zhuan* (Collection of Biographies of the Seal Carvers of Flying Swan Studio) itself is a rich text that can be studied from various perspectives. Most of the seal carvers whom Wang recorded were well educated but had failed the civil service examinations. In this context, Wang played two roles in these seal carvers' lives: intellectually, he appreciated these people's talents, and economically he supported them. Wang was equal to these talented seal carvers on an intellectual level but was superior to them in terms of financial strength.

41 Chang, "A Guide to Ming-Ch'ing Anthologies," 122.

42 Wang stated that "regarding the poems that faithful maidens and chaste wives wrote just before their anticipated deaths, even though the meaning of these poems is simple, they have great spirit which should not be hidden. I worry that the other anthology editors have neglected these poems and not recorded them, so I have collected and assembled them together." See "Editorial Principles," in his *Xie fang ji* (Collected fragrances), 1a. In order to achieve this goal, Wang began his anthology with the biographies and poems of particularly representative chaste wives (*jie fu*) and faithful maidens (*zhen nü*). It is also important to note that the content and the rest of the arrangement of *Collected Fragrances* seems to belie Wang's interest in the moral function of women's poem. Even though Wang positioned moral women's poems at the beginning, he also included the writings of concubines (*shi ji*), nuns (*fang wai*), courtesans (*qing lou*), anonymous women (*wu ming*), and even immortals and ghosts (*xian gui*). In addition, among the eighty volumes of *Collected Fragrances*, only the first thirteen volumes are devoted to moral women. From this perspective, Wang's *Collected Fragrances* greatly contrasts with Wanyan Yun Zhu's anthology *Zheng shi ji*, which recorded only writings by moral women.

43 Wang's anecdote collection titled *Shui cao qing xia lu* (Records of Leisure from a Water Transportation Official) recorded some examples showing a common passion for women's poems. For instance, the Manchu Chenggui once recited for

Wang a sentence from a poem written by the Red Banner Manchu Lady Xiu, only because this sentence was especially beautiful. See Wang, *Shui cao qing xia lu*, 10. Even though there is no evidence—akin to Wang's seal party—showing how Wang and his elite fellows appreciated women's poetry together, other sources prove that this kind of literary appreciation was popular among scholarly elites. For instance, Wang Yuying (1753–76), the wife of the prominent scholar Sun Xingyan (1753–1818), was famous for her "ancient and sharp" (*gu qiao*) poetry. Wang's friends "copied down and passed around her poems [*chuan chao shu pian*]." Because of this, even though Wang was never able to access Yuying's anthology, he was still able to read and record Wang Yuying's poems. Wang and his friends' fascination with Yuying's writing reveals the common interests (*hao*) between Wang and his male friends, as did their shared appreciation of seals. See Wang, *Shui cao qing xia lu*, 78.

44   The original quotation is: "[I] wish friends and especially the people who share my high purpose will send me whatever they see." See "Editorial Principles," in Wang, *Xie fang ji*, 2a.

45   Jiang's mother (née Zhong) was a famous poet. She compiled her poems in an anthology but "was not willing to show them to others." Wang, *Shui cao qing xia lu*, 9. For Jiang's biography, see Hummel, *Eminent Chinese of the Ch'ing Period*, 141–42.

46   For example, the attendant censor (*shiyu*) Wang Shoumo once asked Wang to collect and record his grandmother's poems. See Wang, *Shui cao qing xia lu*, 20.

47   For instance, the official and famous calligrapher Wang Wenzhi (1730–1802), who was granted the *jinshi* degree in the twenty-fifth year of Qianlong's reign, sent Bao Zhihui's anthology to Wang. Bao Zhihui was a famous female poet from Wang Wenzhi's hometown. See ibid., 85. Wang also recorded that his friends sent him a poem written by a talented woman poet of the Kangxi era, Fu Shouzhen (91).

48   For instance, when Lady Wu's husband passed away, she wrote two poems to express her sadness at her loss. The literatus Ni Yiqing sent Lady Wu's two poems to Wang to preserve her moral voice. See Wang, *Xie fang ji*, 2.22a.

49   This book records events that Wang saw or heard about when he served as the director of the Bureau of Waterways and Irrigation on the Board of Works (Gongbu dushuisi langzhong) in Beijing, an official position he obtained by purchase. See Hucker, *A Dictionary of Official Titles*, 301.

50   Zhao originally passed the civil service examination with the topmost rank of *zhuang yuan*. But the Qianlong emperor discovered that the third-ranking graduate in Zhao Yi's year came from a province that had never produced a *zhuang yuan*. Thus, the emperor ordered the names to be interchanged, with the result that Zhao Yi was ranked third. Zhao Yi was an important official, historian, and poet. See Hummel, *Eminent Chinese of the Ch'ing Period*, 75.

51   Yuan, *Sui yuan shi hua bu yi*, 5.692.

52   Huang, "Male Friendship and *Jiangxue*," 149.

53   *Li Chi: Book of Rites*, 472.

54   A comment by one of the women interviewed for Gail Hershatter's chapter in this volume reveals the persistence into the twentieth century of this idea that men (and only men) "travel the world."

55   Also see Huang "Male Friendship in Ming China," 6.

56   See Mann, "The Virtue of Travel."

57   As historians have discussed, it is fair to say the inner-versus-outer division, although relative and situational, did exist as an ideal social order. See Mann, *Precious Records*, 15; Bray, *Technology and Gender*, 54–55.

58   "Editorial Principles," in Wang, *Ji gu yin cun*, 1a.

59   As noted earlier, Wang held several offices in varied locations, including Shandong and Beijing. Also see Wang's biography in *Huizhou fuzhi*, in Min, *Bei zhuan ji bu*, 45.20b–21a; Hummel, *Eminent Chinese of the Ch'ing Period*, 810.

60   For instance, he purchased a considerable number of seals from markets when he served in the capital, Beijing, for just over a year.

61   Shen Chu, preface to Wang, *Xie fang ji*, 2a.

62   Shao Daye, preface to Wang, *Chun hui tang yin shi*, 1b.

63   Zhang Mei, preface to Wang, *Fei hong tang yin pu, ji* 1, 7.2a.

64   Elman, *From Philosophy to Philology*, 6.

65   For example, the famous Wuliang shrine was discovered by the noted scholar and antiquarian Huang Yi in the eighteenth century. See Wu, *The Wuliang Shrine*.

66   Xu Zhi lived between the Hongzhi and Jiajing eras. See "The Biography of *Xu gong* from Pingshan," in *The Genealogy of Xu Clan*, in Zhang and Wang, *Ming Qing hui shang zi liao xuan bian*, 216. Duanmu Ci, styled Zigong, was one of Confucius's best students. He was not only good at learning but was also famous for his business talent.

67   Although his view was that of a merchant, it would have been local elites who recorded this statement and published it, thereby showing that, at the very least, the author of this genealogy approved of this idea.

68   Part of Ni's biography was collected in Zhang and Wang, *Ming Qing hui shang zi liao xuan*, 150.

69   Yu, *Zhongguo jinshi zongjiao lunli yu shangren jingshen*, 189–273.

70   Zhou Xuanwu, preface to *Seal Impressions from the Flying Swan Studio*, 2b.

71   Zhu Zhang, preface to Wang, *Han tong yin cong*, 3a.

72   Sun Chendian, preface to Wang, *Fei hong tang mo pu*, 2a.

73   "Editorial Principles," in Wang, *Ji gu yin cun*, 1a.

CHAPTER FOUR

WRITING LOVE

The *Heming ji* by Wang Zhaoyuan and Hao Yixing

Weijing Lu

Arguably the most noted female scholar in the Qing, Wang Zhao-yuan (1763–1851), attracts considerable interest in her work and life from historians today.[1] Her marriage to Hao Yixing (1757–1825), a leading scholar of philological studies, prompts additional fascination with this upbeat story: Wang Zhaoyuan not only carved out a role for herself in the male world of academia but also fashioned a marital relationship—centered in academic work—that won admiration from her contemporaries. Their successful marriage, however, was not a subject the couple dwelled on in their own writings. In fact, except during the first several years of their marriage, they left behind only scattered personal notes that rarely went beyond showing their satisfaction in studying in one another's company. This shortage of accounts in their own words makes the only work in which they did speak exclusively about their marriage unique and that much more valuable. Titled *Singing in Harmony* (Heming ji), it is a work of poems, all composed by the couple themselves, that they compiled when they were newly married. The only extant source about their marriage, *Singing in Harmony* opens a small window into the emotional and intellectual world of the newlywed couple, bringing to light their understanding of *qing* (emotional resonance) and allowing us to witness the textures and colors of marital intimacy in their early years of marriage.

The marriage of Wang Zhaoyuan and Hao Yixing is a powerful rebuttal to the familiar assertion that men and women in imperial China were deprived of conjugal affection. Since the early twentieth century, the loveless arranged marriage has been the poster child for the repressive patriarchal family system and the suppression of women that supposedly prevailed.[2] This stereotypical argument has begun to lose ground, however. In her seminal study of seventeenth-century female culture in the lower Yangzi region, for example, Dorothy Ko uncovers a wealth of evidence showing the emergence of the companionate marriage defined as "a union between an intellectually compatible couple who treat each other with mutual respect and affection."[3] Romantic emotions were no longer the monopoly of courtesans or concubines.[4] The poetic exchanges between husband and wife, or *changhe*, that came into fashion during this time epitomize this close emotional bond and intellectual compatibility.[5] During the eighteenth and nineteenth centuries, writing continued to be utilized as the primary mode of expressing of conjugal love, as testified by the commonplace of wives and husbands writing together or to each other.[6] Poetry supplied educated women as well as men with a sophisticated and culturally appropriate medium for communication, helping forge emotional closeness between married couples. Compilation of poetry written by husband and wife, and its publication in a single volume, projected in yet another fashion a joyful marriage worthy of public commemoration.[7]

Singing in Harmony is a testimony to this growing trend. But it was an unusual collection even at a time when writing and publicizing conjugal poetry was in vogue: its forty-eight poems came from the couple's first years of marriage, and the volume was created not merely to display a happy marriage but in a jubilant celebration of *qing*, love.[8] This remarkable consciousness of *qing* sheds new light on the changing definition of the term in the eighteenth century, its place in conjugal happiness, and the implications of female literacy for marital relations.[9] Bearing in mind that many more studies are necessary before we can paint a clear picture of the contours of historical change regarding marital ideals and practice, we can say that Wang Zhaoyuan and Hao Yixing present us with an excellent opportunity to take a step in that direction.[10]

Weijing Lu

Wang Zhaoyuan and Hao Yixing were married uxorilocally in 1787 at her mother's residence in Fushan county, Shandong.[11] The Wangs were an influential lineage.[12] Hao Yixing, a thirty-one-year-old widower, came from Qixia, which is also in Shandong. At twenty-five, Wang Zhaoyuan was relatively old for marriage by the standard of the time. The delay, it appears, was due in part to the high expectations her mother, Lady Lin, held for a son-in-law. Lady Lin finally located Hao Yixing in Qixia, her own natal county, where the Lins were a prominent lineage.[13]

Marrying a widower with children (Hao Yixing had two daughters from a previous marriage) may not have been ideal, but the Haos were a respectable household that had boasted low-level degree holders for several generations. Hao Yixing himself had done well in his studies. He was elected as a county-school student at twenty-two and was chosen from among the most promising students in Shandong to enroll in the Taixue, the Imperial University in Beijing. Potential for success in civil examinations was a crucial qualification for a son-in-law.[14]

Lady Lin had lost her husband at the age of twenty-six. Teaching her only child to read the books he left behind had been a means for her to cope with the difficulties of widowhood.[15] Besides personally giving lessons to her daughter, she also had Zhaoyuan study with a tutor and even attend a school for girls.[16] Lady Lin was somewhat unusual, even for supportive mothers of talented girls in that era, in that she wanted her daughter not simply to have a good education but to achieve something great. She said to her daughter that Ban Zhao's commentaries on the *Biographies of Exemplary Women* (Lienü zhuan) had long been lost, and that Zhaoyuan should write a commentary on this classic someday.[17] Zhaoyuan took her mother's wishes to heart. The *Supplementary Commentary on the Biographies of Exemplary Women* (Lienü zhuan buzhu), which she completed in her early forties, would become her signature work.[18] Wang Zhaoyuan had this to say about her mother:

> I lost my father at the age of six, and my mother, née Lin, nurtured me and brought me up with love so that I was able to reach adulthood. When I was ten, she taught me to read the *Classic of Filial Piety* (Xiaojing) and the *Familial Rules* (Neize). When I was twelve, she taught me the *Book of Songs*. I understood their general meanings. As a child, I did not like to study. My mother told me to recite, which I often did well into the night. At fifteen, I

begin to pursue study with determination. I studied both classics and history after I finished womanly work, and wouldn't stop even in sickness.[19]

Lady Lin died only four years into Zhaoyuan's marriage, but she remained an inspiration throughout her life. Her desire to fulfill her mother's instructions and honor her wishes drove Zhaoyuan to work hard.

The uxorilocal marriage was arranged most likely because Zhaoyuan was a beloved only child (although her mother adopted a son to be the family heir). Moreover, as in other Qing elite uxorilocal marriages, having a man of potential marry into a well-to-do and well-connected household conferred benefits on the families of both bride and groom.[20] Even though Lady Lin was a widow, she had the means to provide crucial assistance to further Yixing's education. Yixing had failed repeatedly to pass the provincial-level examination and was frustrated by his lack of progress, which, in his view, resulted from the lack of a good teacher. Lady Lin put enormous effort into his academic training, and she had connections. She found Yixing an excellent tutor, named Wang Gucun, a cousin in her lineage (*zu xiong*).[21] She paid Yixing's tuition and mailed his writings to Wang for commentary and correction. She even personally supervised Yixing's progress. When the essays came back, "she counted carefully the circles the teacher had marked [signs of excellence or approval], and was happy when the circles were many. She also had her adopted son read the teacher's comments to her so that she would know if [Yixing] were making improvements."[22] This went on for more than four years, until her death in 1791.[23] Yixing's progress initially appeared to be rapid. Less than a year after the marriage, he earned his provincial (*juren*) degree. But it would be another eleven years before he gained his national degree (*jinshi*), in 1799.

It was probably shortly after Lady Lin's death that the couple moved to Qixia to live with Yixing's family. They relocated to Beijing upon Yixing's appointment as a secretary (*zhushi*) in the Department of Revenue in 1799, following his earning of the national degree. Except for a short period from 1800 to 1803, during which they returned to Qixia in observation of mourning for Yixing's father, the couple made Beijing their home. Zhaoyuan gave birth to four children, including a daughter who died at seventeen. Only one son survived both of them.[24]

In Beijing, the couple continued to pursue their academic passions. Hao Yixing did not thrive in government service. Promotions to powerful and profitable positions evaded him throughout his career, but he found fulfillment in his studies. An exceptionally focused and productive scholar, he worked on a wide range of topics, from philology and history to Confucian classics and other ancient texts. According to the "yearly records" (*nianpu*) compiled by the early-twentieth-century scholar Xu Weiyu, Hao Yixing's published works consisted of thirty-four titles, and his unpublished manuscripts included as many as twenty-eight titles. His most acclaimed work is *Explanations of the Erya* (Erya yishu), which took him twelve years to complete. Zhaoyuan's scholarship included a draft annotation to the *Book of Songs* titled *Minor Notes on the Book of Songs* (Pajing xiaoji) in addition to the *Supplementary Commentary on the Biographies of Exemplary Women.*[25] It was never published and is believed to have been incorporated into *An Inquiry into the Book of Songs* (Shi wen), a coauthored annotation based on the couple's conversations about the *Book of Songs* during their first years of marriage.[26] Zhaoyuan also seemed to be intrigued by the supernatural and the mysterious. She annotated another old text, *Biographies of Immortals* (Liexian zhuan), and authored a text entitled *Book of Dreams* (Meng shu). Her other works include eleven essays, mostly prefaces and postscripts, which were compiled into a collection called *Extant Prose from the Boudoir of the Hall of Sunning Books* (Shaishutang gui zhong wencun). Besides those in *Singing in Harmony*, Wang Zaoyuan's only known poems are a series of ten stanzas written in a satirical style on the topic of family members offering sacrifice to the God of Wealth, and a separate piece on a portrait of Ruan Yuan's mother, likely solicited by Ruan.[27] Although she produced far fewer scholarly works than her husband, she contributed to his work.[28] For her contributions, including to his *Explanations of the Erya*, Hao Yixing made his acknowledgments. Hao Yixing died of illness at the age of sixty-nine. Shortly afterward, Zhaoyuan and her son moved back to Qixia, where she devoted the rest of her life to compiling Yixing's work. We know virtually nothing about this last phase of her life, which came to end in 1851 when she was eighty-nine.

The couple was remembered as the most accomplished scholarly wife and husband of the Qing period. In the circles of their friends in Beijing, they were known as "the Hao couple of Qixia," analogous to the "Wang father-son of Gaoyou," which referred to the noted contemporary philological scholars Wang Niansun and his son Yinzhi.[29] At a time when female scholars were a rarity, Wang Zhaoyuan came to represent the unusual breed of erudite and accomplished women, and the couple's work relationship captured the imaginations of male scholars. One of their close friends, the scholar Chen Huan

(1786–1863), who specialized in the *Book of Songs*, remarked that the couple "analyzed the doubtful and investigated the difficult as if it were between a teacher and student or two friends." Hao Yixing routinely worked into the early morning hours, and Wang Zhaoyuan often did not sleep. With incense burning, the two "examined and compared the different and the similar and the correct and the mistaken. When they disagreed on something, they would not stop arguing about it."[30]

Wang Zhaoyuan was recognized as a scholar in her own right, but her image as an accomplished scholar seemed inevitably defined through her relationship with her husband. It was the image of the couple working together in a modest study that captured male scholars' lasting imagination. In a handwritten note on the margin of a postscript by Zhaoyuan, Li Ciming (1830–94) compared their companionship in intellectual life to that of Li Qingzhao and Zhao Mingcheng of the Song period, calling it "a beautiful story for eternity."[31] The postscript that touched Li Ciming's heart describes the years when the couple were working on a project on the histories of the Jin and Song dynasties (265–479) (later titled *Jin Song shu gu*). At the time, Yixing was suffering from a chronic illness and taking herbal medicine, but he would not stop working despite his wife's advice. "The medicine pot was often full, and the desk was dusty," Zhaoyuan wrote. As he was also troubled by his declining memory, she took notes for him. As time went by, the notes grew in volume. Yixing added, deleted, or corrected the entries whenever he could manage it, finally compiling them into a manuscript. When he recovered from his illness, Zhaoyuan encouraged him to publish it.[32] Clearly, these scenes of mutual support and shared endurance between the couple resonated deeply with the nineteenth-century educated elite.

SINGING IN HARMONY

Singing in Harmony is a collection of poetry from the couple's early years of life together. Although they continued to compose poetry in later years,[33] few conjugal poems from those days exist. The forty-eight poems appear to be arranged roughly chronologically. The only dates mentioned in the entire anthology, 1787 and 1788, were the first and second years of their marriage. Toward the end of the volume, two poems by Wang Zhaoyuan indicate that she was around thirty years of age and had given birth to a child (Zhaoyuan gave birth to her first child in 1789).[34] The large majority of the collection seems to have been written during the first two years. The preface to the anthology is not dated. Judging by its exuberant tone, it must have been composed not long after their wedding. *Singing in Harmony*, therefore, is a work by newlyweds.

It seems unusual that the couple would stop writing conjugal poems altogether after those initial years.[35] The discontinuation might have something to do with their relocation to Yixing's home following the death of Zhaoyuan's mother, where her maternal duties and new role as a daughter-in-law might have interfered with the leisurely activity of poetry writing.[36] Her mother's death might also have played a psychological role. The exceptionally close mother-daughter relationship no doubt made it much harder to recover from the trauma, and consequently her romantic mood may have subsided. One may also suspect that, as academic research consumed their energy, her (though not his) interest in poetry ebbed.

But in *Singing in Harmony*, Zhaoyuan assumed an active role. Of the forty-eight poems, twenty were authored by Yixing (courtesy name Langao) and twenty-eight by Zhaoyuan (courtesy name Ruiyu). Wang Zhaoyuan also initiated more titles, to which Hao Yixing responded, matching the rhymes (*he*). This may have been a result of having more time at her disposal. Hao Yixing, on other hand, was arduously studying for his examinations all along.

The tone of the couple's conscious presentation of their relationship as one with profound *qing* is set in the preface. Written by Hao Yixing, it speaks with the voices of both. It begins with these analogies:

> If the metal and stone do not have feelings [*qing*], then why do the magnet and needle attract each other? If grasses and trees do not have feelings, then why do their flowers and leaves grow well-matched? All kinds of things are made of yin and yang, and they become responsive by sound and scent; how much more is this true of human beings! Human beings are especially endowed with the refinement of yin-yang essence. They are not like the dull metal and stone or the senseless grasses and trees.

Qing here refers to a specific kind of sense or feeling: mutual attraction between male and female. This sense is not unique to humans. Rather, it is universal, encompassed by all things under heaven. Each and every thing is endowed with the capacity for mutual attraction. Such tendencies are presented as the outgrowth of the yin-yang energies that permeate the universe. However, there is a hierarchal order of things: humans are on the highest end of this hierarchy, and their sensibility separates them from all other objects in the universe. Therefore, only humans are capable of experiencing the deep feeling of love between a man and a woman.

> However, there are exceptions. Some people are perfidious and others drifting. Their hearts are not as firm as stone, and their disposition is colder then that of the metal. People of that sort are probably unmovable. [The poems] "Wild and Windy" [Zhong feng] describes resentment; "Cloudy and Rainy" [Yin yu] depicts ingratitude [*gu en*].[37] If the two persons are not united, then it is like a single string that cannot make music. [If] one looks at the broad sky [to sing] but no one echoes, then even if he sings, the sound will not be beautiful. To use grasses and trees as metaphors for this [kind of unmovable persons], their difference is as striking as that between the aromatic and the foul. How can they hope to have the words of sharing hearts that are fragrant like orchids? The utmost *qing* is often beyond understanding. People in the past said, "There are things that cannot be explained by reason but make sense in terms of *qing*." Now we see it!

Although human beings are, in theory, capable of deep love, variations in disposition make some people unable to achieve it. They lack sincerity and concentration of feeling. Their disposition is such that they are coldhearted and shallow, and they drift and cheat. *Qing* can arise only when two equally sensitive and devoted hearts meet. If one person is concentrated and the other is insincere or adrift in his or her feeling, there will be no *qing* to speak of. But the chances of meeting a person who is just as sincere and devoted as oneself are rare, as demonstrated in the cries of the abandoned women recorded in the poems "Wild and Windy" and "Cloudy and Rainy" from the *Book of Songs*.

Love does not come easily to human beings. It is a privilege of the lucky few, and Wang Zhaoyuan and Hao Yixing, needless to say, were among the fortunate. Moreover, as the preface professes, when it comes to experiencing the most intense kind of *qing*, it is simply beyond logical explanation: *qing* is mysterious and powerful. The text continues:

> Here are two people, Langao and Ruiyu; their feeling of *qing* is indeed deep! This is especially so for Ruiyu. Before she met [Langao], [the auspicious relationship] was confirmed by dreams and her spirit was already in contact [with his]: she had already tied her heart [with his]! Then, wild geese sang

and beautiful jade was presented [metaphors for betrothal], and the two are like guests and friends [*bin you*]![38] Our matching interests were decided after we were born, but our spiritual compatibility already existed before we met. The two of us [coming together in marriage] is really a "miracle encounter" [*qi yu*]!

In characterizing their marriage as a "miracle," the couple suggests that it belongs to a category of phenomena that occurs only extremely rarely; and that when it does occur, it is the result not of human effort but of the intervention of supernatural power. This, of course, underscored the extent of their satisfaction with their marriage. The phrase they used, "miracle encounter," implies that their marriage was not simply an ordinary coming together of two people. In literati writings, the term often carries the connotation of spiritual oneness of two people who met somewhat unexpectedly, or the meeting of soul mates.[39] In the preface, an earlier line elucidates this point: "Our matching interests were decided after we were born, but our spiritual compatibility already existed before we met." For the couple, love was characterized as the complete sharing of intellectual interests and being wholly harmonious in spiritual life. It meant the mutual responsiveness and mutual understanding that bind two souls into one.

This part of the preface also allows us to speculate about their betrothal, for which no information is available. We are told here that Wang Zhaoyuan's feeling for Yixing had something to do with the dreams she had before their engagement. We don't know how Hao Yixing's name was brought to Zhaoyuan's mother as a candidate for a son-in-law, but it seems that the matchmaker's introduction of Yixing made such an impression on Zhaoyuan that it set her dreaming of him and encountering his spirit. The dreams and spiritual encounters, in turn, might have played a part in convincing her mother to seal the engagement. Zhaoyuan had fallen in love even before the official betrothal rites were performed. The beautiful betrothal rituals that followed made her envisioned ideal match a reality.

The preface continues:

Langao [Yixing] said, "These words are beautiful, and we cannot afford not to pass them on. Poetry is what human beings use to express [their feelings]. If metal and stone are not harmonious they would not make sound; grasses and trees do not make sound, and it is the wind that touches them to cause sound. The same can be said of poetry. But why is this collection called *Singing in Harmony*? Yishi [of the Spring and Autumn period] said, "The male and female phoenixes [*feng huang*] fly together, singing back and forth; their sound is clear and crisp"—this is what the title symbolizes. Changli [the Tang poet and thinker Han Yu] also said, "Singing in harmony is to broadcast the prosperity of the country." Although we dare not say that the poems the two of us have written can be disseminated by [inscribing them onto] metal and stones, would they be like the fragrant and the foul that are not suitable to be stored in the same container?" Ruiyu [Zhaoyuan] said, "Very good." Therefore we compiled them.

Concluding the preface, the couple explained why they felt their poems deserved to be passed on and why they named their volume *Heming ji* (Singing in harmony). Employing again the metaphors of metal, stone, grasses, and trees—drawn from a famous essay by Han Yu—they stressed that poetry was the vehicle through which human beings express their feelings; and human feeling was aroused only when one's heart was touched. Their poetry recorded their deep feelings. The title *Singing in Harmony* alluded to a great marital union from antiquity. According to the *Zuo Commentary on the Spring and Autumn Annals*, when Yishi, an aristocrat from the state of Chen, was considering arranging the marriage of his daughter to Chen Wan from the state of Qi, his wife consulted the spirits. She declared that the marriage would be "auspicious," citing the words from the divination: "*Feng* and *huang* [male and female phoenixes] fly together, singing back and forth; their sound is clear and crisp." "Singing in Harmony" signifies not only the auspicious nature of their marriage but also an ambitious wish for their marriage.

Ending an intimate preface with a reference to "the prosperity of the country" may not make much sense to a modern reader. But for the couple, their vision of a successful life together was closely tied to success in the extradomestic realm. As I will discuss further, the motif of striving to make a name in the world was featured throughout their poetry. It was a prospect that they relished. Their citation of Han Yu is noteworthy. Han Yu made his remarks when commenting on three promising poets of his day, suggesting two opposite courses of life that might lay ahead for them: they might have a smooth career, which would prompt them to write in celebration of the glory of the country; or they might suffer a miserable life, which would inspire them to produce great poetry about their misfortune.[40] Wang Zhaoyuan and Hao Yixing chose to omit the second part of Han Yu's speculation: they did not see a setback as part of their future. This conscious choice reveals tremendous confidence and optimism. Inspired by their "magic" union, they were poised to build a promising life together.

Readers could hardly have failed to notice the language of elation and the direct style with which Wang Zhaoyuan and Hao Yixing expressed their mutual attraction. It is especially interesting to note that Wang Zhaoyuan was presented as even more deeply in love than her husband before their marriage—certainly not the innocent maiden that social norms at the time would have us see. *Qing* was identified as a cornerstone to their happy union, the source of their enjoyment and inspiration.

In short, the preface to *Singing in Harmony* reveals in an astounding fashion Wang Zhaoyuan and Hao Yixing's fascination with *qing*. They saw it as an essential source of martial bliss, attesting to the powerful legacy of the seventeenth-century cult of *qing*. However, their ecstatically written manifesto was noticeably fresh in the ways *qing* is characterized. In the fictional world of the seventeenth century, *qing* is a mysterious, awe-inspiring, overpowering, and potentially destructive force, the essential attributes captured by the dramatist Tang Xianzu in his famous declaration in *Peony Pavilion*: "Love is not love at its fullest if one who lives is unwilling to die for it, or if it cannot restore to life one who has so died."[41] In the seventeenth century, *Peony Pavilion* served as a great inspiration for young and idealistic women in their fashioning of marital relationships. Du Liniang, the protagonist of the famous play, was their icon. However, their fantasies of marital love seem to have been inevitably associated with heartbreak and unfulfillment.[42] By contrast, a prevailing sense of optimism marked the spirit of the imagination of Wang and Hao. *Qing,* for them, was just as intense, powerful, and mysterious, but it was also containable and rational. It was essentially a calm, reasoned, and morally validated emotion. The single most important point to note about their rationalization of *qing* is the connection they established between *qing* and the Confucian classical tradition. By constantly weaving references to classics and orthodox writings into their delineation of *qing*— including the *Book of Songs,* the work of Han Yu, and the *Zuo* commentary—they placed *qing* in the context of the revered intellectual tradition and thus legitimized it, while effectively disassociating it from the problematic fictional discourse and its overtones of transgression.[43]

Qing therefore secured a respectable place within the Confucian classics: it was presented as a pure emotion buttressed by ritual. Wang Zhaoyuan and Hao Yixing did not want others to doubt the correctness of their *qing*.

To give another example, while the preface highlights Zhaoyuan's strong feelings for her prospective husband even before the betrothal process was complete, which a moralist would have found somewhat distasteful, she projected her emotion as being, in the end, appropriate: the betrothal process brought her emotion into the realm of ritual, and through ritual the emotion was validated and legitimized. The enactment of the betrothal ritual provides a legitimate channel for expressing the feeling, anchoring *qing* firmly in the Confucian moral tradition.

LOVE, AMBITION, AND COMPETITION

The rational delineation of *qing* in the preface was succeeded in the poems by vibrant displays of conjugal rejoicing that came in various forms. *Singing in Harmony* is a slender volume, but the small size belies its rich content. The poems can be grouped roughly into the following subjects: wedding, travel (mainly by Hao Yixing), appreciation of scenery, daily activities, and expressions of aspiration. There can be little question that the poems were carefully selected to deliver an image the couple desired; but they also represented memories of cherished moments for the newlyweds. The moments, like snapshots, captured real moods and authentic feelings that were at once intensely romantic and delightfully cozy—but not without tensions.

Two poems titled "Hastening the Bride's Toilette" (Cui zhuang) and four titled "Removing the Fan [That Covers the Bride's Face]" (Que shan) open the collection with a somewhat formal celebration of the wedding. Both titles were traditionally supposed to be used by guests and friends to write congratulatory poems, but by the eighteenth century it was not uncommon for grooms and brides to try their hands at them, probably in the days immediately following the wedding. The two titled "Hastening the Bride's Toilette" in *Singing in Harmony* read:

> Heaven grants the coming together of the auspicious union,
> People witness the moment of happy marriage.
> Two stars [the Cowherd and Weaving Maid] hang over the decorated
>   [wedding] chamber,[44]
> The two pages of [the stationery] reflect the new poems.
> How luxuriant is the peach blossom![45]
> The beautiful flower waits at the gate-screen [*zhu*].[46]

She dreamed the dreams of the candles repeatedly making snuff flowers
    [an auspicious sign],[47]
The union of a hundred years is long predestined.

                                                    —Langao

Heaven brings us together,
Today, we wed.
In happiness, we write the sentences of "bringing good to the family"
In our beautiful residence, we compose poems.
Reciting the line "admiring the high mountain,"[48]
Filling our ears is the song of "Zhu."[49]
My mother is joyous, [seeing that] we are respectful and deferential;
I foresee that I will grow old together with you.

                                                    —Ruiyu

Starting with a conventional expression about marriage being the blessing of heaven, the poems were highly celebratory, as both the groom and bride took pains to present good wishes for their marriage. Both repeatedly alluded to the *Book of Songs*, which Zhaoyuan had studied earnestly. The citation of the poem "Zhu" by both Yixing and Zhaoyuan is noteworthy in particular. From the "Air of Qi" section of the *Book of Songs*, "Zhu" relates an ancient wedding ritual; moreover, it came from none other than Shandong, the native region of both Yixing and Zhaoyuan and where their own wedding took place. The repeated reference to "Zhu," therefore, was a nod to a classic ritual and their locality's rich Confucian cultural heritage.

Considering that these were their first poems together, the heavy reference to the *Book of Songs* suggests, on the part of the groom, a painstaking effort to acknowledge his bride's talent while showing his own familiarity with the classic; and Zhaoyuan was probably delighted at the opportunity to show her own learning as well as put her groom to the test. In the second set of wedding poems, "Removing the Fan," the celebratory theme included profuse praises for each other. Evidently they were courting each other carefully.

The silvery candles light up the boudoir,
Incense burns in the precious censer on this auspicious night.
Brilliantly talented, you are skilled at composing the snow stanza,[50]
My ambition is to ascend to the high clouds.[51]

Flowers adorn the respectfully raised tray,[52]
Amid the aroma of the tea we write prose.
Knowing from early on your knowledge of the "Admonitions for Women"
    [Nüjie],
I pull my deer-cart and make known to you my admiration.[53]

—Langao

Two stars unite in this happy evening,
Fragrant incense burns in the precious censer.
My heart does not indulge in drinking wine,
Your ambition can ascend the clouds.
Beautiful writing accumulates, adding to the books' luster;
Like a flower grows out of the tip of the writing brush, you compose won-
    derful prose.
Not worth reading under the lamp,
This poor verse delivers my admiration.

—Ruiyu

Both poets employ cultural icons of learning and talent to sing their praise of the other party, with Yixing comparing Zhaoyuan to the gifted Ban Zhao and Xie Daoyun, and Zhaoyuan relating Yixing to the genius Tang poet Li Bai (701–62), whose success was predicted in a dream he had in which a flower opened at the tip of his writing brush. Also noteworthy are the three iconic marriages to which they allude. The story of Meng Guang and Liang Hong from the Han was perhaps the most frequently cited in Qing literature praising a good marriage. Meng Guang was said to be a rather unattractive maiden who chose to marry the recluse-scholar Liang Hong. At the wedding, she dressed up beautifully only to be rejected by the groom. She therefore did a complete makeover, putting on cotton clothing, wearing an ordinary woman's hairdo, and taking on manual labor, which won the groom's approval. Their idolized marriage is most vividly captured in the image of Meng Guang "holding the tray to the height of her eyebrow" as she "did not dare to look up" when serving her husband food."[54] The second iconic marriage, also from the Han period, involved the poor scholar Bao Xuan, who was chosen by his teacher to marry his daughter. The bride arrived at the wedding with a luxurious dowry, much to Bao Xuan's displeasure. She instantly had it returned and put on the clothing of a working wife. The two pulled a deer-cart and returned to live in his home.[55]

Little in these marriages suggests conjugal affection; instead, the stories champion wifely compliance and service, reaffirming the central principles that defined the husband-wife relation according to orthodox Confucian teaching. Although often the use of historical references was flexible and their interpretations selective (and indeed it appears that in most Qing usages, the two marriages just described symbolized mutual respect rather than wifely service and devotion), a hierarchical relation remains part of the marker of these ideal marriages. It is thus interesting to note that the two stories appeared in Hao Yixing's poems but not in Wang Zhaoyuan's. Zhaoyuan cited only the folklore about the Cowherd and the Weaving Maid, in which their conjugal relationship was free of suggestions of inequality. She may have purposely ignored the male-constructed, conventional icons of a virtuous wife. A submissive role was not what she imagined.

After poems about the wedding celebration, the collection proceeds to those depicting scenes of spring; the pleasures of reading, writing, and play in the wedding chamber; and the couple's high aspirations. In the eyes of the newlyweds, spring was full of vibrant energy and exuberant beauty, which they appreciated with a distinctive sensibility. Spring was the season emblematic of romantic love, but in this case it was natural as well as symbolic that the couple's honeymoon coincided with spring's arrival. Budding plum blossoms, emerging bamboo shoots, the golden-colored new leaves of the weeping willows, and bright peach blossoms—symbol of the bride—all conveyed an air of delight and excitement. The bride was an observer and an integral part of the enchanting spring scene, as seen in her short poem titled "Adorning My Hair with a 'Welcome Spring' Blossom":[56]

Ashes [of the New Year's fireworks] drifting in the air, a new season has
    arrived.
In the little garden, spring flowers open.
Welcoming the warmth [of spring], the golden stamens unwind,
The hairpin reflects [the blossom that adorns] my hair.

While the early spring garden creates a symbolic outer space of conjugal joy, the inner space—the study and the bedroom—was where the intimacy of the newlyweds unfolded. The poems delivered their affection in suggestive language and through images, real and imagined, as they wove literary tropes and allusions into depictions of actual scenes. Occasionally, the affection is expressed boldly. For example, in the following poem, Yixing begins with an affectionate voice, calling his bride "love-crazed," before giving an idyllic portrayal of their new life:

> [People] brag about the charm of a beautiful bride,
> What I like most in my darling is that she is love-crazed.
> By the lamp's light, the "golden flower card" enters our dream,[57]
> Sharing their hearts, the red berries [*hong guo*] hang in the twigs of the jade
>   tree.
> Basking in warm sun, kingfishers play by the orchids,
> The deep snow freezes the ink, so it looks as if glazed.
> Rolling up the bamboo screen, we boil the tea; smoke of the censer arises.
> Finishing cutting the stationery for poetry, we play chess.[58]

The sweet atmosphere of the wedding chamber is created through the fragrance of tea, the smoke carrying the scent of incense, and the bright colors of berries and birds. The "red berries," more commonly known as "red beans" (*hongdou*), were a symbol of love; and the kingfishers invoke marital harmony in the imagery of a pair of birds in each other's company. Amid this beautiful setting comes a hint of physical intimacy: falling asleep late at night and sharing the sweet dreams indicating a brilliant future for the groom. The pleasure of the inner chamber was intellectual as well as sensual: writing poetry, practicing calligraphy, and playing chess all speak to their cultural refinement and intellectual compatibility.

If Hao Yixing was quiet or even reserved in the eyes of his friends,[59] he did not appear so when it came to expressing his affection for his bride. She was under his constant gaze, and once he even injected a bit of humor, joking perhaps about their age difference: "I peep at the bridal mirror before the candle light, 'Please don't call me, in your lowered voice, "the old rascal" ' [*lao nu*]."[60] Wang Zhaoyuan, on the other hand, did not make use of intimate and humorous tones such as this. Gender norms regarding female behavior, it seems, played a part in her guarded demeanor. It would be improper for a bride to speak about conjugal intimacy in that manner. The difference in their ways of expressing intimacy showed again in the few poems they wrote while apart. During a trip to Ji'nan, the provincial capital, Yixing sent Zhaoyuan a poem with a suggestive query: "Sitting deep into the night by the fireplace, are you feeling cold embracing a quilt?"[61] By contrast, in her poems to Yixing, who was away while taking the provincial examination,

Zhaoyuan focused solely on his upcoming undertaking. She expressed her wishes for his success, imagining the glory he would bring home. Moreover, she exhorted him to continue studying diligently even if he fulfilled his hope and passed the examination.[62]

Zhaoyuan had high hopes for her husband, but she also set up ambitious goals for herself. She was a young woman with tremendous drive.

Toward one's ruler and parents, one must be loyal [*zhong*] and filial [*xiao*],
Women can make a name, just as men can.
[My] aspiration soars to the farthest limits of the sky [*jiu xiao*], shining over
    the sun and moon,
The one who wears skirts and hairpins is indeed a hero![63]

Zhong (political loyalty) was a paramount male virtue. When *zhong* and *xiao* appeared together as parallel moral attributes, they signified the greatest possible accomplishment for men. At a time when women assumed no political roles and were not allowed to take a government position serving a ruler, *zhong* was largely (although not always) irrelevant to women, whose virtue was measured instead by chastity and fidelity to their husbands. Zhaoyuan, however, unambiguously rejected the gendered underlining of the notion. She makes clear her ambition: she will not agree to play a lesser role even though she is a woman; she aims to achieve high honor in the world just as a man would.

Wang Zhaoyuan was not unique in her desire to make a name for herself in spite of the limited opportunities afforded women. Seeking achievement and recognition motivated other women to aspire to artistic and literary excellence or extraordinary moral deeds in Qing times. That she "craved fame" was in fact a familiar charge against such women.[64] Zhang Xuecheng, for example, decried the female poets (and their male mentor Yuan Mei) who circulated and published their works for the alleged purpose of "boosting their reputations."[65] Even Yuan Mei remarked, although not negatively, that "women have a greater desire than men to seek fame."[66] Wang Zhaoyuan's blunt declaration of ambition adds to our understanding of the gendered dimension of the idea of making a name. It is possible to argue that the intellectual and moral capacity women demonstrated in the Qing period fostered a more assertive mentality in young women than ever before. Establishing a name was traditionally a masculine ideal, and as Yulian Wu's chapter in this volume shows, it remained a chief motivation for men, including merchants and merchants who turned scholars, to achieve manly distinction. But it appears that, as women became increasingly conscious of their self-worth, the traditional gender demarcation was challenged. Of course, according to men like Zhang Xuecheng, seeking a name was an utterly unwomanly behavior and had to be stopped.

Wang Zhaoyuan, of course, would have none of it. But despite her tremendous drive, she did not delude herself about what a woman was allowed to accomplish. Her goal lay not in serving the court as a loyal official but in the realm of learning, in which remarkable women of the past had set precedents:

> For thirty years I have kept wiping dust from the mirror's surface,[67]
> In it, my appearance of youth has not changed.
> My life goal is to be a woman versed in books [lit., nü jiaoshu],
> One who would make the person of the Wuyi Lane [Xie Daoyun] feel
>   proud.[68]

Entitled "Self-Exhortation" (Li zhi), this poem was written around her thirtieth birthday. Using the metaphor of "wiping dust from a mirror," drawn from Chan Buddhism and referring to steadfast striving for enlightenment, she proudly reflected on her unfailing efforts. From a young age, she had set her heart on becoming a scholar, and she was as energetic in her pursuit as ever. Women had long demonstrated superiority in learning, she suggested; and like the brilliant Xie Daoyun, she believed that her talent, too, would outshine that of men.

In these early years of marriage, the couple's intellectual life merged to a large extent with their love life, and one enhanced the other. The marriage brought to each an intellectual companion who further inspired the ambition for success. From elsewhere we learn that during these years, the couple devoted much of their time to discussing and writing commentaries on the poetry in the *Book of Songs*. This was a project Zhaoyuan had initiated and had been working on, and their marriage turned it into a shared cause.[69] They planned to finish in a couple years, but it would take three times that. The final product of their collaborative labor, *An Inquiry into the Book of Songs*, commemorated their happy and intellectually fulfilling first years of marriage. Yixing wrote a preface for the work, recalling the delight they had shared during those days. Those had been among their most spirited and carefree years: living comfortably in the residence of Zhaoyuan's mother, full of hope, they had yet to face career setbacks (for Yixing) and perennial financial difficulties.

But aspiration had its downside: it gave them purpose but also created anxiety. All this time, Yixing had been working intensely in preparation for the provincial and later the *jinshi* examinations. Wang Zhaoyuan's earnest hopes for him, and her competitiveness, it appeared, put considerable pressure on him. Shortly after the wedding, Zhaoyuan and Yixing had been chatting casually on a beautiful moonlit night, and Zhaoyuan had challenged Yixing to write four poems, for which she had chosen the titles, before a pot of wine was warmed. He was able to finish only two within the time limit. He did get to drink the wine, and he completed the other two poems on another day. A few days later, Zhaoyuan wrote, in response, four poems, with the same four titles that she had chosen for her husband.[70] Yixing probably had not fully anticipated such challenges from his bride. He admitted to Zhao Tongyang, his sister's husband: "I am slow, which often causes me to be ridiculed by my wife."[71] He indicated to Zhao that he had to succeed so that he could expunge Zhaoyuan's taunts (*xue si yan*).[72] *Slow* did not simply refer to things such as the inability to finish poetic composition within the time allowed; his struggle to advance more quickly for a *jinshi* degree was probably the real cause for embarrassment. In a poem titled "To Ruiyu," Yixing praised Zhaoyuan's talent while reassuring her of his own ability: "I do not believe your husband is not a man of outstanding talent; only now I know women are truly heroines."[73]

Therefore, even though the newlyweds were immersed in marital bliss and enjoyed intellectual companionship, the bride's talent and ambition injected some tension into their relationship. The titles of the four poems that Zhaoyuan had chosen for Yixing to write on bespoke the couple's lofty aspirations, but the pressure was on for the groom. Three of the four incorporated symbols of great success (defined as examination success and holding high office): "A River Carp Ascending the Dragon's Gate" (He li deng longmen), "Glory of the Country and Family" (Bang jia zhi guang), and "A Flying Swan Making a Far-Reaching Call" (Fei hong xiang yuan yin). Yixing projected a tremendous sense of confidence and optimism into the imagery. Like a "river carp" ready to jump through the steep, hundred-foot-high "dragon's gate," and "a wild swan" whose sound will "set the country to shake," his talent would carry him to the highest realm of achievement.[74] The most telling of the four poems is perhaps the first, "The Osprey's Cry" (Guanguan jujiu). Taking its title from the opening poem of the *Book of*

Songs, which celebrates courtship and conjugal love, what each spouse wrote responded only in part to that theme. Playing on the imagery of a pair of birds swimming and merrymaking, Yixing ended his poem with a grand scene suggesting, again, a magnificent prospect for success; and in Zhaoyuan's, the ospreys are depicted as "flying to the dragon's pond, freely drinking and eating in the Shanglin Imperial Garden,"[75] invoking images of celebration after a glorious feat.

CONCLUSION

Singing in Harmony is a fascinating, one-of-a-kind work. Compiled in the early years of a marriage, this poetic anthology richly illustrates conjugal love as conception, imagination, and experience. For the newly married Wang Zhaoyuan and Hao Yixing, love presented a rational, morally justified, and passionate emotion. More than anything else, the collection lays bare the idea that *qing* held an essential place in marriage and was a key ingredient in a happy marital union. If, beginning in the seventeenth century, *qing* as a proper component of marriage was increasingly touted in the social circles of the literati, *Singing in Harmony* brought out that ideal in a most telling fashion.

Marital love was not an uncommon literary subject before the seventeenth century.[76] Even in the seventeenth century, however, rarely did a married couple jointly speak of it as forcefully and unequivocally, employing the idea of *qing* as the framework and the vocabulary of their presentation of happiness. *Singing in Harmony* suggests that, since the idea of *qing* had taken the educated public by storm a century earlier, predominantly through theatrical and fictional constructions, it had become even more deeply ingrained in the structures of marital emotion and was the focal point around which married couples fashioned their emotional lives. But Wang Zhaoyuan and Hao Yixing, who would grow into scholars of the classics, did not perceive *qing* as a legacy of the late Ming cult; rather, they persistently delineated it through its connections to orthodox literature such as the *Book of Songs*, thus injecting moral authority into the emotion of *qing*. Confucius had characterized the poems of the *Book of Songs* as "not straying from the path" (*si wu xie*);[77] likewise, the poems in *Singing in Harmony* correctly found their footing in the classic tradition.

For many educated couples of the seventeenth and eighteenth centuries, poetry was the medium of communicating conjugal affection, and harmony was the hallmark of a companionate relationship centered in the intellectual and spiritual realms of life. The conjugal love projected in *Singing in Harmony* attested to this ideal: attraction was manifested in artistic and leisurely activities. But the poetic volume also brings something different to this picture. The power of love in the Wang-Hao case was immensely inspirational as well as joyful, and it even had the effect of disturbing the harmony in marital life. Wang Zhaoyuan was not merely an agreeable companion; her self-confidence and assertiveness occasionally had a destabilizing effect on their love relationship. These traits continued to shape their relationship later in life, as suggested in accounts that describe Zhaoyuan as an assertive intellectual partner. Having been raised by a strong-willed mother, and having lived as an uxorilocally married wife (thus free of control by parents-in-law) for several years, had allowed her to develop an usually independent mind and a keen awareness of the self. But in a broad sense, her assertiveness had everything to do with the culture of the eighteenth century that valorized female education and glorified female talent. Female literacy, it seems, was altering the conventional marital dynamic, at least in some ways.

In the roles that Wang Zhaoyuan envisioned for herself, her supportive social duties took a back seat while her self-worth was emphatically valued. It is tempting to argue that Wang Zhaoyuan might have been articulating a different kind of marital relationship, one that eroded the fundamental gender hierarchy in marriage. Zhaoyuan probably was not representative in this regard. Many learned women did not pursue goals beyond their domestic roles, and managing the household was their preoccupation. Marriage often transformed a precocious young woman into an upright wife who discontinued her writing in order to fulfill her new duties.[78] Gan Lirou (1743–1819), another poet who enjoyed a companionate marriage, was content to be a dutiful wife. Marriage means "the way of the daughter comes to an end, that of the wife begins," she wrote at her marriage.[79] Even so, Zhaoyuan was not alone in expressing a desire to accomplish more than simply the fulfillment of conventional roles. Such desire led to, for example, the deep frustration of Wu Zhao (1799–1862), who lamented her fate as a woman with no opportunities to advance in society.[80] Unlike Wu Zhao, Wang Zhaoyuan was optimistic and hopeful, believing in her ability to achieve greatness even as a woman. If companionate marriage in the seventeenth century did not expand women's space outside the role of helpmate,[81] Zhaoyuan seemed to be pressing to change that limit. If education functioned to some extent as an equalizing force in gender relations, Wang Zhaoyuan seemed to have taken it to a new level.

The refreshing features in the Wang-Hao marriage—the somewhat egalitarian relationship (as far as their intellectual activities were concerned), the notion that the best marriage represented an encounter of heart and soul, and the notion that love was perceived as an essential ingredient of marriage—suggest the possibility of a limited cross-cultural comparison. Whether by coincidence or not, the ideal of companionate marriage was established in early-nineteenth-century England and the United States with the rise of the modern family. In Victorian England, for example, by 1830 it became a norm that marriage represented "the union of soul mates."[82] At approximately the same time in the United States, "many women and men had placed a new value on affectionate ties between family members, particularly within the immediate family, whose nucleus was a married couple joined by romantic love. This new desire for intimacy and companionship displaced a domestic patriarchy in which men wielded authority over the other members of the immediate and extended family and in which an emphasis on harmony and order limited the open expression of affection."[83] Karen Lystra notes in her study of courtship letters of nineteenth-century America that "when the companionate ideal was emotionally charged with romantic love, it was a powerful counterbalance to male dominance in male-female relationship."[84] While illuminating in some respects, *Singing in Harmony* as a historical source is silent on other ramifications of *qing*: for instance, it touches little on the broad significance of family relations, including parent-child relations.

I have taken the West as a point of reference not to show how China measured up to a Western model of progress—and not to use the binary of modernity and tradition as an analytical framework[85]—but rather to draw attention to the fact that ideas about marriage were evolving in China as well. The changes there were not as radical and were certainly not driven by similar historical circumstances, but China did move in a direction that emphasized emotional and spiritual bonding in the conjugal relationship.[86] It is of course impossible to surmise retrospectively where the changes would have led had the historical trajectory of nineteenth-century China been different, but perhaps the love that Wang Zhaoyuan and Hao Yixing so consciously celebrated would not have been drowned out by an all-out denunciation of the so-called Confucian past in the early twentieth century.

Earlier drafts of this chapter were presented in 2010 at the annual meeting of the American Historical Association, the University of Virginia, California State University at Long Beach, and UC Davis at the colloquium "Moving Forward: Gender and Chinese History." I am grateful for Zhang Cong, Guotong Li, and Beverly Bossler for providing me with these wonderful opportunities, from which I received helpful comments and suggestions. I also extend my appreciation to Beverly Bossler for her tireless work on this volume; to the anonymous reader; and in particular to Susan Mann and Cathy Kudlick, whose comments have greatly shaped my thinking on this project.

1   Wang Zhaoyuan and her work have been the subjects of many article-length studies. A leading historian in English language publication is Harriet T. Zurndorfer. See "The 'Constant World' of Wang Chao-yuan," "The *Lienü zhuan* Tradition," and "Wang Zhaoyuan (1763–1851) and the Erasure of 'Talented Women.' " Another recently published work is Sufeng Xu, "Domesticating Romantic Love." For Chinese language publications, see Di, "Hao Yixing yu Wang Zhaoyuan"; Xu, "Qingdai Wang Zhaoyuan"; and Song, "Qingdai cainü."

2   During the New Cultural movement of the early twentieth century, whereas the image of the bride who killed herself while being carried to her wedding in a sedan chair captured the evils that the feudal society had done to the younger generation, free choice and a loving marriage represented a key promise of modernity.

3   Ko, *Teachers of the Inner Chambers*, 179.

4   Beside Ko's work, also see Ropp, "Love, Literacy, and Laments"; Duan, "Xiu dao renjian"; Lui, "Li Shangzhang"; and Xu, "Domesticating Romantic Love."

5   Two such cases have been studied by Xiaorong Li. See "Singing in Dis/harmony" and "Fuchang fushui."

6   Collections of poetry from the early Qing through the nineteenth century commonly feature poems exchanged between married couples. In recent years, historians have made use of these valuable sources to explore marital relations. One case, that of Zhang Wanying and Wang Xi, is described in Susan Mann's *The Talented Women of the Zhang Family*. See also Mann, *Precious Records*, 111–12; Fong, *Herself an Author*. For works in Chinese, see Chen, *Qingdai jiadao*.

7   See Liu, "Qingdai zhi fufu hegao."

8   The word *qing* is translated in this paper as "love and affection." Depending on the context, *qing* has different meanings. See Epstein, *Competing Discourses*, 62–65.

9   These issues are explored in Sufeng Xu's article "Domesticating Romantic Love during the High Qing Classical Revival." Xu argues that "the cult of *qing* that characterized the subversive late Ming literati culture" was "domesticated, ritualized, and transformed into conjugal love" and "integrated into the High Qing "familistic moralism" (220). The article, which is also a close study of the *Heming ji*, came out when this chapter had gone into production, and as a result I have been unable to fully incorporate its arguments here.

10 The relationship between the High Qing classic revival and changing marital rela-

tionships is one of the issues that needs further examination. Sufeng Xu argues that "classical scholars saw *qing* as residing within the husband-wife relationship, and also elevated the status of this relationship" ("Domesticating Romantic Love," 246). My sources suggest that classical scholars were far from unanimous in their stance on cultural and social issues, including those related to the marital relationship.

11 They were married in the winter of the fifty-second year of the Qianlong reign, which fell either at the end of 1787 or in early 1788. Xu, *Hao Langao (Yixing) fufu nianpu*, 8. That the marriage was uxorilocal is indicated in the biography of Wang Zhaoyuan's mother written by Mou Moren (a close friend of Hao Yixing). Xu, *Hao Langao (Yixing) fufu nianpu*, 9.

12 Among the influential figures the Wang lineage produced was the late Qing scholar Wang Yirong, who would call Zhaoyuan a "lineage grand aunt" (*cong zugu*). Wang Zhaoyuan was a cousin of Wang Yirong's paternal grandfather.

13 Xu Weiyu states that "Lin looked for a husband for Wangquan [Zhaoyuan], and she found Hao Langao [Yixing] of Qixia." *Hao Langao (Yixing) fufu nianpu*, 9. All translations in this chapter are mine unless otherwise noted. According to Zurndorfer, Wang Zhaoyuan met Hao Yixing while working as his daughter's instructor. I have been unable to verify this information. "The *Lienü zhuan* Tradition," 62.

14 Xu, *Hao Langao (Yixing) fufu nianpu*, 1–7.

15 Ibid., 9.

16 Lady Lin's biography written by Mou Moren notes that Lady Lin "respected the teacher and encouraged [Zhaoyuan] to study." Xu, *Hao Langao (Yixing) fufu nianpu*, 9. The term *nüxue* appears in Wang Zhaoyuan's "Pajing xiaoji xu," in which she stated that her mother pressed her to enter *nuxüe*. *Nuxüe* could mean a "girl's school" or "women's learning." Wang, *Shaishutang gui zhong wencun*, 1a.

17 Wang, *Shaishutang gui zhong wencun*, 2a.

18 Her own preface to *Lienü zhuan buzhu* was written in 1805. See Wang Zhaoyuan, "Lienü zhuan buzhu xu." Two contemporaneous scholars, Zang Yong and Ma Guanchen, contributed prefaces to it, praising the work. Its influence can also be seen in the fact that influential scholars at the time added commentaries and corrections to *Lienü zhuan buzhu*. See Wang Zhaoyuan, *Lienü zhuan buzhu*; and Zang et al., *Lienü zhuan buzhu jiaozheng*.

19 Wang, *Shaishutang gui zhong wencun*, 8a.

20 On Qing elite uxorilocal marriages as a social mobility strategy, see Lu, "Uxorilocal Marriage among Qing Literati."

21 It is unclear why the surname of this cousin in her lineage differed from hers.

22 Hao, *Meisou xianping*, 2.23a. Peiyuan was Yixing's father. Given that Lady Lin was literate, it is somewhat puzzling that she would have someone read to her the teacher's comments. One possibility was that she was in poor health at the time.

23 Wang Zhaoyuan's mother died when she was twenty-nine. See ibid., 2.23a.

24 According to Xu, *Hao Langao (Yixing) fufu nianpu*, their first child, a son, was born in 1789 and died of smallpox in 1792, together with a daughter from Yixing's previous marriage. Wang Zhaoyuan gave birth to their second son in 1794, who died in

1804, and her third son in 1801. Their youngest child was a daughter born in 1807, when Wang Zhaoyuan was forty-five *sui*.

25 Wang Zhaoyuan's preface, written in 1808, stated that a draft of *Pajing xiaoji* had been completed more than twenty years earlier.

26 Xu, *Hao Langao (Yixing) fufu nianpu*, 47. The work's coauthored nature was made clear by Hao Yixing's own preface to *Shi wen*, although publishers and authors in later times have attributed it either to Hao Yixing (for example, *Qingshi gao*, Xu Weiyu's *Yearly Records,* and the *Xuxiu siku quanshu*) or to Zhaoyuan (the version presented by Shuntian prefecture to Emperor Guangzu).

27 The ten stanzas on sacrifice were attached to *Heming ji*. The poem on the portrait of Ruan Yuan's mother was included in Wanyan Yun Zhu, comp., *Guochao guixiu zhengshi ji*, 17.3a–b.

28 Zhao et al., *Qingshi gao*, 13245.

29 Ibid.

30 Chen, *Sanbaitang wenji*, 611.

31 This copy was housed in Central Library of China in Beijing.

32 Wang, *Shaishutang gui zhong wencun*, 6a.

33 Hao Yixing has a separate collection of his own that totals over five hundred poems, titled *Shaishutang shichao*, included in his collected works, *Shaishutang ji*.

34 See "Li zhi" and "Qu wen." Wang and Hao, *Heming ji*, 657, 656. In the latter, Zhao-yuan describes the scene of burning herbs to expel mosquitoes to protect a baby.

35 Few in Hao Yixing's poetry collection are conjugal poems.

36 After marriage, an educated woman was expected to stop writing and devote her time and energy fully to household work, although in reality some did manage to do both. See Mann, *Precious Records*, 77–78.

37 "Zhongfeng" is a poem in the "Bei feng" section of the *Book of Songs*; *yin yu* is a phrase from another *Book of Song* poem titled "Gu feng" that was believed to have been authored by an abandoned wife. See Chen, *Shijing zhijie*, 90, 104.

38 The term *guests and friends* signifies a high level of mutual respect. In Confucian teaching, respect was a core principle of the conjugal relationship.

39 As in the phrase *yuhe*, "meeting of two minds."

40 Han Yu, *Han Yu quanji*, 1465. Han Yu's essay is a famous work in the literary history of China.

41 Ko, *Teachers of the Inner Chambers*, 79. Also see *Competing Discourses* by Maram Epstein, which provides an insightful analysis of the notion of *qing* in the literary, historical, and philosophical contexts of the Ming-Qing period. See chapter 2.

42 Ko, *Teachers of the Inner Chambers*, 89–91.

43 See Epstein, *Competing Discourses*. The notion that excessive *qing* would lead to desire, an inappropriate emotion, was also noted in the seventeenth century discussion of *qing*. See Ko, *Teachers of the Inner Chambers*, 80.

44 The Cowherd and the Weaving Maid were mythical lovers.

45 "Peach blossom," alluding to the "Peach Tree" poem in the *Book of Songs*, is a metaphor for the bride.

46 This line plays on the poem "Zhu" from the *Book of Songs*.

47 When the charred part of a candlewick accumulates on the top of a burning candle, it looks like "flowers." The phenomenon was commonly interpreted as an auspicious sign.

48 This alludes to another poem from the *Book of Songs*. The poem describes a man longing to marry a beautiful girl. Chen, *Shijing zhijie*, 790–94.

49 This line again plays on "Zhu" from the *Book of Songs*, using phrases from that poem. In the original, the phrase *chonger* (filling the ears) refers to "ear-plugs," a type of jewelry or decoration.

50 This is a reference to the famous story about the female poet Xie Daoyun. See Mann, *Precious Records*, 83.

51 Ascending to the high clouds is a metaphor for great achievements.

52 Literally "the tray that is being raised to the height of the eyebrow," this is a reference to the iconic marriage of Liang Hong and Meng Guang. See discussion later in the chapter.

53 The "deer-cart" refers to the Bao Xuan story discussed later in the chapter.

54 Fan, *Hou Han shu*, 2766–68. In the original story reported in *Hou Han shu* (Latter Han History), Meng Guang dressed beautifully at her wedding to test her husband's moral character, and her "holding the tray to the height of her eyebrows" was meant to help establish his standing after they moved to a new area, where he worked as a hired laborer (the idea was that a person of such low status who could command such respect from his wife must be an extraordinary man). These meanings, however, seem to have been diluted in the Qing usage of the story.

55 Ibid., 2781–82.

56 Wang and Hao, *Heming ji*, 655.

57 During earlier dynasties, men who had passed the *jinshi* examinations were presented with the "golden flower card" (*jinhuabang*) to announce the good news.

58 Wang and Hao, *Heming ji*, 653–54.

59 Zhao et al., *Qingshi gao*, 13245.

60 Wang and Hao, *Heming ji*, 653. The term *lao nu*, which first appeared in stories in *A New Account of the Tales of the World* (Shi shuo xin yu) by Liu Yiqing, is a playful term for addressing one's husband.

61 Wang and Hao, *Heming ji*, 656.

62 Ibid.

63 Ibid., 657.

64 Faithful maidens—i.e., betrothed women who lived as chaste widows or who committed suicide after their fiancés' deaths—were examples of women who demonstrated exemplary moral integrity. See Lu, *True to Her Word*, 137–39.

65 Zhang, *Bingchen zhaji*, 98. Also see p. 58. For more on Zhang Xuecheng's criticism of Yuan Mei and the debate about proper learning for women, see Mann, "Learned Women in the Eighteenth Century," 28–32.

66 Wang, *Qingdai guixiu*, 53.

67 Wiping dust from the mirror's surface is a reference to a verse written by the famous Chan Buddhist Shenxiu, recorded in the *Platform Sutra of the Sixth Patriarch*.

68 Wang and Hao, *Heming ji*, 657. Wuyi Lane (*Wuyi xiang*) was the residential area for

the prominent Wang and Xie clans of the Eastern Jin dynasty. Here Wang Zhao-yuan was referring to the female poet Xie Daoyun of the Xie clan.

69 See Hao Yixing, preface to *Shi wen*, 172–73.

70 Wang and Hao, *Heming ji*, 654.

71 Hao, *Shaishutang ji*, 672.

72 Other poems to Zhao Tongyang also hint at his anxiety. In one, for example, he sighed when noticing his white hair. He wrote, "It is shameful that the golden list does not have my name on it," and regretted that he "previously did not read books (i.e., he did not read widely)." Ibid.

73 Wang and Hao, *Heming ji*, 654.

74 Ibid.

75 The Garden of Shanglin (Shanglin yuan) was a Han dynasty imperial garden.

76 To give a few examples, one enduring tale of marital love was that of Qin Jia and Xu Shu from the late Han period. Their poetry exchanges were recorded in the sixth-century anthology *Yutai xinyong*; another popular story, recorded in *Shishuo xinyu*, tells of Xun Chan of the Three Kingdoms period. Xun was so deeply in love with his wife that when she fell ill with fever, he laid his bare body on ice in bitter winter and then cooled her body with his. He died of sorrow about a year after her death. In the Qing, both stories were frequently cited as cultural icons of marital devotion and love.

77 Stephen Owen, foreword to Waley, *The Book of Songs*, xxiii.

78 Mann, *Precious Records*, 117–20.

79 Fong, *Herself an Author*, 23.

80 Volpp, "Drinking Wine," 239–50.

81 Ko, *Teachers of the Inner Chambers*, 180–83.

82 Marcus, *Between Women*, 6.

83 Jabour, *Marriage in the Early Republic*, 2.

84 Lystra, *Searching the Heart*, 233.

85 Haiyan Lee's book, *Revolution of the Heart: A Genealogy of Love in China, 1900–1950*, offers an extensive discussion of how the nature of love evolved from the "Confucian structure of feeling" to a modern sentiment.

86 Legal cases examined by Janet Theiss point to a shift in state policy in the eighteenth century that increased the control of husband or wife over some aspect of his or her life while limiting the authority of parents or in-laws. At the same time, she argues that conjugal love was difficult to achieve, because it was in conflict with ritual propriety and patrilineal interests. "Love in a Confucian Climate," 205–9.

PART TWO

"Cloistered Ladies"
to New Women

CHAPTER FIVE

"Media-Savvy" Gentlewomen of the 1870s and Beyond

Ellen Widmer

M

IGHT there be a lacuna in the study of Qing women, specifically during the period between the end of the Taiping Rebellion in 1864 and the publication of the first women's magazines of the 1890s? Whereas the 1890s was a time of transition for women—from the old world of privately circulated poems and correspondence to a new one of dedicated women's magazines[1]—signs of such a transition are also evident in material from four literary magazines of the 1870s. The first three of these are essentially the same periodical twice renamed, and the titles of all three can be translated as *Miscellaneous Accounts of the World* (Yinghuan suoji, Huanyu suoji, Siming suoji). They came out between late 1872 and early 1876 and were supplements to the early Shanghai newspaper *Shanghai News* (Shenbao), which began publication in 1872. The fourth, *New Delicacies* (Houqing xinlu), came out in four issues, all published in winter 1876, in imitation of the first three.[2] These supplements were published in small numbers, about two thousand per issue,[3] and none lasted more than a few years.

Of the thirty or so women whose names appear in these magazines, many cannot be identified because of the pseudonyms they use. Of the roughly one dozen who published under what appear to be their real names, only five have entries under these names in Hu Wenkai's historical bibliography of Chinese women authors.[4] Another two can be accessed in that bibliography via their pen names.[5] Two other woman, who appear in the supplements as recipients of someone else's poems, have entries in Hu's bibliography; but since they do not appear as writers in the supplements, they are not included here.[6] Similarly, since the focus of this chapter is on living women who actively sought these new means of publication, women who had clearly died before our story begins are also not included.[7]

Despite the small number of searchable names, in combination with other evidence, this material allows us to begin to fill in a gap in our understanding of late Qing literary women. It permits us to assert that the new media did not supplant old-fashioned women's literary culture but, rather, enabled it to move in new directions. There were seasoned women writers of the 1870s who took an interest in these literary journals and sought to publish in them. Many brought their old literary habits with them, but even in the first and more conservative of the two cases that I present here, there are small signs of receptivity to a rapidly changing world. At the same time, the Taiping Rebellion was very much on the minds of writers in this period, male and female, particularly the older ones. A full study of all periodicals from 1872 until the end of the Qing might someday allow us to draw up a scheme in which the rebellion receded as new themes and practices arose—in women's writings, as well as in men's.[8] The goal in this chapter, however, is merely to introduce this material and propose how it might fill in a blank in our understanding.

The source materials I used present certain difficulties. The four literary journals are actually in good physical shape and, in that sense, are not difficult to work with, but because they have no modern reprints they can be difficult to obtain.[9] Even more of a problem is the thicket of pen names used by authors of both genders whose works were published in them. Many used nothing but pen names, making them impossible to trace without evidence from other sources. Another difficulty is that authors changed their pen names as they moved from genre to genre or as other circumstances changed. It is often quite a challenge to assemble one individual from the various pieces that one finds. Complicating the picture further, *Shanghai News*, too, published women's literary submissions, which were sometimes

Ellen Widmer

the same as, or in conversation with, those in the literary journals.

How does one arrive at the figure thirty women? In the total of fifty or so issues from the four journals, approximately that number of authors use the title "Woman Historian" (*nüshi*) as part of their self-identification, or else claim to have written from the women's quarters. Certainly some other writers who do not identify themselves as such were also women. But to keep matters simple, these two criteria are the ones I have used in identifying female authors. Some of them appear only once in the entire set of materials. Others recur, a few or many times.

Scholars familiar with the Chinese literary tradition might wonder whether some of these "women historians" were men. We know that during the very late Qing it was not uncommon for men to write in the voice of women.[10] However, since some of the thirty are identified as women by Hu Wenkai, it is reasonable to assume, at least for now, that these "women historians" are indeed women. Many of the thirty give scant hope they can ever be identified. It is pointless to pursue names like "Woman Historian of Heavenly Fragrance" (Tianxiang *nüshi*) or "Woman Historian of the Eastern Pearl (Dongzhu *nüshi*), let alone "Woman Historian Whose Name Has Been Lost" (*Nüshi* shiming"), until other evidence emerges. However, more than ten names aside from the five already located in Hu's bibliography consist of surname, given name, and hometown. There is a reasonable chance that they will eventually be located in gazetteers and similar sources. Here I am concerned with just two of the women who can be identified in Hu's bibliography and who were alive in the 1870s.

WOMAN HISTORIAN OF WEAVING CLOUD: WANG QINGDI

About Wang Qingdi (1828–90), we know a fair amount.[11] She used the pen names "Beautiful Immortal" (Nongxian) and "Woman Historian of Weaving Cloud" (Zhiyun nüshi). She was the mother of Zhan Xi (1850–1927) and Zhan Kai (c. 1860–c. 1910), both of whom wrote late-Qing-style modern novels. In addition to these two brothers, other family members were writers, notably a third brother, Zhan Lang, as well as their father Zhan Sizeng (1832–94).[12] The latter two both have entries in one of the four literary magazines. The family came from Quzhou in western Zhejiang, but Wang Qingdi herself was from Hangzhou. As a girl she had traveled with her father, Wang Baohua, a national-degree holder (*jinshi*) and member of the Hanlin academy, to Sichuan, where he performed his official duties.[13] During her girlhood there, she wrote well enough to be broadly acclaimed.[14] Her poems lamenting her departure from that province appear at the beginning of her collected poems.

Wang's poetry collection, titled (from her pen name) *Poems of Weaving Cloud Tower* (Zhiyun lou shi ji), was published in 1857. About 120 poems of Wang's poems are extant, of which a majority come from this published collection. In addition, in the 1960s a descendant copied much of the collection by hand and added some of Wang's later poems. Both the original and the copy are preserved in the Quzhou Museum.[15] The same material was also recently reprinted in a slightly altered format.[16]

Perhaps the most notable among the collection's poems are those describing the Taiping Rebellion, from which the family had to flee several times. Another interesting set was written to Wang's sons Zhan Xi and Zhan Lang (Zhan Kai was born after the collection was published). Predictably, Wang exchanged a fair number of poems with her husband, Zhan Sizeng, who was part of the effort to put down the Taipings in the Quzhou area. In taking her to Quzhou, Wang's marriage removed her from the main branch of Lower Yangzi culture, but she seems to have frequently traveled back to Hangzhou.

It was most likely from Quzhou that Wang submitted her work to the new-style journals *Siming suoji* and *Houqing xinlu*. All three of her entries in these two journals are found in sets of poems assembled by a man named Du Jinqing, courtesy name Du Qiukui, pen name Fanke shanqiao (Woodcutter of Fanke Mountain). In two of these three cases Du appears to have been the organizer of the set, in the third he was just one among several who submitted poems.

Du's life circumstances are rather obscure. He was apparently well known in the Haichang area, and he traveled widely, including to Shanghai. He lived some of his life in Longyou county, on the easternmost side of Quzhou. He passed the county-level *shengyuan* examination.[17] He was a friend of the late-Qing, early-republican writer Zou Tao (1850–1931). Zou wrote for the four journals I discuss here, using the name Zou Hanfei.[18] Zou was a friend of Zhan Kai and almost certainly of Zhan Xi, as well.[19] Du was perhaps the most frequent contributor of all to the four journals, and he also published frequently in *Shanghai News*.[20] Du is further known to have assembled several collections, including a group of short stories in classical Chinese called *Strange Stories Heard during Travels* (Kezhong yiwen lu).[21] A few of the names associated with this short-story collection can be linked with Du or his friends from the literary journals.[22] Dated 1879, *Strange Sto-*

Ellen Widmer

ries Heard during Travels interests scholars because it is an early instance of classical language influenced by the vernacular (*baihua*), and because of its relatively open attitudes toward women. Another point of interest is its descriptions of the Taipings.[23]

Du's contributions to the journals consist mainly of regulated verse (*shi*) and lyrics (*ci*), although he also has a brief "Talks on Poetry" (*shihua*) section at the end of *New Delicacies*. Moreover, he frequently organized sets of poems by himself and other writers. The writers whose contributions he organized consisted of both male and female friends. Some of these sets could have been assembled over time. This is the case with all three of the sets in which poems by Wang Qingdi appear and which I discuss here. At other times they appear to represent face-to-face exchanges of poems by coteries of poets. Whether they consist of poems produced all at once or assembled over a longer period, they can probably still be encompassed under the heading "coterie publishing," a phenomenon that Tobie Meyer-Fong has described.[24]

At least one other man is important in relation to Wang Qingdi's submissions, her son Zhan Xi. Zhan and Du were acquainted, and they may have been good friends. We can say for certain that they moved in similar circles and were the same age. (Zhan Xi's collected poems do not survive.) Along with two of Wang Qingdi's three submissions, Zhan Xi submitted a piece in the same set, and in one of these her second son, Zhan Lang, is also represented. For both of the sets in which she appears along with her sons, Wang used her full identification by hometown, name, and pen name: Hangzhou Gentlewoman Wang Qingdi, Beautiful Immortal (Qiantang *guixiu* Wang Qingdi Nongxian) or Female Historian Wang Qingdi of Hangzhou, Beautiful Immortal (Qiantang *nüshi* Wang Qingdi Nongxian). For the third submission Wang used the pen name Historian of Weaving Cloud.

However, a problem arises at this juncture. This is because another woman in Du's set of poetic friends used the pen name Weaving Cloud (Zhiyun). She is clearly someone else. She has a different name (Xu Songjin)[25] and husband (surname Chen, pen name Gongman). Still, we know that this poem by Historian of Weaving Cloud is by Wang, and not Xu, because it appears almost verbatim in the poems copied by Wang's descendant, the only difference being a few wrong characters that crept into the printed version. The same is true of the two poems that came out under her full name.[26]

Unlike in the other two cases, it is not clear whether Zhan Xi published a poem in the third set. However, we can identify one of the poems in this set as the work of Wang's husband, Zhan Sizeng. Complicating matters is the fact that he did not use his real name or any of his usual pen names. Here, as with Wang herself, we can identify the author only through a match with a poem in Zhan Sizeng's collected poems.[27] Likewise, Zhan Xi could have authored one of the poems in this set, but if he did so, it was under a name too obscure to be recognizable at this time. Surprisingly, from what we know at present, it is Du, rather than Zhan Xi or Zhan Sizeng, whose work visibly accompanies all three of Wang's submissions. Du's appearance in all of these cases prompts us to ask whether and how she could have known him. Her husband definitely knew Du, and two of Wang's three published poems mention him.[28] Yet it is not likely that Wang ever traveled to Haichang, which was Du's home town. Zhan Sizeng or Zhan Xi were the most likely intermediaries. Or Du may have traveled occasionally to Quzhou during this era. His long-standing tie to Longyou county would have put him close to Qu county upon occasion. In any event, whereas it would have been natural to assume that the main reason Wang Qingdi submitted her work to journals related to *Shanghai News* was that her son encouraged her, now that we see Du's prominence in all three cases we have to assume that he, too, helped Wang's publication efforts. It appears that Du, Zhan Xi, and very possibly Zhan Sizeng worked together to publish Wang's poems.

Let us now look at the three poems. The first poem published under her own name came out in the second issue of *Siming suoji*, which is to say, in the third month of 1875 (second month of the year designated as *yihai* on the lunar calendar). It is the last poem in a set that begins with Du's biography of a virtuous woman surnamed Mao, whose maiden name was Chen. The virtuous woman did not die as a direct result of the Taiping Rebellion, but her death was indirectly related. She was from a good family of Haining (Haichang) county in Jiaxing prefecture and respectful of the old virtues. When the Taipings arrived in 1861, she took her mother to safety in nearby Tongxiang. There she met the mother and grandmother of the Mao family, who were impressed with her virtue and lined up a marriage for her with their son. The mother and grandmother soon died. Afterward Mao became pregnant, but her husband declined and died in the wake of the Taiping disaster, and the circumstances for bringing up a child deteriorated. Although she did everything she could to manage the household, she was uncomfortable surviving her husband. Once the child was old enough, she turned him over to a relative and killed herself, at the age of twenty-two *sui*.

This type of sad story about a virtuous wife or mother whose death was Taiping-related occurs frequently in the four journals. As often as not they

Ellen Widmer

were written by men. In this case, several of the seven *shi*-style poems that follow are quite long, including those by Zhan Xi and Zhan Lang. This may imply that the Zhans knew this woman personally. Wang Qingdi's "Poem on the Biography of Virtuous Woman Mao," the last in the set, is brief:

> All vie to honor her virtue;
> She had a noble character, who can compare?
> Pure as ice and frost, her heart never wavered.
> Like metal and stone, her will could not be changed.
> It is fitting that all in the inner chambers should look up to her.
> She expects her body to follow her husband in death.
> She has lived up to the highest standards.
> Her good name will last for all the ages.[29]

The focus on typical female virtue in this poem is not surprising. Many of Wang's other poems are more lively, but this one falls within a range that would be expected from someone of Wang's station. So far we can conclude that although this poem appears in a new print medium, it has all of the trappings of old-fashioned women's publishing. These include the coterie context, the subject matter, and the moral underpinnings.

The second poem appeared in *New Delicacies*, second issue, in the winter of 1876 (as previously noted, all five issues of *New Delicacies* came out at the same time). It was written as an endorsement of a painting by Du. The painting was titled *Picture of Studying by a Tree in Autumn* (Qiushu dushu tu). Fifteen endorsements of the painting are printed together in this issue. Especially because another poem about the same painting appeared earlier, in the tenth issue of *Siming suoji* (1875, eleventh month), we need not assume that all these endorsements were written at the same time, nor must we assume that Wang and Du were directly acquainted. In this case Wang went against the prevailing pattern and wrote her endorsement in song lyric form. This endorsement, like the previous ones, is brief, and it, too, occurs last in the set. This time, because there is no explanatory introduction, and because it is a poem about a painting, the meaning is more obscure. The subject of the painting by Du is traditional: a moment of teaching that took place in a natural setting. Likewise, as in Wang's poem in honor of the Virtuous Woman Mao, the coterie context and the song lyric style add to the impression of a traditional-style poem.

"Tang Duo ling" (Picture of studying by a tree in autumn):[30]

> The red leaves have already fallen
> But the lonely, secluded person is still engaged.
> He takes fine writings
> And turns to forest and streams.
> In a place surrounded by chrysanthemum fence and plantains,
> A nice landscape,
> Grass well trimmed [to make an abode?].
>
> The frost is quiet, the blue sky is high.
> The sounds of autumn whistle, the evening rustles.
> They aid him with chanting.
> His poetic spirit must be expansive.
> He sits a long time and does not realize from the slanting rays of sun that it
>   is getting late.
> The shadow of the brightening moon
> Moves up the valley between the mountains.[31]

Except for Zhan Xi and Wang Qingdi, virtually all the other endorsers are from Jiaxing, not Quzhou.[32] This was also the case with the first poem.

The third poem, written under a pen name, came out in the fifth issue of *Siming suoji* (1875, fifth month). Again the set is prefaced by Du, whose account of an 1874 trip from Longyou to Shanghai provides the context for the eleven endorsements. The contrast is jarring between the peaceful scenery Du sees on the trip and the hubbub and electric lights of Shanghai, and the big city strikes Du as otherworldly. Afterward a painting of the trip was made. From a poem by Zhan Sizeng, we learn that the painter was Zhan Xi, even though he had not yet met Du.[33] Du says he especially enjoys looking at the scenes in the painting, which remind him of his travels. Again Wang comes last in the series of endorsements, and again she writes in song lyric form, although this time four of the other poems, including one by her husband, are also song lyrics. Here is Wang's poem "Jinlü Qu: Inscription on a Painting of a Small Boat Seeking Beautiful Scenery, for Mr. Du Jinqing of Haining":

> A secret enthusiasm, who can know it?
> You avail yourself of a boat.
> You travel to north and south of the river.

West lake, eastern Zhe.
You do not rely on mountains and rivers to feed your creative powers.
You have your colorful brush that reaches heaven [i.e., ambition and talent].
One would guess that you are
An immortal riding on the raft to heaven.
Having toured all the famous sites
You must personally have visited all the ones with fine views.
As I unroll the painting
It describes everything from the beginning.

On a sheet of raw silk is evidence of your trip:
Most appropriately,
Spring sail, fine rain,
A lonely boat in the setting sun.
Drifting away with an oar in a boundless expanse of misty water.
How many times will you have this experience?
Making one whistle and laugh
Are the clear wind and bright moon;
They everywhere tell of Shaoling's [Du Fu's] words.
But your brocade bag
Has long since filled with a thousand poems.
He wielded a jade brush
And sang of refined tunes.[34]

Wang's poem has nothing to say about the hustle and bustle of Shanghai, but we can infer from her acquaintance with the route traversed by Du, if nothing else, that she knew something about the city's qualities.

What conclusions can we draw from these poems? Most obviously they add to the information we can glean from Wang's poetry collection. Thus, they chronicle her venture into the new media and introduce her relationship with Du, although they are silent about other details of her background. The three poems may not seem radical compared to what develops in women's poetry and prose of the 1890s; but the mere fact that Wang allowed her work to be submitted to these journals must mean that she enlarged her field of readers, if nothing more. For a number of reasons, then, Wang Qingdi's venture into the new media did not turn her into a modern writer. And yet we cannot completely dismiss the transformative potential of this woman's debut on the late Qing publishing scene.

The trends identified in Wang Qingdi's case appear to have intensified over time, as we see in the case of another poet with ties to Du Jinqing, about whom much less is known. In the supplements she is identified only through her pen name, Recluse of Buluo Mountain (Buluo Shanren). Buluo Shanren was clearly part of a group of women who responded to one another's poems but who were also in touch with Du and his circle of male friends. This group appears to have been better known for its interactions with each other than with Du,[35] but members joined Du's groups upon occasion. They also had poetical interactions with men other than Du. Among this set, only Buluo Shanren has (to my knowledge) been identified. Her name is Zhang Qingsong, and she has an entry in Hu Wenkai's bibliography (p. 527). I will refer to her as Buluo Shanren, since that is the name through which she became best known.

Hu's account can be amplified with information from a work by Huang Shiquan (1853?–1924), *Account of a Dream Journey to Shanghai* (Songnan mengying lu), written about 1877: Buluo Shanren was from Shanghai and was characterized by her extreme filial piety. She took care of her ill father for six years. She had a male tutor and learned to write so well that, reportedly, all traces of feminine style were purged from her work. (This was intended as a compliment.) She was also praised for the naturalness of her writing and was widely regarded as the outstanding woman writer of the 1870s and 1880s. She is a far more allusive and sophisticated writer than Wang.

Buluo Shanren was known especially for her complaints about the feminine condition. Chief among her laments were those about her unreliable fiancé, who was so unreliable that her marriage did not work out.[36] At some unspecified time, she set up a school and taught students for decades, dying at the age of fifty-six *sui*.[37] Her life dates cannot be pinned down with precision. She turned out two poetry collections, but these seem not to have survived. Like Wang, she wrote poems for the three literary supplements. Unlike Wang, she had many poems published in *Shanghai News* itself. Numbering well over seventy, they extend from 1872 until 1887. She must have been younger than Wang, but perhaps not much younger.[38] Even if her age was not much different from Wang's, as a resident in Shanghai she would have had an experience of China's modernization that was far more extensive and immediate. Her poems indicate that she was a gentlewoman confined to the inner chambers, but unlike in Wang Qingdi's case, there is clear indication that she was an avid and frequent reader of *Shanghai News* and the literary supplements. (Wang Qingdi had no known submissions to *Shanghai News*.)

Beginning with Buluo Shanren's poems in the literary supplements, we immediately see a far greater level of independence than we saw with Wang. Buluo Shanren's first poem, published in 1874, was not part of a group of poems but stood entirely on its own. We cannot know what happened behind the scenes; but to all outward appearances, this was work directly submitted by the poet, not by a helpful man. It had the title "Thirty Regulated Verses, without a Title." It is too long to reproduce in full, but here is a brief excerpt.

> It seems as though there are little words when she moves her red lips,
> But tears stream through her makeup, wetting her silken scarf.
> She does not master her regrets before more regrets arise.
> How many loves and sorrows are combined in her person?[39]

The poem as a whole establishes her loneliness, unhappiness, and isolation in the women's quarters. I know of no poetical responses, but there could have been some in periodicals of which I am unaware.

Buluo Shanren's second and third submissions were both published in the same issue of *Huanyu suoji* in the next year (eleventh month, 1875). One answered a poem by her frequent poetical correspondent Yaosheng *nüshi*, the other was presented to two women friends, Yaosheng *nüshi* and Danjuan *nüshi*. It built on a reworking (*die*) of the rhyme of an earlier poem. Whereas the first of these three poems shows us Buluo Shanren's ostensible independence from any male supporter, the second and third demonstrate how she and her friends made use of the new media to further poetical exchange.

Further evidence on these two points is found in Buluo Shanren's work in *Shanghai News* proper, as opposed to the supplements. A daily newspaper like *Shanghai News* would have made a better forum for interactivity than a journal that came out monthly or, as in the case of *Houqing xinlu*, in a set of five issues published simultaneously. Buluo Shanren's first poem to *Shanghai News* was two years earlier than any of her poems in the literary supplements. It was apparently through *Shanghai News* that she first made her name.[40] "Changhuai ci" (Dispirited words) was her first *Shanghai News* poem. It appeared on November 5, 1872. Here is the final couplet, from a set of four regulated verses:

In the end I try to cast off worries but I cannot.
All alone at night, with a green light illuminating half my wall, I chant
    poems.

Incidentally, this kind of sensitivity to light is a hallmark of Buluo Shanren's poems.

A long prose note at the end of this poem gives particularly clear evidence of the way the new medium encouraged an interactive frame of mind. It may be a first for a woman in this regard. Here is the note:

> A sad, dusty dream that seems so far away. Rancor tied up over three lives; when resentment ends, life is over. Delicate autumn wind adds to myriad thoughts. The beautiful figure in the mirror is half taken over by ultimate vanity. The beauty in the painting is really living out her miserable fate. A fragrant flower of the past will end up scattered and dispersed. The dark orchid of today will soon deteriorate into worthlessness. How can my grief be abated, where can I find sympathy? Holding a pen and writing words—indeed the stone cannot hope to fill the void left by sorrow. I let my words follow my mood as I grieve over autumn. The flower really is like a brokenhearted person. How dare I resort to a poetry group to give vent to my hidden anger? It is just that I let this drawn-out song be my cry. I would not dare call this poetry.[41]

What is striking about this note is its outreach to *Shanghai News*'s readership as a potential poetry group, one with the capacity to give the author comfort and generate new poetical friends, both male and female. Over the course of the next three months *Shanghai News* published six poetical responses to this poem.[42] The first was by a Shanghai woman, but at least some of the later responses were by men, among them Shanghai writer Ge Qilong.[43] It is likely that some if not all of these six poems were by writers who did not initially know Buluo Shanren. During the next seventeen years, quite a number of Buluo Shanren's other poems elicited responses. This was especially true of her poems complaining about women's condition. Buluo Shanren, for her part, often responded to other women writers' poems, many of which were as plaintive as her own.

It is interesting that the group of women poets I refer to did not all live in Shanghai. Even though we cannot identify such respondents as Yaosheng *nüshi*, Zhifang *nüshi*, Shujuan *nüshi*, or Danjuan *nüshi*, *Shanghai News* usually identified their hometowns. Of these particular four, the first two were from Haichang and the second two were from Suzhou (although Shujuan was temporarily living in Shanghai). We can further establish that the two from Haichang (Yaosheng *nüshi* and Zhifang *nüshi*) were members of the poetry group in Haichang in which Du Jinqing played such an active role.[44] It is possible that Buluo Shanren never met any of these respondents face-to-face, even though they sometimes behaved like a cluster of friends in their poems published in *Shanghai News*. Occasionally, we are told, a more distant follower of the "group" sent her submissions to *Shanghai News* by mail.[45] Buluo Shanren's chief respondents changed over the fifteen years of her submissions, and although there are many others besides the ones I have listed, Yaosheng *nüshi*, Zhifang *nüshi*, Shujuan *nüshi*, and Danjuan *nüshi* are among those most frequently listed as her friends.[46] Another interesting feature of Buluo Shanren's and her fellow poets' submissions to the new media is the publicly stated plea for help with and corrections of the poems. A number of poems include an invitation for correction by readers at the end of the title; also, quite a few poems between what appear to be people who did not know Buluo Shanren invite her to submit her corrections to their poems.[47] Traditionally construed as gesture of modesty, requests for help like these take on a new valence when they are in a form that all the world can see.

The women in Buluo Shanren's sphere of influence in the new media can be compared to poetically linked groups of women from the late Ming through the mid-Qing. Then, too, women might hear of one another entirely through written work and submit poems over long distances, even without any face-to-face meeting. The tendency to ask for corrections is another holdover from women's poetical culture of an earlier time. But when transferred to into a late-Qing newspaper-based culture, these practices were altered. The most notable alteration is from private to public interactions. Whatever was published in the supplements or *Shanghai News* became known to a wide readership. The same was not as true in earlier periods, when the medium of exchange was privately circulated poems or privately published collections. Such work was not as fully in the public sphere. Moreover, by publishing poems in a public format, later women poets like Buluo Shanren increased the chances that their work would become known to male poets from outside the family and that they might find themselves receiving poems from men like Du Jinqing and Ge Qilong. A third important difference is Buluo Shanren's emphasis on the difficulties of women's existence. Buluo Shanren's unmarried state and her confinement in the women's quarters became a topic of public discourse at this time. Her poems on these subjects can be contrasted with the three poems of Wang Qingdi that appeared in literary supplements, which are not plaintive or personal at all.

Let us now consider the full text of one of Buluo Shanren's poems in *Shanghai News*. Like "Dispirited Words," "In Praise of Chrysanthemums" is one that drew responses. It is as long as "Dispirited Words" (four regulated verses in eight stanzas) and is full of allusions—to poets Li Qingzhao, Du Fu, and Tao Yuanming, among others too numerous to deal with here:

> In the old garden of yellow flowers bisected by a path;
> Their faint fragrance, their thin shadows struggle against the west wind.
> Rolling up a curtain, I stand at a distance from the clean frost.
> I am holding a glass of wine in the lengthening autumn as the sunlight
>   declines.
>
> The cold beauty cannot bear to find solace in vulgar companionship.
> The lone blossom is just right for the one visiting secluded branches.
> This is the face of autumn, do not complain about its plainness.
> Would you think of the lofty spirit east of the fence?
>
> Because I regret that autumn light dims easily with the setting sun
> I sit under a pine in the dampness of its pure splendor.
> As my chant ends I sink in a glorious dream.
> Having recorded the mountain's shape, the silk for painting is now chilled.
>
> Coldness invades my green sleeves along the moonlit path of the recluse.
> Green vines secretly guard an arbor of flowers.
> Frosty grace and white hair face each other in leisure.
> Sparse music and distant poundings hardly make for a real commotion.
>
> Why does it matter if the branch is high when the hand reaching out is
>   cold?
> When I pick it the frost still remains.
> Most suitable for adorning a vase, how much autumn adds.
> I also enjoy watching the moon through the open curtains as it nears the
>   balcony.

My pure shadow is listless, hat askew,

Finding a friend in the lone blossom, I yet fear that my clothes are too thin.

The eagle flies, the locusts sing, they do not prattle on and on.

With their true meanings one forgets words. I want to debate them but am
deterred.

I do not regret the flowers of spring, I regret the branches of fall.

With strong stems and sparse fragrance, they have an otherworldly
beauty.

The form and feelings of a recluse should show proper detachment.

The beauty may be old, but how can she not deign to sigh.

Suitable for delicate refinement and simplicity, [life in the women's quar-
ters] can change [baleful customs.]

As in a clean prison, how can [an occupant] be said to disdain the times?

Would one send tears for the homeland from the frosty branches?

By the fence my thoughts are tied to [officeholders like Tao Yuanming].[48]

The poem is followed by the line "In fall, listless in the women's quarters, walking along the eastern fence and chancing to work out four regulated verses on chrysanthemums."[49]

As is usual in this poet's poems, there are many allusions, the poet is depicted in the isolation of the women's quarters, and the seasons and changing light of day and night are closely observed. The poem as a whole conveys loneliness and learning, and there is an immediacy to its description of the cold, cloistered garden in the autumn of the year. The link between reclusion and the isolation of the women's quarters is noteworthy, as is the self-portrait, another distinguishing feature of Buluo Shanren's poems. "In Praise of Chrysanthemums" was one of two poems by Buluo Shanren (the other was "Dispirited Words") to be reprinted in *Shanghai News* in 1917, as part of a retrospective on "Old Shanghai."[50]

A few of Buluo Shanren's poems depart from the themes of feminine confinement and disappointment. One is a fantasy of life in the immortal realm.[51] Another, one of five poems from a set titled "Reading at Night," details the poet's reactions to a sequel to the novel *Honglou meng*.[52] From it (and elsewhere) we learn of Buluo Shanren's long familiarity with the parent novel and her identification with ill-fated heroine Lin Daiyu. Interesting though such poems may be to us today, however, the poems of pure lament were the ones most often answered by Buluo Shanren's contemporaries, especially those identified as women.

The relationship between poems in *Shanghai News* and those in the four journals can be complicated. In at least one case the same poem (Du Jinqing's) appears identically in both *Shanghai News* and *Huanyu suoji;*[53] at other times, conversations between or within a group of poets appear to carry over from *Shanghai News* to the journals and vice versa. For example, five lyrics on the theme of dispelling cold (*xiaohan ci*), by or inspired by Yaosheng *nüshi*, are split between *Huanyu suoji* 11 (November 1876) and *Shanghai News* of August 1876. Here we can see a new level of intertextuality, one not found with Wang Qingdi. To keep up with all the poems that were cross-referenced and responded to, one would presumably have to read *Shanghai News* as well as all the journals. There is no need for such adroit reading when it comes to Wang.

Other differences can be found in geographical range and readership. If Buluo Shanren stayed in Shanghai and corresponded with the newspaper by mail, as seems most likely, she would nonetheless have been reaching out to women and men from Jiaxing, Suzhou, and other cities nearby. In contrast, Wang Qingdi's newspaper-based interactions are more narrowly addressed to Du Jinqing in Haichang, and they do not seem to invite responses. Furthermore, by adding *Shanghai News* to the mix of public venues, Buluo Shanren essentially doubled her number of readers, for *Shanghai News* is said to have published four thousand copies per issue, as opposed to the journals' two thousand.[54] We cannot know whether or how often Buluo Shanren and her poetical friends communicated through nonpublic channels, nor can we know how often their published poems had first been exchanged privately. But in the case of Wang's poems, no such questions can even be raised, because her level of interactivity is so low.

One final difference is the way Buluo Shanren caught the attention of readers through *Shanghai News* and the associated publications. Although she published two collections of poetry,[55] it was probably not through these collections that most readers came to know her; rather, they likely became familiar with her as the star of a group of women poets publishing in the literary journals and in *Shanghai News*.[56] Conceivably, Wang, too, reached some new readers via the new print media rather than through her published collection or privately circulated poems. But we have no evidence that she made her primary impression through new media.[57]

In a sense, Wang and Buluo Shanren can both be regarded as hybrids.

Ellen Widmer

Wang's three poems in the *Shanghai News* supplements almost certainly first appeared in those supplements. However, much if not all of the rest of her work seems to have reached readers through published collections or private correspondence. In Buluo Shanren's case, by contrast, it is safe to assume that her primary reputation was made in the new periodical outlets and that all or most of her published collections were reprints of what had already come out in such places. Even in Buluo Shanren's case, though, some readers may have first made contact with her writings through printed collections or privately circulated poems.[58]

THE IMPACT OF THE NEW MEDIA

Evidence regarding Wang Qingdi and Buluo Shanren allows us to propose that *Shanghai News*, its three literary supplements, and *New Delicacies* represent a new stage in the conditions under which women published and, in that sense alone, had an impact on later developments. Some scholars would go even farther. According to at least one, the growing visibility of women writers in the new print media helped paved the way for the changes in women's schooling that would go into effect during the last years of the Qing.[59] As this logic would have it, writings by women in Shanghai newspapers and journals provided important proof of women's intellectual ability to a skeptical (male) public. These writings would not have been disseminated so broadly without the journals. In addition, future research may allow us to conclude that the many instances in which Du Jinqing and others like him helped women to publish (or somehow stood beside them in print as they appeared in public) were part of a conscious effort on their part to bring women's talent to public attention. Such a conclusion would be premature at present, but it accords with the tone of Du's *Strange Stories Heard during Travel*, the short-story collection of 1879, which takes a relatively enlightened view of women. At the same time, the legacy of Yuan Mei, the famous eighteenth-century patron of women, hovers over our subject. Not only were Du and his friends sympathetic to Yuan;[60] also of interest is the fact that both Wang Qingdi and Buluo Shanren used pen names that may reflect Yuan's influence.[61] The two poets under discussion here made use of new media, but they were still under the spell of this important leader of the mid-Qing.

One topic needs further elaboration: the broader impact of the poems in *Shanghai News* about the plight of women. I have already proposed that the women's poems found in *Shanghai News* and its supplements might have helped male reformers understand the need for women's schooling. Now we turn to the effect they might have had on women writers themselves. For this we return to the life and poems of Wang Qingdi.

When we look at Wang's work as a whole, we find many despairing poems. These appear most frequently in her writings of the 1870s and 1880s. This part of her work was not published during her lifetime, and it was apparently never submitted to the *Shanghai News* supplements or *Shanghai News*. It would seem at first glance to bear no connection to the despairing tone of poems turned out by Buluo Shanren and her friends. I have discussed these poems elsewhere and will give just one example now, "Listening to Rain":[62]

> I must regret ever having sown plantain near the pavilion.
> In fall the rain [on the leaves] makes an endless dripping sound.
> Best if a grieving person not listen.
> In the depths of night I'm unable to sleep, I am heartbroken.[63]

This poem probably was written around 1874 or 1875, around the same time as the one on the virtuous woman Mao.[64] Compared to the three poems Wang published in the *Shanghai News* supplements, this and her several poems like it from the same time project a much darker tone.

One cannot be certain of the reasons for this dark mood, but Wang's life circumstances appear to have grown more difficult during the 1870s. One important source of concern was her "companionate" husband's departure, first for the examinations and then for a job in Jiaxing. On the surface, these might seem like positive developments, but they increased Wang's isolation. The Republican-period local history of Quxian, *Gazetteer of Qu County* (Quxian zhi) adds a little more detail. In its words: "Late in her life her family's great poverty and her many grievances led her to write poems overcome with depression."[65] So far, then, we can explain Wang's despairing poems of the 1870s and 1880s without resort to Buluo Shanren's (and others') dark poems of around same time. Should we conclude that Wang merely submitted poems to the *Shanghai News* supplements without reading what was published there or in *Shanghai News*? Should we conclude that she was never influenced by Buluo Shanren and her friends?

There is a little evidence to counter this line of speculation. As it happens, both Wang's and Buluo Shanren's work are discussed in a retrospective on talented poets of the late Qing. It was published as a short piece in *Women's Eastern Times* (Funü shibao) of 1911.[66] The author is Zhou Guoxian

(1882–1969), who was originally from Suzhou but was later based in Shanghai.[67] Here we find excerpts from two poems that do not appear in either the hand-copied or the recently republished set of Wang's poems. One of the two "new" excerpts has no bearing on our story. In it she refers to her children as young. The poem is very similar to an extant poem that frets over how her children will fare during an onslaught by the Taipings. It was probably written in the late 1850s. The other "new" excerpt is titled "White Chrysanthemum." It seems to echo the wording of Buluo Shanren's poem "In Praise of Chrysanthemums," although it is not a match in terms of rhyme. The excerpt is very short, just two lines:

> Along the moonlit path of the recluse, thin shadows move.
> Along the fence the heavy mist is penetrated by cold fragrance.[68]

In this isolated couplet, terms found in Buluo Shanren's poem—"moonlit path of the recluse" and "thin shadows"—recur; the mist is another carryover. Could Wang have been writing here along the general lines set down by Buluo Shanren?[69] Partly on the basis of the wording in this couplet, I regard it as somewhat conceivable that Wang knew "In praise of Chrysanthemums" or some other of Buluo Shanren's many works along the same lines,[70] even though her surviving collected works contain no direct responses, and even though she never published in *Shanghai News* itself.

A second piece of evidence from this article is no less shadowy. When it mentions how much other women appreciated receiving her poems, the article suggests that Wang Qingdi may have been better known in Shanghai than we would otherwise have reason to believe. This is because of the likelihood that Zhou collected the evidence for his article through outreach to women's poetical societies in Shanghai.[71] Wang's own collection reveals no more than a small handful of correspondents in Quzhou and Hangzhou. In hinting at a larger, Shanghai-based group of fans, as well as some hitherto unknown poems, Zhou's piece may signal that the circulation of poems from Wang to Shanghai, as well as from Shanghai to Wang, was greater than we can currently prove.

The vague nature of these two findings rules out hard and fast conclusions, but we can still explore the implications of the possibility that Wang knew *Shanghai News* and was known in Shanghai's poetical circles. First, if this were so, *Shanghai News*'s influence could be said to have extended broadly, even to Quzhou. Certainly Wang could have been in Hangzhou (or somewhere else) and read Buluo Shanren's poem there instead, but from what we now know, the chances are strongest that she would have been in her Quzhou home. On this particular point, however, we do not need Wang's example in order to make the point. *Shanghai News* itself gives evidence of a fairly wide catchment of influence. Thus, we can show that Buluo Shanren's "In Praise of Chrysanthemums" reached at least as far as Zhenzhou (near Nanjing). Two poems from there, published on December 14, 1874, both by women, were written in response to this poem; and we know the poem reached Hong Kong as well.[72] A second possible conclusion is that a woman like Wang with much to lament did indeed take heart from reading *Shanghai News*. In this scenario, her surge of complaining poems of the 1870s and 1880s could have been a response, even if indirect, to Buluo Shanren's and others' poems.

To be sure, neither *Shanghai News* nor Buluo Shanren could have been Wang Qingdi's only inspiration when it came to writing of her unhappiness. Well before the 1870s, her collected poems already contained a few unhappy poems.[73] However, the quotient of despairing works increased in the 1870s and 1880s. It is this coincidence of timing, more than the couplet from her poem on chrysanthemums or the vague evidence on Shanghai readers, that suggests some linkage to *Shanghai News*. *Shanghai News* alone may not have caused this change, but it could have enlarged Wang's vocabulary of complaint about the feminine condition as experienced in remote Quzhou. In the changing climate of the 1870s and 1880s, having somewhat feminist periodicals like *Shanghai News* and its supplements enter women's cloisters on a regular basis could have transformed the way their occupants wrote about their lives.[74]

No doubt men like Du Jinqing and Zhan Xi also benefited from the new trends and ideas they read about in the newspaper, and they took comfort from newly formed, newspaper-based communities of far-flung "friends." But men like Du and Zhan had the freedom to travel to one another's places of residence, whereas women like Wang Qingdi and Buluo Shanren were not free to leave their homes. It was the self-portrait of the cloistered woman at the heart of Buluo Shanren's most famous poems that most consistently evoked responses from other women, and the fact that such women received *Shanghai News*–based literature from the outside world is clear evidence that their cloisters were not as isolated as they had once been.

Writing of an earlier era, Deng Hongmei has argued that a new, dejected tone in lyric poems of the early nineteenth century was actually empowering for women.[75] Seven or eight decades later, in the pages of *Shanghai News*, we have evidence of how much it meant for women poets to read one another's laments and answer them in kind. Buluo Shanren is one important case in point, and her close friends are others. Perhaps there are many others, a possibility that needs to be researched over time.[76] Even the more ambiguous case of Wang Qingdi leaves no doubt that she was at least somewhat engaged with the new ways of reaching audiences brought about by the literary journals, if not *Shanghai News*; and the chance that she knew *Shanghai News* as well is great.

In many ways it is amazing that a gentlewoman like Wang from as far away as Quzhou could have published three poems in the literary journals of Shanghai. Wang's submissions are important, but the story of what she did not submit, and its conceivable debt to Buluo Shanren, may be more consequential still. Once again, though, even without Wang's example we can make a case in this regard. *Shanghai News*'s own pages give evidence of many other women poets over a fairly wide area who were moved by the new despondent mood of women's published poems and were eager to respond in kind.

Twenty years before the major transformations in women's publishing of the 1890s and 1900s,[77] *Shanghai News* and its supplements yield tantalizing clues about how the earliest new media helped to bridge the distances between individual cloisters. It is possible, then, that when it comes to broad consequences, women's writings in the new media did more than simply impress male readers with the authors' skill at writing and their intelligence. By creating a way for cloistered women to communicate with one another, these publications may have encouraged the idea of a national forum for women. Without ever calling for anything so specific, these new media may have anticipated the onset of dedicated women's magazines. In this context, Buluo Shanren's public description of her private pain may have paved the way for major change.

NOTES

An earlier version of this chapter came out in Chinese under the title "1870 niandai yijiang jingtong meiti de guixiu" (Media-savvy *guixiu* of the 1870s and beyond). Also, one portion of the argument is recapitulated in chapter 2 of my forthcoming study, *Fiction's Family*.

1   Mittler, *A Newspaper for China*. This work mentions pictorials as being targeted

to women but does not bring out the potential of the literary supplements in this regard. See also Judge, "Reforming the Feminine," and Hu, "Naming the First 'New Woman.' "

2   See Wagner, "Women in *Shenbaoguan*; his "Joining the Global Imaginaire"; and an unpublished draft titled "China's First Literary Journals," supplied to me by the author. Wagner does not discuss *New Delicacies*. For its relationship to the other three, see Shanghai Tushuguan, *Zhongguo jindai qikan*, 1:431.

3   Wagner, "China's First Literary Journals," 4.

4   Hu, *Lidai funü zhuzuo kao*. Those with entries under their proper names are Wang Qingdi, 253; Ni Fengying, 452; Pan Suchun, 727; Xu Songzhu, 564; and Zhang Yunyu, 551.

5   Buluo Shanren is Zhang Qingsong, 527. Wu Pingxiang is Wu Zao, 317.

6   Zhu Peiqiu, 278 (under the name Zhu Dizhen); and Wu Qiongxian, 316 (under the name Wu Shanshan).

7   This includes such women as Wu Qiongxian and Wu Zao, disciples of Yuan Mei (1716–97) and Chen Wenshu (1771–1843). This principle further eliminates the otherwise unidentifiable Wang Ruixian, whose husband claims to have discovered some of her poems in a letter box in 1874, long after her death in 1860. *Siming suoji*, 1.

8   Susan Mann's study of women's responses to the Taiping Rebellion might become the opening chapter in such a project. See "The Lady and the State," 2010.

9   My thanks to Rudolph Wagner and Yasushi Ōki for supplying me with *Siming suoji* and *Houqing xinlu*, respectively. To date I have not seen all of *Yinghuan suoji* and *Huanyu suoji*, only the partial copies available in the Harvard-Yenching Library.

10 On the supposedly female author of the important novel *Dong ou nühaojie* of 1903, see Wang, *Fin-de-Siècle Splendor*, 166.

11 Wang's life dates are given in local histories as 1816–90, but it is obvious from her and her husband's poetry that she was born in 1828. The dates are off by one branch of the sexegenary cycle.

12 Zhan Sizeng's age at death is given in Quxian Zhi Bianzuan Weiyuan Hui, *Quxian zhi*, 557. The year of his birth is determined by a poem by Zhou Shici, a friend, which celebrates his twentieth birthday in 1851. This would mean that he was born in 1832. See Zhou, *Danyong shanchuan shiji*, 3.9a.

13 Quxian Zhi Bianzuan Weiyuan Hui, *Quxian zhi*, 556.

14 Ibid.

15 Zhou Guoxian, "Shihua," presents two poems drawn from the collection that do not appear in the handwritten copy.

16 Wang Qingdi, *Zhiyun lou shici*. The reprint does not separate the poems published in 1857 from the later poems the way the hand-copied edition does.

17 Zheng Yongxi, *Quxian zhi*, 40.32b–33a.

18 Qian, "Shiluo yu mianhuai," 32 and 53.

19 On his friendship with the former, see Zhan Kai, *Rouxiang yunshi*, *shang*, 29b–33a.

20 He had over three hundred submissions to *Shenbao* under one name or another between 1872 and 1889.

21 The collection can be seen in the National Library in Beijing.

22 The pen names of the author of the preface to *Kezhong yiwen lu*, Hongxing *ciren* or Bitao Hongxing *ciren*, appear frequently in the journals. One of the authors, Fanke shanqiao, is Du himself, as is easily gleaned from the journals. Huanhua *ciren* appears to be another person. He appears in both the *Shenbao* supplements and the fiction. However, it is possible that Huanhua *ciren* and Du are one and the same.

23 See for example Hou, *Zhongguo wenyan xiaoshuo, xia*, 25–27; and Shi, *Zhongguo gudai xiaoshuo*, 212.

24 "Packaging the Men of Our Times." See also Ōki, "Mao Xiang and Yu Huai."

25 See *Siming suoji*, 5. Xu Songjin could be the sister or cousin of Xu Songzhu, also of Haizhou, who is rather widely published. See Hu, *Lidai funü*, 564.

26 Thus, even though all three of Wang's poems in journals were produced after 1857, the date of her poetry collection, they have been preserved through the efforts of her descendant, as well as in supplements to *Shenbao*.

27 The manuscript edition is in the Shoudu Library in Beijing.

28 The manuscript version contains a poem of 1874 by Zhan Sizeng to Du.

29 題毛烈婦傳: 節烈人爭敬, 清風孰可追. 冰霜心獨矢, 金石志難移. 德合閨中仰, 身期地下隨. 綱常真不愧, 千古令名垂. *Collected Poems and Songs of Weaving Cloud Tower*, second set, 20a–b. All translations in this chapter are my own. My gratitude to Wai-yee Li for help in translating the poems. Needless to say, any mistakes are mine.

30 The title in Wang's own collection is slightly different from that of the poem in *Siming suoji*. But except for one small change in the wording, it is the same poem.

31 唐多令, 題秋樹讀書圖: 紅葉已蕭條. 幽人逸興饒. 把芸編. 誦向林皋. 籬菊芭蕉團繞處, 風景好, 此誅茅. 霜肅碧天高. 秋聲嘯暮濤. 助吟哦, 詩思應豪. 久坐不知斜陽照晚. 明月影, 上山坳. *Zhiyun lou shici*, songs 6a–b.

32 Haichang (Haining) is a county in Jiaxing prefecture.

33 See the poem to Du in the manuscript version of Zhan's poems. I have analyzed this situation more fully in my study *Fiction's Family*. This time only three of the eleven poems are clearly from the Jiaxing area.

34 金縷曲－題扁舟覓勝圖, 為海寧 杜晉卿茂才作: 幽興誰能織. 趁扁舟, 江北江南, 西湖東浙. 不藉山川才思助, 自有凌雲彩筆. 應猜作, 乘槎仙客. 勝地名區游 已遍. 想亭臺佳景 曾親涉. 披圖處, 從頭說. 生綃一幅留行跡, 更宜人, 春帆細雨, 孤蓬落日. 泛棹蒼茫烟水裡, 此景幾番經歷. 供笑傲, 清風明月. 共說少陵詞翰 富, 錦囊中, 早滿詩千帙. 揮翠管, 歌白雪. *Zhiyun lou shici*, songs 5b–6a. Du Fu (712–70) was one of China's most famous poets.

35 Li, *Jindai Zhongguo*, 1:436.

36 Huang, *Songnan mengyinglu*, 102–3. According to the Harvard-Yenching Library catalogue, the original probably came out in 1877. This source relates that she had a male tutor named Zhang Xunting; but whether this was the same person as her father Zhang Yiting is not known. On Zhang Yiting, see Hu, *Lidai funü*, 527. See also Wang Jingyue, *Zhongguo gudai minsu*, 186. Huang was a longtime reporter for *Shenbao*. He also wrote for the literary supplements. See for example Song Jun, *Shenbao de xingshuai*, 58.

37 Wang Jingyue, *Zhongguo gudai minsu*, 186; and Hu Wenkai, *Lidai funü*, 527.

38 If she died at age fifty-five and was writing until as late as 1887, the earliest she could have been born was 1832. Wang was born in 1828.

39 無題三十絕. 似有微詞動絳唇. 淚沿紅粉濕羅巾. 不勝惆悵還惆恨. 幾許悲歡併在身? From *Yinghuan suoji* 15, no. 1 (1874).

40 I know of no earlier publication. However, her reputation may have been building by 1872, whether in published poetry or private exchange.

41 悠悠塵夢, 恨結三生. 嫋嫋秋風, 愁添萬斛粲. 鏡中之麗質, 半屬空花. 圖畫裡之紅顏,真成薄命. 昔年香草. 竟作飄蓬. 此日幽蘭, 將為蕭艾. 儂愁何補. 儂緒堪憐. 搦管陳辭, 石固難期於填恨. 悲秋遣興. 花真有類於斷腸. 敢政吟壇以誌幽憤. 亦當歌當哭之意. 匪敢言詩也.

42 The dates of the six responses are November 12, 1872, November 15, 1872, November 23, 1872, November 26, 1872, December 3, 1872, January 1, 1873. It is possible that some among these were just pretending to be women.

43 He is the respondent of November 15. He used the name Longqiu *jiuyin*, which is a pseudonym of Shanghai writer Ge Qilong.

44 We can determine this through the literary supplements.

45 See for example April 22, 1875, where a reader talks of using a postal tube (*youtong*) to mail a response to *Shenbao*.

46 Buluo Shanren had no direct poetic change with Du, but both poets appeared on the same occasion in the same issue (11) of *Huanyu suoji*.

47 There is a poem that does this in *Shenbao* of August 15, 1887.

48 The publication date is October 30, 1874.
詠菊: 老圃黃花一徑通. 疎香瘦影鬥西風, 捲簾人立清霜外. 載酒秋延落照中. 冷艷未堪諧俗侶. 孤芳端合探幽叢. 秋容如此休嫌淡. 想得高懷籬落東? 為惜秋光日易斜. 坐來松下浥清華. 吟殘騷些沈瑤夢. 譜就山容冷畫紗. 翠袖寒侵三徑月. 青蕪幽護一籬花. 霜姿素閒相對. 疎籟遙砧未嚴譁. 何慮枝高出手寒? 摘來猶是帶霜看. 最宜瓶供秋添幾. 且喜簾開月近欄. 清影無聊依帽側. 孤芳有伴怯衣單. 鷹飛蚤語休多絮. 真意忘言欲辨難. 春花不惜惜秋枝. 勁節疎香出世姿. 逸士形情原酒落. 佳人遲暮肯嗟咨. 偏宜雅淡能移俗. 若較清狂豈嫉時. 誰遣霜叢鄉國淚. 折腰籬畔繫人思.

49 Ibid. 秋閨無緒散步東籬偶擬菊花詩四律錄呈.

50 October 10, 1917. See also March 22, 1917 and the June 28 and June 29, 1917.

51 November 10, 1876.

52 "Yedu," *Shenbao* December 25, 1880. The poem in the set to which I refer is titled "Du Honglou mengbu you gan er zuo."

53 See *Huanyu suoji*, 10, "Yaosheng nüshi sishi guixing changhe shixi;" it also appears in *Shenbao*, February 10, 1877.

54 Wagner, "China's First Literary Journals," 8.

55 *Huayunju shicun* and *Buluo Shanren shigao*. See Hu, *Lidai funü*, 527.

56 Wang Jingyue, *Zhongguo gudai minsu*, 186.

57 Zhou Guoxian's "Shihua" of 1911 incorrectly identifies Wang as a Hangzhou writer. He mentions how much *guixiu* prized her poems when they received them. In context this could mean women of Shanghai and environs. He also mentions her

printed collection. It seems that Wang had a reputation outside Quzhou. For more on this point see later in the chapter.

58 Zhou Guoxian's "Shihua" mentions *Huayunju shicun*, and it cites poems that are not found in *Shenbao*-related publications.

59 Li Changli, *Jindai Zhongguo*, 1:436.

60 See Du Jinqing, "Huanhua guan shihua," in 5.

61 Yuan Mei had a male friend named Buluo Shanren. See Yuan Mei, *Yuanmeii quanji*, 7:274. One of Yuan's female disciples, Liao Yunjin, used the pen name Zhiyin, but this is a much more common pen name than Buluo Shanren and need not have been an influence on Wang.

62 See my *Fiction's Family*, chapter 2.

63 聽雨： 庭前應悔種芭蕉, 秋雨聲聲不住囂. 獨有愁人聽不得, 夜深無寐魂黯消. This is from the modern reprint *Zhiyunlou shici*, 45.

64 The placement suggests it was written just before the poem on the virtuous woman Mao. However, this collection is rather roughly ordered.

65 Zheng Yongxi, *Quxian zhi*, 25.10 a-b. 晚年以 迫於家境多窮愁抑鬱之作.

66 Zhou Guoxian, "Shihua."

67 Zhou was a writer of "mandarin duck and butterfly" fiction." Li, *Zhongguo xiandai*, 197.

68 白菊： 三徑月明移瘦影. 一籬霜重透寒香.

69 She has two other poems on chrysanthemums, both in her published collection of 1857, that do not use the same terms.

70 Such as "Yedu," mentioned earlier.

71 This is how Huang, author of *Songnan mengyinglu*, claims to have gained access to poems by Buluo Shanren and one other woman poet (102–3).

72 See eleventh month, eighteenth day, and twelfth month, fourteenth day, of 1874.

73 A notable example was written just after her marriage, when she missed her family.

74 Rudolph Wagner comments on *Shenbao*'s feminism. See his "Women in *Shenbao guan* Publications," 229.

75 Deng, *Nüxing cishi*, 339–55.

76 Huang, *Songnan mengyinglu*, says that many Shanghai women knew how to read and write, and that their writings were not in conventionally feminine styles. See 102–3. He lists Buluo Shanren as preeminent among these, but there were others too.

77 On women's magazines of the 1880s and 1890s, see Nanxiu Qian, "The Mother *Nü xuebao* versus the Daughter *Nü xuebao*."

CHAPTER SIX

THE FATE OF THE LATE IMPERIAL "TALENTED WOMAN"

Gender and Historical Change in Early-Twentieth-Century China

Joan Judge

T HE fate of the late imperial "talented women" (*cainü*) was deeply implicated in the complex gender and historical changes that took place in the lead up to, and in the wake of, the 1911 Revolution. Much of this complexity is captured in the story of Zhang Mojun (Zhaohan, 1884–1965), a remarkable figure who belongs both to the first, pivotal generation of respectable, professional, public women in early twentieth century China, and to one particular female lineage—the Zhang women of Xiangxiang in Hunan—that was deeply implicated in the changes of the era.[1]

The matriarch of the Zhang family, He Chenghui, was an archetypal late imperial woman of talent. An accomplished poet from a cultured family of Hengyang, Hunan, she was the daughter of the renowned Confucian scholar He Tongyin and shared in lyric exchanges with her talented sisters and brothers throughout her life.[2] She entered into a companionate marriage with Zhang Tongdian (Bochun, Tianfang Louzhu, 1859–1915), a provincial-level degree holder from Xiangxiang, also in Hunan, in the late 1870s. Together she and Zhang had three surviving sons and four surviving daughters.[3]

He's second daughter, Zhang Mojun, left the deepest mark in history and serves as the linchpin of our story. Her life, which began in the Guangxu era (r. 1875–1908) and ended in Taiwan in 1965, intersected with the major turning points in modern Chinese history and Chinese women's history. She resisted foot-binding from a young age after witnessing her older sister's suffering, not only refusing to have her own feet bound but encouraging her parents to support the missionary-led anti-foot-binding movement.[4] She entered Sun Yat-sen's Revolutionary Alliance (Tongmeng Hui) in June of 1906, was active in the 1911 Revolution in Suzhou, and remained engaged in Nationalist politics over the succeeding decades. She became a fixture in the Nationalist Party (Guomindang) government from the 1920s and would be the only woman to serve on the Nationalist Central Committee. Of greater concern than Zhang's formal political career, here, are her informal political contributions through the fields of journalism and women's education in the first decades of the twentieth century. In her writing and social practice, Zhang took a public position on the full range of issues the republic faced: from women's suffrage to the assassination of the first leader of the Nationalist Party, Song Jiaoren (Dunchu, 1882–1913); from the Twenty-One Demands in 1915, through and beyond the May Fourth Movement of 1919.[5]

Although Zhang Xiahun (1895–1938), known as He Chenghui and Zhang Tongdian's eighth daughter, was Zhang Mojun's sister, the two women may be considered as representatives of two different generations. This is because of the eleven-year age difference between them, a gap that was accentuated by the exponential pace of change in women's lives in this period.[6] Much of Xiahun's life trajectory followed in Mojun's wake. She was educated in and later taught at a school Mojun founded, and she passionately discussed issues on which Mojun was also outspoken in a journal Mojun edited. Mojun even arranged Xiahun's marriage to the Harvard-educated meteorologist, geologist, and educator Zhu Kezhen (1890–1974) in 1920.[7]

Zhang Xiahun did leave her own imprint in history, however. She became known as a female adventurer, one of the few roles that Mojun did not assume. In 1916, Xiahun visited a demonstration at the Nanyuan Aviation School (Nanyuan Hangkong Xuexiao) in Beijing in the company of her brother-in-law, General Jiang Zuobin (1884–1941) and her sister Zhang Shujia (Zhang Chu, the fifth sister, ?–1938) who remains in the shadow of our story as she does in the sources. Once at the airfield, Xiahun insisted on going up in the airplane despite protestations by the head of the school. Although—or perhaps in part because—the airplane crashed, Xiahun (who broke her left leg and a number of teeth in the fall) became a much-celebrated heroine. She was lauded in the mainstream and the women's periodical press and praised by President Li Yuanhong and premier Duan Qirui. She was also featured in a household encyclopedia published in 1919, as an icon of "advanced womanhood" (*nüjie xianjin*), along with the Guangdong doctor and athlete Chen Yili (Liqing) and the Hunanese national expert on physical education, Teng Chao.[8] And she continues to be celebrated in China's list of historic firsts today.[9] Even in this instance, however, Mojun was the keeper of Xiahun's image. It was she who first sent a photograph of Xiahun to the editor of the *Women's Eastern Times* (Funü shibao).[10]

THE HISTORICAL FATE OF THE WOMAN OF TALENT

The trajectory from He Chenghui, gentlewoman of the inner chambers, to Zhang Xiahun, adventurer and media sensation, constitutes one thread in the unfolding fate of the late imperial woman of talent. Central to this trajectory are the changing aesthetic and institutional contours of women's talent and women's learning.

Textual and Visual Technologies of the Self

The historical status of the woman of talent was inextricably linked to the cultural status of the literary genres with which she was associated, most notably, the poetic *shi* and *ci*. The arc of the Zhang women's writing practices maps the unsteady course of women's poetry in this era: its persistence within new media of the early twentieth century, its changing function as old forms were invested with new content, and its shifting prominence as it went from being the primary genre of female literary self-expression, to one among an expanding repertoire of literary forms, to near eclipse by expository writing.

He Chenghui's principal mode of self-expression was *shi* poetry, as represented in her major work, the *Poetry Collection from Yixiao Hall* (Yixiaotang shiji). He Chenghui published twelve poems serially under this title from December 1912 to February 1913 in a journal her daughter Mojun had founded, *Chinese Women's Journal* (Shenzhou nübao).[11] In response to Mojun's impetus, the entire collection was published in a two-*juan* (two-part) volume in 1917 to commemorate the matriarch's sixtieth birthday.[12]

The two *juan* of the collection are divided into ancient-style or "Guti" poems in the pre-Tang-dynasty style, and "Jinti" or Tang and post-Tang-dynasty "modern-style poetry." As Tan Yankai (1880–1931) emphasized in his preface to the collection, He Chenghui had not "become intoxicated" with recent poetic trends, unlike many contemporary women writers. Instead, she continued to trace her literary lineage back to the "eight dynasties."[13] Many of the poems in the compilation are direct imitations of past masters, including, in the first section, Jin-dynasty poets Tao Yuanming (Tao Jingjie, ca. 365–427) and Xie Tiao (Xie Xuanhui, 464–99), and in the second section, Tang- and Song-dynasty luminaries Wang Wei (699–759), Du Fu (712–70), and Su Shi (1037–1101).

Other *shi* poems in He's collection can be broadly characterized as poems of intimate and social exchange. Many are addressed to her husband or her older brother Puyuan, to a close female friend, (Xie) Junyu, and to her fifth elder sister. She also wrote poems that reflected on womanly virtue—more than one was written in honor of faithful maidens who had remained chaste to their fiancés, for example—and on visits to scenic spots such as Hunan's famous Yuelu Mountain (*Yuelu shan*).

Known for her classical-style poetry, He was, however, also capable of expository writing on topical themes. She penned the inaugural essay (*fakanci*) for Mojun's *Chinese Women's Journal*, in which she declared equal rights for men and women to be a crucial precondition for reaching an advanced civilizational state (*wenming*). While celebrating the new era of mechanical print production in endorsing the journal, her referents continued to be those of the scholar's study: she invited like-minded writers to "dip their brushes in ink" and contribute to the newspaper.[14] The only expository essay I know of in He's repertoire, the *fakanci*, nonetheless suggests that "nineteenth-century *guixiu* [gentlewomen] were becoming 'new women' all along."[15]

While He tentatively adopted the essay form, Zhang Mojun wrote confidently and prolifically in at least five genres. Poetry remained foremost among these: over six hundred *shi* and *ci* constitute the overwhelming majority of the writings included in Zhang's collected works.[16] Mojun's poetic style was a complex amalgam of various strains of influence and of her own evolving literary voice. She was first trained by her classically attuned mother and by adherents of the highly allusive Tong-Guang School (Tong-Guang ti, or style of Tongzhi [1862–74] and Guangxu [1875–1908] eras), who, like He Chenghui, rejected the more experimental forms of poetry advocated from the late Qing. At the same time, however, she joined the revolutionary poetry society, the Southern Society (Nanshe).[17] Mojun's poems range from the highly personal to the incisively political. Her *shi* and *ci*, her preferred technology of self-expression throughout her life, include reflections on a spectrum of topics ranging from reading Laozi to New York City and express a gamut of emotions from grief over the death of loved ones to frustration with the vagaries of Republican politics.

Other genres of Mojun's writings, not all of which appear in her collected works, include biography, most notably the "record of deeds" (*xinglüe*) she wrote to commemorate her father shortly after his death in 1915.[18] She also published numerous essays (together with letters, commentaries, poems, and songs) in the periodical press, especially in women's journals. Her earliest writings appeared in the journal *Women's World* (Nüzi shijie) beginning in 1904, and she published topical essays in her own journal, *Chinese Women's Journal* (1912–13), in the *Women's Eastern Times* (1911–17), and in the *Ladies' Journal* (Funü zazhi, 1915–31). She submitted articles to nongendered early-Republican periodicals as well, among them *Citizen's Monthly* (Guomin yuekan). Zhang also authored a number of extended essays or treatises on social, cultural, and political themes. These include women's social responsibilities, education in Europe, China's historic ruins, and the people's livelihood.[19] Zhang even contributed to one of the most popular new genres in the late Qing and early Republic: translated fiction, serially publishing her translations of foreign detective novels in the periodical press.[20]

The prominence of *shi* and *ci* in the literary oeuvre of talented women sharply receded by the "third generation" of the Zhang family. Whereas He Chenghui published poetry and at least one expository essay, and Mojun published poetry together with expository essays, treatises, and translated fiction, Xiahun left no extant poetry. As a young student and teacher she wrote a handful of essays on topical themes—on suffrage, on religion and

張默君女史油畫

圖　獅　醒

FIGURE 6.1. Zhang Mojun's *Awakened Lion* (Xingshi tu). From *Women's Eastern Times* (Funü shibao) 4 (November 5, 1911), n.p.

national strength, and on the assassination of Song Jiaoren—but she appears to have stopped writing, or at least publishing, in her later married years.[21]

The Zhang women expressed and represented themselves visually as well as textually. Mojun was, again, the most public and prolific in the use of visual media. Her highly regarded calligraphy graced the cover of the eleventh collection of the Southern Society, and a number of her paintings were featured in China's first national exposition, the Nanyang Exhibition (Nanyang Quanye Hui) held in Nanjing in 1910.[22] Three of her paintings were reproduced in *Women's Eastern Times*. As was the case with her poetry, Mojun reconfigured this classic woman-of-talent artistic practice in tandem with contemporary cultural forms and political concerns. She painted in oil rather than in brush and ink, and her artworks depicted not only serene landscapes but also symbols of renewed national strength. They include *Awakened Lion* (Xingshi tu; figure 6.1), and a beauty with a sword leaning on a horse.[23]

We can assume her mother, He Chenghui, painted and possibly even instructed Mojun in the medium, but I have found no direct references to

影攝歲三十五人主堂孝儀

FIGURE 6.2. He Chenghui, age fifty-three, from Zhang He Chenghui, *Poetry Anthology from the Hall of Rites and Filiality* (Yixiao tang shiji), n.p.

He's artistic skills. Similarly, although the author of an account of Zhang Xiahun's flying incident noted that Xiahun was particularly talented at drawing, no reproductions of her work appear to be extant.[24]

All three of the Zhang women used the new photographic medium as a mode of self-representation. Although one photograph of the patriarch, Zhang Tongdian, dates to 1905, the first extant portrait of He Chenghui, a modest head-and-shoulders portrait included in her poetry collection, is from 1910, when she was fifty-three years of age (figure 6.2).

The only other published photograph of He is a classic studio portrait: she is seated next to a table with a potted plant and, befitting a matriarch about to celebrate her sixtieth birthday, has a grandchild on her lap (figure 6.3).[25] Most of the photographs of Zhang Mojun that appeared in the contemporary periodical press or in later publications are also portraits of her head and shoulders. She is identified as the editor of the journal she founded in 1911, the *Suzhou Journal of the Great Han* (Suzhou Da Han bao), in two sharply contrasting portraits. In the first, she is wearing Victorian-style Western dress and, despite the look of focused resolve on her face, appears more like a debutante than a revolutionary (figure 6.4). In the second picture she wears simple Chinese attire and an equally earnest expression.[26]

影攝孫抱近最人主堂孝儀

FIGURE 6.3. He Chenghui with grandchild, from Zhang He Chenghui,
*Poetry Anthology from the Hall of Rites
and Filiality* (Yixiao tang shiji), n.p.

蘇　州　漢　昭　張
筆　主　報　漢　大　女　士

FIGURE 6.4. Zhang Mojun (Zhaohan), editor of the *Suzhou Journal
of the Great Han* (Suzhou Da Han
bao), *Women's Eastern Times* (Funü
shibao) 5 (January 23, 1912), n.p.

Photographs of Zhang that appeared much later in her career, in the 1930s,
continued to be mostly portraits of her head and shoulders rather than full-
length portraits. These include one photograph that appeared in the journal
Dangdai funü (Contemporary women) in 1936 (figure 6.5), and another that
was the frontispiece for a photographic record of Zhang's journey to a number
of key historic sites, titled *Xichui yinhen* (Hymn to the ancient Northwest). The
latter album includes a full-length portrait of her, on both sides of the Republican lens: the photo shows her in the act of taking a photograph.[27]

Zhang Xiahun's photographic practices, like her writing practices,
diverged radically from those of Mojun and He Chenghui. The most widely
reproduced portrait of her, a photomontage that commemorates her historic
flight, is tinted, includes her entire body, and nods to current fashion: the
white scarf around her neck is a near ubiquitous accessory in portraits of
fashionable Republican ladies (figure 6.6).

FIGURE 6.5. Zhang Mojun, from *Contemporary Women* (Dangdai funü), 50.

FIGURE 6.6. China's female flier Zhang Xiahun (1895–1936), n.p. *Women's Eastern Times* (Funü shibao) 20 (November 1916).

The portrait is not only stylish but also distinctly heroic. The painted backdrop of the central inset, with its rocks and oceanic tides, evokes romantic notions of lone bravery. Both of Xiahun's hands are held behind her back in a vaguely masculine pose, a posture which contrasts with that found in most photographic portraits of women from this period, in which the subject places only one hand behind her back while the other holds a white handkerchief. The montage that the editors of the *Women's Eastern Times* created around this striking portrait further accentuates the drama of the defining incident in Xiahun's life. A World War I airfield serves as the background on which a small, oval photograph of Xiahun in the cockpit of an airplane is superimposed (figure 6.7).[28]

A second, less dramatic but equally fashionable photograph of Xiahun appears in the final issue of *Women's Eastern Times*. There is no caption to the photograph, but Xiahun is mentioned in the article by Zhang Mojun that

FIGURE 6.7. Zhang Xiahun (unidentified), from Zhang Mojun, "Dingsi chun," *Women's Eastern Times* (Funü shibao) 21 (April 1917), 101.

appears on the same page. In the article Mojun introduces the American stunt-flier Katherine Stinson (1891[6]–1977), who gave widely attended flying exhibitions in Japan and China in 1917. At the end of the article, in which she lauds the Stinson family tradition of aviation and praises the heroic nineteen-year-old Katherine for her flying skills, her patriotism, and her chivalry, Mojun briefly describes Xiahun's own Nanyuan Aviation School stunt.[29]

FROM WOMEN'S LEARNING TO WOMEN'S EDUCATION

Education was one of the principal threads that bound the lives of the Zhang women to one another. In addition to instructing her young daughters in *shi* poetry, He Chenghui financially contributed to the founding of Mojun's girls' school, Chinese Girls' School (Shenzhou Nüxue), in 1912 and helped conduct classes at the school on singing to the accompaniment of stringed instruments (*xiange*).[30] Xiahun first attended and later taught at the school.

He Chenghui brought valuable experience to the Chinese Girls' School initiative. She had served as head teacher and administrator at two early schools for women, the Hunan Girls' School in Ningbo (Hunan Zhu Ning Diyi Nüxue) and the Wuhu (Anhui) Public Girls' School (Wuhu Gongli

Nüxue), respectively. This experience earned her the title of "Teacher within the Four Seas" (Hainei *nüshi*).[31]

He's most famous student, her daughter Zhang Mojun, is depicted in biographical sources with the classic tropes used to describe the late imperial talented women: she knew six hundred characters by the age of three *sui* and could read three hundred Tang poems by the age of four. Her later intellectual formation was the product of both formal and informal schooling. Instructed in poetry by her mother and in the classics by her father, she also read voraciously in the works of Song dynasty sages and Ming loyalists — Huang Zongxi (1610–95), Gu Tinglin (1613–82), and, most passionately, her Hunan co-native Wang Fuzhi (1619–92). While her formal education began in 1901, when she reached the age of eighteen, her most formative educational experience was the degree she earned in the teacher-training program at the Shanghai School of Fundamental Women's Learning (Wuben Nüxue) between 1904 and 1907. Upon graduation she was immediately offered a position at the Girl's School of Pure Intelligence (Cuimin Nüxuexiao) by the Manchu viceroy Duan Fang (1861–1911). After the 1911 Revolution she was finally able to establish her own school in Zhabei (the present-day downtown district of Shanghai), the Chinese Girls' School, which had trained over a thousand girls and women by the time it was destroyed by fire in 1927.[32]

As one of the most prominent women in the field of education in the early Republic, Mojun was sent by the Ministry of Education to investigate women's schools in Europe and America in 1918. She spent much of that year studying at Columbia University and then went on to investigate educational practices in France, Switzerland, Germany, and other European countries in 1919. When she returned to China, she began to hold important government portfolios in education. In 1921 she was appointed to the Chinese Educational Reform Association (Zhongguo Jiaoyu Gaijinshe) as head of female education.[33]

After Mojun's earliest years of instruction in the home, her education diverged sharply from that of the late imperial woman of talent. She attended formal schools, took classes in foreign languages, and studied abroad. The most historic shift was, however, in her conceptualization of the objectives of women's learning. While she continued to write and teach poetry herself,[34] she did not believe women's schooling should serve as a gateway to rarefied modes of self-expression or allusive dialogues with past poetic masters. Aware that illiteracy was the greatest impediment to a successful Republic and to women's full participation in it, she turned her energies, beginning in the early 1920s, to universal education and the establishment of schools and curricula for commoners.[35]

Zhang Mojun also reconceptualized the relationship between education and the home. In the imperial period, women's learning had been sharply divorced from their domestic work, to the extent that the two were considered mutually incompatible: cultivating talent took time away from a woman's more pressing household duties. In contrast, early-twentieth-century intellectuals and social activists like Zhang considered the valorization and scientization of the gendered practices of everyday life as central to China's modern transformation.[36] She advocated elevating household knowledge to the level of formal pedagogy and science, as well as tying formal pedagogy and science to domestic work.[37]

GENDERED FAMILY HISTORY AS METHODOLOGY

The historical method of tracing one lineage of women over multiple generations can be highly productive.[38] The limitations of focusing on one elite family are overcome by the advantage of controlling for such contingencies as geographic location, social status, and family background in mapping historical change over time. Premised on the notion that women are a particularly important locus for examining historical tensions, this approach opens up a valuable microhistorical vantage point for reexamining broad historical trends and critical historical moments.

From "Genteel Ladies" to New Women

The story of the Hunan Zhangs offers a microperspective on the historical process that has been described as the transition from "genteel ladies" (*guixiu*) to New Women, or more sweepingly, as the passage from tradition to modernity.[39] It brings into sharp relief a crucial social demographic and a complex historical reality that overdrawn characterizations such as these elide. More fully understanding this demographic—the talented woman— challenges and enriches our understanding of important aspects of not only Chinese women's history but also late Qing and early Republican history.

The pivotal generation in a study of the shift from the world of He Chenghui, poet and mother-instructor, to the world of Zhang Xiahun, would-be pilot and occasional essayist, is the generation of Zhang Mojun. This cohort of women, born between the late 1860s and the early 1880s, includes Qiu Jin

(1875–1907), Wu Zhiying (1868–1934), Xu Zihua (1873–1935), and Shi Shuyi (1876–1945).[40] Through their politically motivated cultural production and their culturally grounded social activism, these women demonstrated the capaciousness of the culture of their late imperial mothers. Faced with unprecedented global challenges, they did not shed the cultural practices that critics were already declaring obsolete. Instead they adapted and mobilized existing literary and artistic resources while simultaneously accumulating new ones, expanding the repertoire of the woman of talent to include journalistic polemics, expository essays, translated fiction, and oil painting.

Ironically, these women who so deftly made the practices of the woman of talent relevant to twentieth-century geopolitical challenges would also be key architects of the new education that would spell the demise of these very practices.[41] Committed to uplifting their twentieth-century descendants and universalizing basic and political literacy, they both defied the characterization by Liang Qichao (1873–1929) of the apolitical woman of talent and heeded his 1896 call for a new kind of women's education.[42] They thus embodied a profound historical bind that has long outlived them. Their own practices serve as testimony to a range of aborted historical possibilities and forms of cultural accommodation that could have helped avert the totalizing upheavals that have punctuated modern Chinese history. At the same time, however, they helped advance a historical trajectory from Liang Qichao through the New Culture Movement and the Cultural Revolution that would violently denigrate China's cultural resources in the name of serving the nation and the people.

The 1911 Revolution

The vantage point of the Zhang family women also offers a unique perspective on critical historical moments, among them, the 1911 Revolution and the early years of China's first Republic.

The consensus on the historiography of the 1911 Revolution is that it was a nonevent. The revolution preserved the status quo—many Qing bureaucrats stayed in their positions, for example—and while preexisting trends may have been accelerated by the revolution, no form of radical change could be directly attributed to it.[43]

The revolution certainly did not produce as lasting a cultural or social rupture as did the Taiping Rebellion with its traumatic dislocations and dramatic loss of life so poignantly recorded in the writings of the Changzhou

Zhangs, and particularly of Wang Caipin (d. 1893).[44] The writings and activities of the Hunan Zhangs, and principally of Zhang Mojun, nonetheless challenge commonly held assumptions about the inconsequentiality of 1911 and the failure of early Republicanism.

With the blessing of her mother, Zhang Mojun followed her father into radical politics in the first years of the twentieth century. She joined the Revolutionary Alliance in 1906 and was allegedly both a fellow traveler of Qiu Jin and a participant in violent anti-Qing activities.[45] She and Zhang Tongdian were instrumental in the restoration of Suzhou, and she became the editor of the *Suzhou Journal of the Great Han* shortly afterward (see figure 6.4).

Zhang Mojun was not the only woman to actively support regime change, either in her own day or in Chinese history: heroic women were prominent and much eulogized figures in all periods of dynastic transition.[46] But unlike these earlier woman warriors, including Hua Mulan (ca. 500), who was repeatedly invoked as a model in this period, Zhang and her 1911 comrades were not willing to return to hearth and home after the Qing was overthrown. Instead, they were committed to institutionalizing and expanding the political and social space they had opened for themselves at the time of the revolution. Marking a sharp departure in Chinese women's history, they sustained their political momentum and refused to retreat from their objective of more fully integrating women into Chinese public and political life.

Most studies of women active in the 1911 Revolution and the early Republic have focused on the more radical suffragists, including Tang Qunying (1871–1937) and Zhang Hanying (1872–1915), who stormed parliament, broke windows, and outraged their male counterparts.[47] Zhang Mojun initially collaborated with Tang and others in establishing the first women's suffrage organizations, and she personally hosted the American head of the International Women's Suffrage Association, Mrs. C. C. Catt, in 1912.[48] Revealing her sophisticated understanding of what Republican citizenship entailed, she did not agitate to immediately gain the vote, however. Instead she focused on what she considered to be crucial presuffrage work: universalizing women's education and augmenting women's knowledge of law and politics.

Zhang actively carried out this presuffrage work, founding the Chinese Girls' School and the *Chinese Women's Journal* in the first year of the Republic. The journal, which was the first and perhaps the only Republican women's journal to include detailed sections on national and international news,[49] is an invaluable and as yet untapped source for assessing the state of Republican consciousness shortly after the 1911 Revolution. It features several

Joan Judge

articles on topical issues, including women's suffrage, penned by prominent men—Sun Yat-sen, Wu Zhihui, Jiang Zuobin—and by women, including Tan Sheying, Yang Jiwei, Zhang Xiahun, and Zhang Mojun. The nature of early Chinese Republicanism is best revealed not in these polemical essays, however, but in various columns published over the course of the journal's history that focus on the preservation of historical memory, the cultivation of critical political consciousness, and the promotion of engaged activism.

The women who wrote for the *Chinese Women's Journal* seemed to anticipate both the ban by President Yuan Shikai (1859–1916) on women's involvement in Republican politics beginning in late 1913, and historiography's later verdict of the insignificance of the 1911 Revolution. A series of articles titled "A History of Women's Activities at the Time of the Restoration" (Guangfu shidai nüjie huodong shi), written by one of Mojun's closest colleagues, Chen Hongbi (1884–1966), meticulously documents women's participation in that event. The series, for which the editors repeatedly solicited contributions, was designed to serve both immediate and long-term political objectives. It would legitimize women's demands for fuller political participation by detailing their significant contribution to the Republican victory, and it would preserve an intimate record of the revolution for posterity.[50]

The *Chinese Women's Journal* itself focused on critiquing rather than on celebrating the new Republic. Satires printed in its pages bemoan that "our nation is not a Chinese Republic [*Zhonghua minguo*] but a Chinese male-public [*Zhonghua nanguo*], a dictatorship that deprives women of freedom."[51] Discursive essays repeatedly emphasize the republic's incompleteness. Based on a *geming* (revolution) but not a *gexin* (change in consciousness), it was "yet to be consolidated . . . still unstable."[52] Caustic criticism of the tragic political failures of the Republic's first years include Zhang Mojun's lament, in both essay and song, over the assassination of Song Jiaoren, Yuan Shikai's most threatening political rival.[53] Boldly outspoken, the writers and editors of *Chinese Women's Journal* thus reveal a critical Republican consciousness rather than a lack of Republican consciousness, as well as their resolute refusal to compromise on their vision of what the Republic of China could and should be.

This vision was articulated in the journal's detailed record of the activities and regulations of the Chinese Women's Cooperative Society (Shenzhou Nüjie Xiejishe), the umbrella organization for both the *Chinese Women's Journal* and the Chinese Girls' School. The organization was to be run like a mini Republic of women: it would unite members of the five races of the Republic

(Han, Manchu, Mongolian, Hui, and Cang [Tibetan]) and be divided into various departments, such as education and professionalization. Its objectives included universalizing education, studying law and politics, promoting various professions (including sericulture, banking, photography, and commerce), endorsing national products, cultivating competent female citizens, and assisting the nation. Unlike in the broader society, women were granted the vote within the Chinese Women's Cooperative. The heads of the association and of each department were to be elected by the whole body for one-year terms, and voting regulations were carefully outlined.[54]

Not all activities that the Chinese Women's Cooperative initiated came to fruition: the Jiangwan Animal Husbandry and Horticultural Experimental Site (Jiangwan Xuzhi Shiyan Chang) was quickly aborted, and owing to a lack of funding the *Chinese Women's Journal* itself ceased publication after twelve issues and six months of publication. Mojun's efforts, which He Chenghui financially and actively supported, nonetheless established a legacy of sustainable female activism in journalism and education. This provided crucial momentum for the next generation of women, who, like Zhang Xiahun, were anxious to develop their own modes of heroic Republican engagement.

SILENCES AND SENTIMENTS

There is a relatively high volume of what Susan Mann would call noise in the records of the lives of the Xiangxiang Zhangs.[55] This is particularly true of Zhang Mojun, who left us essays, a periodical, and over six hundred other works, which include poems, paintings, biographies, and translated fiction. Mojun was also committed to ensuring that other women in her family were brought out of the still shadows. She published poems by her mother, He Chenghui, in both the *Chinese Women's Journal* and a 1917 collection, and she ensured that the world had visual and textual evidence of Xiahun's historic flight.

But even, and in some ways especially, Mojun's life remains shrouded in silence. We can document her political evolution from early revolutionary activist to member of the Nationalist Party's Central Committee. We can trace her trajectory as a public intellectual from her first writings in *Women's World* through her treatise on jade in postwar Taiwan. We have few records to guide us, however, in understanding the concomitant unfolding of her sentimental journey.

Mojun's intimate life is one of the more extraordinary parts of her story.

She remained single until the age of forty, when she married Shao Yuan-chong (1890–1936), who was six years her junior. Mojun and Shao had known each other at least since 1912, when they both took positions in the recently founded Nationalist Party. They also shared textual space on more than one occasion: Shao wrote for *Chinese Women's Journal*, and he and Zhang had essays published sequentially (hers first) in *Citizen's Monthly* in 1913.[56] Their conjugal bliss is recorded in Shao's diary and poetry, Mojun's poems, and records of their work and travels together.[57] Their happiness was cut short in 1936, however, when Shao was killed, the only fatality in the Xi'an Incident, when the Nationalist leader, Jiang Kai-shek, whom Shao and Mojun supported, was kidnapped by two of his own generals.[58] Personal details such as these remind us of the ways human tragedy has been folded into dramatic historical change.

It is indisputable that Zhang Mojun was able to achieve much of what she did in the first decades of the twentieth century because she was unmarried. In contrast to late imperial talented women, who were dependent on male family members to make their poetry—and thus their very existence—publicly visible, early-twentieth-century women who left a mark in history were generally unencumbered by husband and family. With the exception of Qiu Jin, who left her husband, most of these women, including Tang Qun-ying, Xu Zihua, and Shi Shuying, were widows. Their status as chaste widows endowed them with the moral capital necessary to participate in public life.

Although Mojun lacked this protective social layer, she was undeterred in her public efforts to achieve her educational and political goals. She directly asked powerful men for money to support women's education, traveling to Nanjing shortly after the revolution, for example, to request funds from the provisional government for the faltering Shanghai Wuben School.[59] She collaborated with men in political and cultural associations—the Nationalist Party, the Southern Society—and in her journal and essays she openly criticized prominent politicians.

Zhang's social activism raises a number of questions central to understanding the fate of the late imperial woman of talent in the early twentieth century. How did this very public woman inoculate herself from social criticism? Did her close political relationship with her father maintain at least the veneer of the three obediences until Zhang Tongdian's death in 1915? Did her repeated emphasis on high standards of female virtue in both her writings and the regulations for the potentially threatening institutions she founded—the Chinese Women's Cooperative and the Chinese Girls' School—preempt public censure? Was her persona sufficiently masculine and asexual that she appeared above reproach? What, in short, were the criteria for unimpeachable female public conduct in the immediate post-1911 era?

While orthodox sources are silent on these questions and on the details of Zhang Mojun's private life, online sources—the twenty-first-century unofficial histories, or *waishi*—are not. According to more than one account, Mojun remained single until the age of forty not out of political or feminist conviction but because of a painful experience of thwarted love. Shortly after the 1911 Revolution, Mojun allegedly brought Jiang Zuobin, a returned overseas student with a promising military career, home to meet her mother. Jiang then promptly fell in love with Mojun's fifth sister, Zhang Shujia.

Unaware of Mojun's feelings for Jiang, He Chenghui agreed to Jiang and Shujia's marriage, which took place in 1912. At that moment Mojun purportedly swore she would never marry.[60] In the following years, when Shao Yuanchong repeatedly expressed romantic interest, Mojun equally persistently put him off, insisting that she would not even consider his overtures unless he successfully fulfilled certain criteria (which would essentially make him Jiang Zuobin's clone): complete a program of study abroad and attain a high military position.[61]

These rumors will most likely remain unverifiable. Shujia is a mute presence in the historical sources, and Jiang Zuobin has left no record of the incident recorded here. Jiang is, however, a ubiquitously noisy presence in Zhang Mojun's family history. He penned one of the inaugural essays for *Chinese Women's Journal*, a patronizing discussion of why Chinese women were not yet ready for suffrage.[62] He allowed his young sister-in-law (together with his wife) to accompany him on his official visit to the Nanyuan air show in September of 1916, the occasion of Xiahun's historic flight and accident. He solicited the preface for and included his own calligraphy in the collection of He Chenghui's poems that Zhang Mojun compiled in honor of her mother's sixtieth birthday.[63] Most bizarrely, Zhang Xiahun is identified as Jiang's wife in the caption to a photograph of Xiahun published in the March 20, 1919, issue of the *Women's Weekly* (Funü zhoukan, a supplement to the newspaper *Eastern Times* [Shibao]).

This photograph is the upper portion of the full portrait of Xiahun that had appeared, unidentified, in *Women's Eastern Times* two years earlier (see figure 6.7). The *Eastern Times* (Shibao) was also the publisher of *Women's Eastern Times*, which had featured not only this unidentified photograph of Xiahun but also the green-tinted montage (see figure 6.6) she had appeared in and the Nanyuan story, in 1916. Presumably its editors would have been familiar with the conjugal arrangements in the Zhang family and known that Shujia, rather than Xiahun, was Jiang's wife.[64]

Finally, and most poignantly, when the forty-year-old Mojun could not conceive after her marriage in 1924, she adopted one of Jiang and Shujia's daughters as her own.[65]

None of these details should appear strange given the closeness of elite Chinese families. All are made stranger, however, if we allow ourselves to fill in the silences in the historical record with the white noise of Mojun's unrequited love.

Gifted historians depend on more than rumors and unofficial histories to fill in historical silences and re-create historical moments. Once they have amassed historically verifiable and credible details, they use their imaginations, first, as Susan Mann puts it, to "set a scene," and then to connect disparate facts and ask penetrating questions. One such scene that begs for noise is a solemn family portrait taken five months after Shao Yuanchong was killed by a stray bullet in Xi'an.[66] Another, also haunted by absence, would take place two years later, when Mojun received news of Xiahun's death. Zhu Kezhen, the husband Mojun had found for her beloved eighth sister, and the current president of Zhejiang University, had moved the university and his family to Ji'an in Jiangxi to avoid the Japanese bombing in 1938. Living under harsh conditions with poor medical support, Xiahun's son succumbed to dysentery. She died of the same illness less than a month later. Zhu Kezhen, who would remarry less than two years later, was not with her when she died.[67]

Predeceased by her two younger sisters (Shujia too would die in 1938) and her younger husband, and having buried her mother in 1941, Mojun left mainland China for Taiwan in 1948. Again, the historical record is silent. From what port did she leave? With whom, and with what? Was she pressed with other refugees, fighting chaos and panic as she rushed to board ship, or did she stealthily make her way toward a Nationalist liner in a black limousine in the calm of night? And what were her thoughts on the moment of departure—a twentieth-century woman of talent forced to leave the country whose gender and political systems she had struggled to reform, and whose lyric and cultural traditions she so tenaciously upheld?

1   I discuss various aspects of Zhang Mojun's life and activities in *Republican Lens: Gender, Visuality, and Experience in the Early Chinese Periodical Press*, particularly chapter 5, "Practical Talent" (Berkeley: University of California Press, 2015).

2   Tan, "Xu," 1–1a. Some online sources identify He Tongyin as He Chenghui's older brother. Tan notes, however, that when he was fourteen he had been dependent on He Tongyin's support so I assume he is correct in identifying He Tongyin as Chenghui's father.

3   For the family genealogy see Zhu, *Zhu Kezhen quanji*, 12:577–78. See also Zhang, *Xiankao* 10.

4   Gao, "Daningtang," 519–20; Liu, "Shiji suidong," 69.

5   On Zhang Mojun's life, see Gao, "Daningtang," 515–55. For an abbreviated account in English, see Edwards, "Zhang Mojun." Edwards also focuses on Zhang's engagement with the suffrage issue in *Gender*, 50–51, 70–79, but she mistakenly calls her Zhang Shaohan.

6   The educator Li Lihua, who was born in 1900, claimed, for example, that her sister who was five years older than she had been "born in a different era." Wang, *Women in the Chinese Enlightenment*, 165.

7   Liu, "Shiji suidong," 70.

8   *Zhijia quanshu, shang.* Cheng was also a female representative in the Guangdong parliament; see *Funü shibao* (Women's eastern times; hereafter *FNSB*) 10 (May 25, 1913). All three women were featured in *FNSB*, which was, quite likely, the source for the photos. For Teng's photo see *FNSB* 12 (January 10, 1914). All translations are mine.

9   "Zhang Xiahun feixing yuxian jinxun." Liu, "Zhongguo zhi nü feixingjia." I discuss this incident at length in "Portraits of Republican Ladies." Zhang Xiahun continues to be celebrated in contemporary China for her daring airplane incident. See Hao, *Shenzhou diyi ren*, 310–11.

10   "Bianji shi zhi tanhua."

11   See *Shenzhou nübao* (Journal of Chinese women; hereafter *SZNB*), *xunkan* 7, January 1912, *yuekan* 4, June 1913.

12   Chenghui, *Yixiao tang shiji*. The volume is included in the *Fanshu ouji*. It is also included in Hu, *Lidai funü*, 229. Tan Yankai had served as military governor of Hunan and had special ties to He's father.

13   Tan, "Xu," 1a. The term *eight dynasties* refers to the period from late Han through the Sui.

14   He, "Fakanci," 1–2. Cited in Liu, "Ou Mei," 29. This is the one issue of the *Shenzhou nübao* of which I do not have a copy.

15   Mann, *The Talented Women*, 200.

16   Zhang, *Zhang Mojun*. This volume includes approximately 602 *shi* and *ci* (poems), 16 commentaries (*lunzhu*), 14 lectures (*jiangyan*), six documents (*gongdu*), and 42 pieces of miscellaneous writings (*zazhu*).

17   On Zhang Mojun's training by practitioners of the Tong-Guang style such as Chen Sanli and Chan Yan, see Liu Feng, "Wan Qing," 99.

18   Zhang, *Xiankao.* This volume is held in the Shanghai Library.

19   Examples include Zhang, "Xiandai"; *Zhanhou; Xichui; Zhongguo.*

20   Zhang Mojun translated (using the penname Mo) installments of a detective novel entitled "Tongying an" (The case of the reflection in the pupil of an eye) in the first seven issues of the *xunkan* edition of *Shenzhou nübao.* On other novels she translated, see Zhu, *Xiandai Hunan nüxing wenxue shi,* 32.

21   Zhang Xiahun's essays include "Shenzhou," "Song xiansheng," and "Zongjiao."

22   For a contemporary account of the exhibition in English, see "The Nanyang Exhibition." According to Doris Sung, Zhang's paintings were among the limited number of works in the Western medium exhibited at the Nanyang exhibition. For a near contemporary review, see Wu Bonian. I am indebted to Doris Sung for the sources on Zhang's participation in Nanyang.

23   The "Awakened Lion" painting appeared with two of Zhang's landscapes in *FNSB* 4. The painting of the beauty, sword, and horse was not reproduced, but Zhang's colophon to the painting was. See Zhang, "Ziti 'meiren.' "

24   Liu, "Zhongguo zhi nü feixingjia," 81.

25   Both photographs of He were published in He Chenghui, "Fakanci."

26   See "Xinhai geming shihua."

27   Zhang, *Xichui yinhen,* n.p.

28   For a fuller interpretation of this photograph, see Judge, "Portraits."

29   Zhang, "Dingsi chun."

30   Gao, "Daningtang nianpu," 528.

31   Liu, "Shiji suidong," 68.

32   Gao, "Daningtang nianpu."

33   Ibid.

34   For example, Mojun taught Chinese poetry at Jinling Nüzi Daxue in 1935. Ibid., 541.

35   In 1921, together with Zhu Qihui, the wife of Xiong Bingsan (Xiong Xiling), Mojun created the Chinese Commoners' Education Movement (Zhongguo Pingmin Jiaoyu Yundong).

36   On male intellectuals engaged in this enterprise of valorizing the women's everyday practices, see Judge, "Everydayness."

37   Zhang wrote that the basis of household education was science and discussed the need for such courses as household chemistry (*jiating huaxue*), common medical knowledge (*yiyao changshi*), and household industry (*jiating zhiye*), together with sewing, cooking, and gardening. Zhang, *Zhanhou,* 32–34.

38   Susan Mann has most successfully used this method in *The Talented Women.*

39   See, for example, ibid., 200.

40   Qiu Jin and Shi Shuyi have been the subjects of recent penetrating studies by Hu Ying and Hu Siao-chen: Hu Ying, *Burying Autumn*; Hu Siao-chen, "The Construction of Gender."

41   According to Hu Siao-chen ("The Construction of Gender," 361), "When women at the turn of the century began to publish their prose writings, they fundamentally changed the nature of women's education in language and literature, a topic that needs more exploration." Hu analyzes this line of thought more fully in *Xin lixiang.*

On efforts to sustain the study of poetry in the age of the new women's education, see Tang, "Nüzi shi ci jiangxi she."

42 Liang made this call for the new women's education, and his critique of the woman of talent in the subsection on "Women's Learning" (Lun Nüxue), in his 1896 essay "On Reform" (Bian fa tong yi lun nüxue). Xue Shaohui explicitly challenged Liang's characterization of the *cainü*. See Judge, *The Precious Raft*, 92; Qian, "The Mother *Nü xuebao*."

43 Zarrow, "China in War and Revolution," 30.

44 Mann, *The Talented Women*, 130–64.

45 There is much discussion of but little hard data on Zhang Mojun's radical late-Qing activities. According to Gao ("Daningtang nianpu," 524), she entered the Tongmeng Hui in 1906. Chen Hongbi gives the date as 1904, which is questionable since the organization was not formally founded until 1905 ("Guangfu shidai," 7). A number of sources mention several encounters with Qiu Jin (see Gao, "Daningtang nianpu," 524–25) and even Zhang's financial support for Qiu Jin's bomb-making activities (see Chen, "Guangfu shidai," 7). Liu Feng ("Shiji suidong," 65) describes an incident in 1909 when Zhang received a shipment of firearms.

46 Judge, *The Precious Raft*, 143–62.

47 See Edwards, *Gender*, 65–102; Strand, *An Unfinished Republic*. Both Edwards and Strand discuss Zhang Mojun as well.

48 "Jiade furen."

49 News was under various columns titled or subtitled "Jishi" (Recorded events).

50 The series appeared in issues 1, 2, 5, and 7 of the *xunkan* edition of *SZNB*. The request for submissions was included in the "Benshe qishi" (Society announcements) under "Zhengwen" (Manuscript request) in most issues of the *xunkan*.

51 Shen Jikai *zhiyan*.

52 See, for example, Zhang Mojun's comment at the end of the essay by Song Cen ("Zhengji," 10). Also see Yang, "Shiping" and Chen, "Guangfu shidai," 9.

53 Zhang, "Ku Song." See also Zhang Xiahun, "Song xiansheng."

54 See, for example, "Shenzhou nüjie."

55 Mann, "Biographical Sources"; *The Talented Women*.

56 Shao, "Nüquan." Zhang, "Ai Song Dunchu" is followed by an article by Shao also eulogizing Song.

57 See, for example, Shao, *Shao Yuanchong riji*; Zhang, *Xichui*.

58 Gao, "Daningtang nianpu," 542.

59 "Benshe jishi."

60 Baidu Baike, "Zhang Mojun," http://baike.baidu.com/view/477464.htm.

61 Ibid.

62 Jiang, "Jinzhu *Shenzhou nübao*."

63 Tan, "Xu," 1a-b.

64 *Funü zhoukan*, 1.

65 Zhu, *Zhu Kezhen quanji*, 12:577. The girl Shao Yingduo (Nengneng) was adopted in 1926. Mojun and Shao also adopted a boy.

66 The portrait is reprinted in Zhu, *Zhu Kezhen quanji*, vol. 1.

67 Zhejiang Sheng Zhengxie Wenshi Ziliao, "Yidai zongshi Zhu Kezhen."

CHAPTER SEVEN

MOVING TO SHANGHAI

Urban Women of Means in the Late Qing

Yan Wang

I N the autumn of 1891, the seventeenth year of the Guangxu emperor's reign, a young woman of the Zhuang family married Sheng Xuanhuai (1844–1916), the leading official-merchant of the late Qing era and a pivotal figure in China's history of capitalism, as his successor wife.[1] It had been more than ten years since Sheng's first wife, Lady Dong (1846–78), had died. The successor wife's name was Zhuang Dehua (1866–1927), styled Wanyu.

Such a match was satisfactory for both the Zhuang and the Sheng families. The former, a Changzhou local gentry family, had prospered for several generations in the high Qing period. In the family's twelfth generation, ancestor Zhuang Peiyin (1723–59) had won the highest score, the first rank (*zhuangyuan*) of the *jinshi* metropolitan degree, in the civil service examination in 1755; but unfortunately, the talented scholar died young, in his thirties. Zhuang Peiyin's elder brother Zhuang Cunyu (1719–88) acquired his *jinshi* degree in 1745 and started the Changzhou School of New Text Confucianism along with his nephew Zhuang Shuzu (1751–1816) and grandson Liu Fenglu (1776–1829). The Changzhou school planted the seeds for the late-nineteenth-century radical thought of Kang Youwei (1858–1927).[2] As a Changzhou gentry family, the Zhuangs also maintained a close relationship with the local Zhang family, whose talented women (*cainü*) had been brilliant poets for generations.[3] But the glorious Zhuang clan had undergone a gradual decline in the late nineteenth century. By the fifteenth generation, no names ranked high in the civil service examinations. Zhuang Peiyin's great-grandson Zhuang Yuying merely achieved the title of *linsheng*, which means "the most distinguished among those who passed the county-level examination."[4] Zhuang Yuying produced three sons and three daughters, of which the two elder sons and two elder daughters all died before reaching their teens. Only the youngest son and the youngest daughter by his concubine Lady Jin survived. In 1887, when the family composed its genealogy, the youngest daughter was not yet engaged.[5] But several years later, she married upward into the powerful Sheng family: she is the protagonist of this chapter. The Sheng family felt content that they had found a suitable match, because the Zhuang family with its glorious past came from the same local county. In addition, the new bride was more than twenty years younger than the bridegroom.

Lady Zhuang stood on the margins between the tradition of the "talented woman" and the modern "new woman." She emerged from the place and time in which "talented women" had flourished. But unlike the Zhang women described by Joan Judge in chapter 6 of this volume, she had not acquired the education and political awareness that marked new-style talent in the late Qing.[6] As an ordinary gentlewoman (*guixiu*)—a woman of means in the transitional period when "new women" superseded "talented women," in the final twenty years of the Qing—Lady Zhuang was caught in an awkward position. She was not a poet and seldom expressed her talent through writing. She did write, however, mostly in family letters. These letters were written to her husband, her mother, her brother, and friends. Her handwriting in the letters seems unsophisticated, and the writing contains numerous errors. Rather than a valorized "new woman," she belonged to the category of "leisured lady of means," the type of woman who was harshly criticized by late Qing reformers for living off her father or husband, for having no idea what was happening in the contemporary world, and for paying attention only to jewelry and cosmetics.[7] The histories of women like Lady Zhuang have been neglected owing to such discourse and to the scarcity of historical sources written in their own hands. Her story, however, provides a continuous and vivid picture of the transformation of leisured ladies in the late Qing urban world. It demonstrates their critical role in the success of their families and their quick adaptation to and engagement with the modernizing urban world.

MOVING TO THE SHANGHAI CONCESSIONS

Most of Lady Zhuang's married life was spent in Shanghai's "concessions," the city districts controlled by foreign governments. Leaving the old house in Changzhou, a city that had long been a Confucian cultural center in the late imperial era, and migrating to and settling down in a modern commercial setting were experiences never undertaken by other Zhuang family ladies. Was the future predictable? Did she long for the relocation? How would she confront the moral "decline" in Shanghai? Would she still be able to uphold her position in the family hierarchy and maintain her wifely authority over the restless concubines in a complex urban environment? Would Shanghai be a good place to make money and spend it? At that moment, no one could answer these questions.

Shanghai in the 1880s and 1890s had grown to be a new political, economic, and cultural center in the Lower Yangzi area. In 1843, the city's population was barely over 250,000; it ranked twelfth among all Chinese cities.[8] By 1900, however, its population had reached 1 million, making it the largest city in China; a mere fifteen years later, the figure had doubled.[9] Politically, although Beijing continued to be the capital, where the Manchu court was located, Shanghai in many ways had more impact as a result of its modern media, its progressive ideas, and the protection it afforded various political figures. In the economic sector, modern enterprises like the machine-manufacturing industry, the Merchants' Steam Navigation Company, modern weaving companies, new media such as newspapers and magazines, and telegraph companies all appeared first, and operated successfully, in Shanghai. In the late nineteenth century, Shanghai's total import-export value was more than 50 percent of that of the entire country. Its modern banks outnumbered those of any other city throughout the country. The economic environment of late-Qing Shanghai provided numerous opportunities and wide networks for people to take advantage of. Culturally, the city anxiously absorbed and even institutionalized Western learning. For example, Shanghai built Western schools, employed Western technology to manage the municipal government, adopted the seven-day work-and-rest schedule and the solar calendar, and established libraries, museums, and so forth.[10] Even upper-class women were permitted to socialize among strangers, walk freely in public spaces, have their pictures taken in photo shops, and purchase commodities advertised in newspapers or magazines.

The Sheng family lived adjacent to the Bund, the Westernized waterfront district where most modern enterprises were constructed. The family owned numerous houses and villas in Shanghai. But according to the archives, Lady Zhuang spent most of her time in the British and American concessions. Before the end of 1899, the family lived on Second Avenue in the British concession, the core of the downtown area along the Bund. Shortly after, they moved into the famous villa of Slanting Bridge (Xieqiao), situated at the intersection of today's Nanjing Road and Wujiang Road, not far from their previous home. One block distant from their home stood the offices of the *Shanghai News* (Shenbao). This district incubated China's modern media and publication enterprises. By 1900, the district was the location of China's top publication organizations, including *Shanghai News*, the Commercial Press, and so forth. On its eastern edge, the Merchants' Steam Navigation Company faced east, toward the Bund. Right next to it was the China Telegraph Bureau. The high concentration of modern projects nearby connected the ladies of the Sheng family to the modern pulse of the city and enabled them to receive the most up-to-date information. The only critical modern enterprise established outside the urban core was the Machine Weaving Company. After its destruction by fire, it was reconstructed in the old industrial area of Yangshupu in Zhabei district, northeast of the British and American concessions. In 1894, officials expanded it and renamed it the Huasheng Textile Mill.

THE CONTINUITY OF INNER-QUARTER RESPONSIBILITIES

Lady Zhuang diligently managed family affairs in the concessions as assigned by her traditional role as manager of the inner quarters. Married ladies of means were inevitably given one of the major inner-quarter tasks: managing the family's consumption.[11] Sheng Xuanhuai's first wife, Lady Dong, who had spent most of her life in the old house in Changzhou, revealed her control of the family's consumption in a letter. She was in charge of the expenditures on all servants and on her own daily needs. One of the largest expenditures was for holidays. Every holiday required extravagant outlays. In 1878, when the Sheng family was not yet as prosperous as it was to become in the 1880s and 1890s, the sum for preparing the celebration for one Dragon Boat Festival reached three hundred taels of silver. Lady Dong had protested that she was not stingy, but that this amount of silver was half of her savings and so was too much for her to spend on one festival.[12]

The successor wife, Lady Zhuang, had a stronger personality, and she controlled the family consumption more freely than her predecessor had. One reason she was able to do this, of course, was that the family had grown richer and their status had risen considerably since the time she married into it. The other reason was that Lady Zhuang maintained a good relationship with the men who controlled the outer accounting office (*wai zhangfang*) of the household. This office was responsible for the accounts of the whole Sheng extended family. Every family member's monthly allowance was paid through this office. But the principal wife supervised and managed the accounting office. Although principal wives like Lady Zhuang had no power to control the use of each member's allotment, especially that of the concubines, they could easily ask the outer accounting office for more money, since they were responsible for maintaining the daily life of the whole household. Lady Zhuang's step-granddaughter Sheng Peiyu still remembered some seventy years later that Lady Zhuang had had two "grand councilors," the accountant (*zhangfang*) and the "private advisor" (*shiye*), to help manage the family income and expenditures under her supervision day and night.[13]

The money available to Lady Zhuang was often more than ten thousand taels. Some of her major costs were incurred while receiving visiting relatives, especially during holidays when relatives traveled to Shanghai from Changzhou, Suzhou, and even faraway provinces to enjoy a family reunion. Lady Zhuang's father-in-law traveled frequently between Changzhou, Suzhou, and Shanghai in his retirement years. A reception for him and his entourage required not only energy but also a large amount of money from Lady Zhuang. When her father-in-law once spent the Dragon Boat holiday in Shanghai, Lady Zhuang claimed that she sent him sixteen hundred taels of silver as a monthly allowance, along with an additional thousand taels of silver as a holiday present. Beyond that, Lady Zhuang decided to display her inner-quarter management abilities in a public space. She hosted a party in the famous Zhang Garden, a public garden integrated with Chinese and Western styles, to celebrate the holiday as well as to pay formal respects to her father-in-law. The whole family had dinner in the Zhang Garden and watched a movie there after dinner. In her letter, she expressed her filial piety and respect to her father-in-law, showing off by stating that all the expenses for food and entertainment were on her own account.[14]

Managing servants' consumption was an important aspect of the principal wife's monthly responsibility. Payments to servants constituted a moderate but regular expenditure in the family budget. The payment lists preserved in the Sheng Xuanhuai archive show that the servants' total salaries reached about 260 taels of silver each month. The Sheng household accommodated a fairly large group of servants, including cooks, gatekeepers, runners, seamstresses, tailors, nannies, gardeners, tomb watchers, guards, and those doing various other jobs.[15] More than seventy servants are listed by name. With the addition of those who provided irregular services, the total number of servants could reach one hundred. Apart from the regular monthly payments, the servants in the Sheng family had many irregular expenses. Since the family members resided all over the empire—especially the family head, Sheng Xuanhuai, who was variously stationed in Hubei, Tianjin, Shandong, or Beijing—Lady Zhuang constantly dispatched servants to them, who sometimes carried prepared foods or fresh fruits, and sometimes brought letters, clothes, or even large sets of furniture.[16] Each trip cost a considerable amount, since it included expenditures for boat tickets, foods, lodging fees, and telegrams sent back and forth.[17] Although sometimes there was no charge for boat tickets and telegrams owing to her husband's position, the whole expenditure was significant. More than one servant was on his way at the same time, all over the empire. Whereas Sheng paid for the trips he dispatched, Lady Zhuang was responsible for trips carried out under her own orders.

In a big compound like the Shengs', wives also had to keep an eye on all sick people who might need special treatment or special medicines and nutrition. Out of her love for her husband, Lady Zhuang repeatedly sent him fresh foods, bird's nest, or ginseng.[18] And she had to prepare sufficient ginseng for her father-in-law whenever he needed it. Meanwhile, she also had to preserve some for other women in the household who might need it, in order to help maintain good relationships with them.[19]

A big family like the Shengs also encountered frequent weddings, birth celebrations, and burial ceremonies. The principal wife was responsible for arranging these festivities and ceremonies, including financing and staffing. Lady Zhuang complained to Sheng about the exorbitant cost of this constant round of ceremonial events. When her eldest stepson had his first son, Lady Zhuang considered giving children's clothes and gold pieces to the couple as birth gifts. At the same time, her second stepdaughter, Sheng Xiaoyi, had just married into the elite Feng family. In order to marry her off properly, Lady

Zhuang decided to present her with sixty garments made of silk, cotton, and foreign cloth, plus hats with gold and silver decorations. Moreover, her third stepdaughter was about to give birth and the family anticipated reporting the coming birth very soon. Lady Zhuang had to prepare gifts for this as well. As a stepmother, she was not merely worried about the expenditure but also concerned about the satisfaction of the family members and relatives who would receive the gifts, for they always believed that the wealthy Sheng family should send more and better gifts.[20] Another case from the archives further reveals women's managerial roles in household finance. Right before the 1911 revolution, when Sheng Xuanhuai and Lady Zhuang moved to Beijing, the principal wife of Sheng Xuanhuai's first son assumed Lady Zhuang's role and functioned as the manager of the big household. At that time it was she who had access to the family account, and it was under her authority that the expenditures for various ceremonies were paid from the household budget. In addition to the eldest daughter-in-law, married-out daughters—who were themselves principal wives of other families—were asked to help their natal family. Sheng Zhihui, Sheng's fourth daughter, helped manage her natal family's wedding ceremonies, which required great effort on her part. She frequently reported her progress to her parents. According to Sheng Zhihui, she prepared all the clothes, embroidery, silver utensils, and jewelry carefully and diligently. But Sheng Zhihui had no access to the family accounts; customarily, that authority belonged to her married-in sisters-in-law, and major domestic matters in the Sheng family's Shanghai compound remained under the control of the eldest daughter-in-law.[21] Still, with the funds disbursed to her by the daughter-in-law and the family accountant, Sheng Zhihui played an active role as a filial daughter and a capable woman of means.

EXERTING POWER IN THE MODERN COMMERCIAL MARKET

As Sheng Xuanhuai rose to power, he influenced and extended control over every aspect of Qing modern enterprise. Mining, shipping, telegraphing, textile enterprises, and modern banks, in all of which Sheng Xuanhuai was involved, were among the critical ventures that the late Qing government attempted to develop. Sheng worked with Li Hongzhang (1823–1901), the most famous leader of the Self-Strengthening Movement (1861–94), and functioned as an influential sponsor of all these enterprises on behalf of the government. In 1873 Sheng was appointed general manager of the Merchants' Steam Navigation Company. Although he was challenged by influential compradors, Sheng fought back and was able to take over the company. In 1875 he began a coal-mining project in Hubei. Because of the low quality of the coal, that first coal-mining venture was not very successful, but the experience paved the way for his later success in the Hanyeping mining project.[22] In 1881 Sheng was assigned to manage China's Telegraph Bureau, an assignment that he successfully pursued with Jing Yuanshan (1840–1903), the renowned gentry-merchant. In addition, he kept an eye on the Shanghai Machine Weaving Company, which was headed by Wei Lunxian in 1876 and then Zheng Guanying from the early 1880s to the early 1890s. Sheng Xuanhuai kept in close contact with them and their textile enterprise from the very beginning, offering suggestions and arranging financing. As we will see, he eventually took over the company and became the de facto owner.[23] Finally, Sheng masterminded the opening of China's first modern bank, the China Merchants' Bank, in 1896. These activities indicate the breadth of his economic empire and his enormous contribution to the late Qing modernization process.

In such a family, whose household head shaped the modern economic tides of the empire, the womenfolk too became actively involved in commercial investments. Lady Zhuang was well known for her participation in commercial activities, which included management of the textile mill and silk factories and investments in raw materials such as grain, cotton, and silkworm cocoons on the wholesale market.

Lady Zhuang regarded the modern mill enterprise as one of her responsibilities. Sheng Xuanhuai's longtime involvement in textile enterprises paved the way for him to open his own family-run textile mill. Especially after 1893, when Zheng Guanying's Machine Weaving Company burned to the ground, Sheng took over Zheng's enterprise and opened the Huasheng Textile Mill, which linked him directly to the late-Qing textile modernization project. Lady Zhuang spent considerable time in the family textile mill, which was nominally managed by Sheng Xuanhuai's eldest son, Sheng Changyi. As it turned out, Sheng Changyi was an opium addict and he seldom carried out his responsibilities effectively. Lady Zhuang complained many times to Sheng Xuanhuai that his eldest son "knew nothing but mahjong, gambling, and flirting with courtesans."[24] Whether or not that was the truth, Lady Zhuang had determined to have a say in the mill's daily management. From her point of view, none of Sheng Xuanhuai's three older sons were capable of helping to manage the family-run factories; all were opium-addicted dandies. This left even more responsibility to the women in the household.

Yan Wang

Lady Zhuang devoted herself to the wholesale market enthusiastically. She eagerly purchased tons of cotton and yarn and stored them in the textile mills. When the prices went up and reached a level satisfactory to her, she ordered an employee to sell these stores off quickly. If prices were not to her liking, she simply saved the raw materials for her own textile mills. In the busy year of 1899, when Lady Zhuang and Sheng Xuanhuai exchanged letters most frequently, they struggled over how to invest in the raw materials markets more effectively to preserve the family's fortune (*caiyun*). Lady Zhuang wrote confidently to Sheng detailing her decision to buy cotton at a cost of 40,000 *yuan*, which she wanted to borrow from her husband. Assuming that her transaction made a profit, she wrote, she would return the original sum to her husband and keep the profit for her own use.[25] In his response, Sheng Xuanhuai endorsed Lady Zhuang's investment and praised her for her acuity and financial talent. But he also cautioned her about avarice. Apprehensive about market uncertainty, Sheng urged Lady Zhuang to sell her stores of raw materials as soon as possible, noting that his own market sensibility was sharper than hers.[26] Sheng's suggestions did not always win Lady Zhuang's approval. In fact, it seems that she was seldom happy with her husband's advice. She criticized Sheng because she believed that he was making excuses not to lend her money. To persuade her husband, she often declared her self-confidence and impressed him with her careful plans.[27]

Lady Zhuang invested in grain as well as cotton and yarn. Unlike cotton and yarn, grain was a basic need. Lady Zhuang was fully aware of its special market qualities. During normal harvest years, the public considered investment in the grain market a legitimate strategy. But in bad years, such investment could bring public criticism and even blame for contributing to food shortages. Both Lady Zhuang and Sheng Xuanhuai were careful to conceal information about their investments in grain during bad years.[28]

Aside from investing in the market for raw materials, Lady Zhuang made loans and bought stock in Shanghai. Her letters rarely mention loans; perhaps she was not that fond of making them. Sheng Xuanhuai kept reminding her of the stable return on loans, but she seldom responded readily to requests for loans.[29] Investing in stock was widespread particularly among late-Qing gentry families, gentry-merchants, and merchants. Sheng Xuanhuai's family participated: Sheng was one of the pioneers in organizing modern enterprises by creating joint stockholding firms. Lady Zhuang herself pawned stocks occasionally in order to obtain cash in emergencies. In the early spring of 1899, she decided to speculate on cotton, but she lacked sufficient cash to purchase the raw material. In order to accumulate enough money, she pawned her stock in a gold ore company for six thousand taels of silver. Shortly afterward, she repeated the speculation and pawned her stock for forty thousand taels of silver.[30]

Lady Zhuang also kept an eye on the real estate market in Shanghai. Since the Little Sword and Taiping Rebellions, Chinese migrants had poured into the Shanghai concessions for protection, after which the real estate market kept prospering to accommodate the large number of newcomers. No evidence proves that Lady Zhuang constructed houses to lease out. But obviously, she was aware of the real estate market in the Shanghai concession areas, for she constantly mentioned her desire to purchase villas, sometimes for the family to live in, and sometimes as pure investment.

The Sheng family had maintained an old villa in Shanghai's concession area, but as more family members came to reside in Shanghai, the old villa became crowded and uncomfortable. Since the family head, Sheng Xuanhuai, spent most of his time in other provinces, Lady Zhuang replaced him as the de facto head of the household, making decisions about everything, including buying, designing, and decorating the purchased villas, though sometimes consulting with her husband and other relatives about the structure and geomancy of them. Since her eldest stepson was supposed to be supervising the Huasheng Textile Mill operations, she focused on supervising the construction of the new buildings. If the textile mill were to earn more, the construction project would have more funds to devote to decoration, she indicated.[31]

Lady Zhuang also attempted to buy another renowned villa, the Yu Garden, because of its potential for rising value. This time, her goal was purely investment.[32] In her letters, there is no indication that she purchased land, although that had been a common practice among late Qing rural women of means.[33] Perhaps as an urban resident confronted with a flourishing real estate market, she was not very interested in land anymore.

ACCESS TO THE MODERN WORLD: CONVENTIONAL AND MODERN NETWORKS

As Lady Zhuang extended her power to the modern commercial world, she skillfully manipulated two different approaches to accomplish her goals. One was the conventional strategy of deploying personal and family networks; the second approach, however, was new: use of the modern print media, the telegraph, and modern shipping and transportation.

Yan Wang

A large family network enabled Lady Zhuang to receive the most current price information. She frequently consulted with her husband and other relatives to get the most current prices of raw cotton and yarn. When Sheng Xuanhuai was stationed in Hubei, he reported the Hubei grain prices to Lady Zhuang. If prices were low enough, then Lady Zhuang would arrange to move grain from Hubei to Shanghai.[34] If the empire's capital was short of grain, Sheng or Sheng's relatives would quickly send this message back and order another long-distance transaction. Lady Zhuang might also be informed of the timing of the winter freeze along the Yellow River, enabling her to sell her grain for better prices after the freeze set in.[35] One of her major consultants was a male relative, Xu Shaoping, who closely monitored the wholesale market. Xu often brought the most recent prices of cotton and yarn to Lady Zhuang and gave her his predictions for the market. In addition, her father-in-law would arrange to buy grain in Wuxi, near their native place, if necessary.[36] Female relatives were another major source of price information for Lady Zhuang. They wrote or gossiped to each other, exchanging the most recent information, including the market prices of grain, cotton, and yarn.[37] Her wide access to price information from all over the empire empowered Lady Zhuang to invest successfully in wholesale markets. She always proclaimed confidently to her husband that she was so well informed that no one could cheat her.[38] In fact, by constantly maintaining a network with relatives, Lady Zhuang was able to keep her hand on the very pulse of the market, which helped her make additional money. Her financial success in turn secured her position as a family manager and a confident principal wife.

Generally speaking, a principal wife's financial success contributed greatly to the family property. In times of financial shortage, her successful investments could tide the family over. If the husband did not earn sufficient income, a good female investor could support the whole family without any additional help. Zeng Jifen (1852–1942), the youngest daughter of the distinguished governor general Zeng Guofan, invested in land, stock, and various other businesses to overcome her own family's difficulties, illustrating this point.[39] Although her natal family was a frugal Confucian one, her husband's family made efforts to invest in modern enterprises. Taking advantage of family connections with merchants and modern enterprises, urban upper-class women like Zeng Jifeng and Lady Zhuang could earn more than they would have from needlework.

Networking of this kind could also increase women's financial independence within the family context, especially of those women who had strong personalities, for networking in the commercial market could enrich their own purses. They could either purchase things they liked, patronize someone of whom they were secretly fond, or give money to a daughter as dowry. With additional money in their own pockets, they could further invest in things they appreciated without consulting with the nominal family head or leaving any record in the family accounting office.

Other modern networks, too, were available to Lady Zhuang. Newspapers, a modern medium, were widely accepted in Shanghai's concession culture. Leisured women were important consumers of newspapers because of the high literacy rates among them, and because they could afford to purchase newspapers. They may be considered heirs of the literate ladies of the late Ming who enjoyed reading so much that the commercial printing industry produced large numbers of illustrated books and didactic books just to cater to their tastes.[40] By the late Qing, leisured women were reading newspapers regularly, alongside their male counterparts.

Even ladies of means from remote areas of the empire made regular use of newspapers. For example, Jing Yuanshan's advertisements promoting the China Girls' School (Zhongguo nüxuetang) were published in newspapers in 1897, with the result that he successfully recruited many influential female readers who lent the school personal and financial support.[41] A gentry lady from Guangxi, far inland from Shanghai, mailed a letter to Jing Yuanshan and his collaborators expressing her happiness at reading the announcement about the school in the newspaper. She donated 10 *yuan* to the Shanghai reformers who were leading the school, a sum that was forwarded to the reformers by her son-in-law, one of Kang Youwei's (1858–1927) disciples.[42] In the meantime, after reading the newspaper, another lady from Shandong forwarded her resume and poetry collection to Jing Yuanshan's group in hopes of securing a teaching position in the China Girls' School.[43]

Living in the concessions, the Sheng family women were no exception. Employing the modern print media, they could absorb all kinds of market information, including rice prices, cotton prices, and news of various recent commercial activities. Sometimes, by reading newspaper accounts of the weather or disasters in a certain province, they were able to predict commodity prices and make decisions on their investments. Lady Zhuang once read an account about her eldest stepson's rice-purchasing business. She clipped the article out of the *News Journal* (Xinwen bao) and delivered it to Sheng Xuanhuai in a letter.[44]

Yan Wang

Women of means also collected useful information from the newspaper for their personal causes. Lady Zhuang often read newspapers to learn the most recent whereabouts of her husband and other family members.[45] She frequently criticized Sheng Xuanhuai for not telling her his true plans: whether he was coming back to Shanghai for the holidays, whether he was dispatched to another post and for how long—none of this was ever clearly passed on to Lady Zhuang. She was once provoked by a notice in the newspaper reporting that her husband had decided to bring his concubine Miss Liu with him to his new post. The report was notable because Sheng's letters to Lady Zhuang had attempted to persuade her not to follow him to his new post on the grounds that the roads north were obstructed by freezing weather. When Lady Zhuang realized from reading the newspaper that Sheng had brought the concubine with him and avoided the freezing temperatures by taking a boat, she became furious. In her letter berating him, she enclosed the newspaper article.[46]

The Sheng family's female newspaper readers were also keen to pick up any information that could affect the family's status. Political struggles, foreign invasions, signed treaties—all were included in their daily concerns. Lady Zhuang paid close attention to the political struggles in Beijing and the local uproar right before the 1911 Revolution, when her husband was accused of several crimes.[47]

Ladies of means not only acquired information from reading newspapers; they also grasped the influence of print media and utilized newspapers to enhance their families' reputations. The Sheng household in Shanghai was in jeopardy just before the 1911 Revolution, when rumors circulated that they had received a 6-million-*yuan* kickback when the government borrowed money from foreign countries. In order to save the family reputation and prevent attacks by a furious public, Lady Zhuang suggested that the family report the truth in a newspaper statement endorsed by the embassies of four foreign countries.[48] Both Lady Zhuang and Sheng Xuanhuai were fully aware of the effect of public opinion represented by this medium. If they used it correctly, they could promote their interests. Otherwise, they could be victims of press coverage: on another occasion Lady Zhuang warned her husband to be careful since the newspapers might accuse the Sheng family of hoarding rice to make a profit.[49]

In addition to newspapers, the telegraph was another critical modern medium employed by urban women of means. Thanks to Sheng Xuanhuai's telegraph project initiated at the end of 1870s, the Sheng family ladies were among the first groups of women who began to share the convenience of this modern technology.

Considerable evidence shows that Lady Zhuang used the telegraph frequently—indeed, to an astonishing extent. Although she is the only woman for whom I have found archival evidence of telegraph use, she was by no means the only woman who employed the technology in the late Qing. The Sheng archive preserves a considerable number of telegraphed messages from Lady Zhuang. Since her husband's telegraph project achieved great success in the 1880s, she fully understood its effectiveness. In fact, she enjoyed sending telegrams in place of letters. During times of emergency, she used telegrams for quick responses. But more often she sent telegrams simply for convenience. In other words, the telegraph had become an ordinary method of communication for her, a woman whose wealth permitted her to enjoy the most advanced technology of the time. When she was worried about fine goods she had shipped to her husband, she would telegraph her relatives or her husband, asking them to look for the shipment's arrival.[50] She also telegraphed her husband to keep an eye on the local real estate in Tianjin.[51] In her telegram, Lady Zhuang discussed not only family affairs with her husband or helpers but also the prices in the market, the harvest in the United States, and other recent commercial trends.[52] Without the modern telegraph, Lady Zhuang's activities in the commercial world would have been much less efficient.

The modern shipping industry initiated by the Merchants' Steam Navigation Company in 1873 brought further convenience to Lady Zhuang's life and enhanced the success of her investments. At the time she married into the family, her husband successfully controlled this shipping company and it had just reached its peak.[53] The branches of the company extended to many important coastal and inland cities, such as Tianjin, Hankou, Hong Kong, Tongzhou, Zhifu, Yichang, Jiujiang, Wuhu, Zhenjiang, Ningbo, Wenzhou, Fuzhou, Macao, and Canton.[54]

With such a wide transportation network, Lady Zhuang was able to ship her goods widely, and she profited from her speculation activities. In the autumn of 1899, she learned that if she sold Wuxi rice in Shanghai, she could earn forty cents for every bushel (*dan*). She asked Yang Tinggao, a Shanghai local merchant and friend of her husband, to buy twenty thousand bushels of rice on her behalf. Furthermore, she added, her husband could also help her transport the rice to Shanghai from Wuxi.[55] At other times, she would ask her male relatives to purchase rice or cotton from Hubei or Changzhou.

She did not explicitly refer to the shipping company that her husband commanded every time, but in her letters she frequently mentioned the ships she employed from that company to transport her desired goods from one place to the other.[56]

The 1898 reform paved the way for women, respectable ladies in particular, to participate actively in the public realm. Their activities centered on disaster relief and educational projects, especially girls' public education. What divided the post-1898 activities from their predecessors was that women in the post-1898 period learned to launch projects by organizing on their own, writing letters, and employing the modern medium of newspapers.

It was customary in late imperial China for men to donate to disaster relief in behalf of female relatives, for which they received acknowledgments and rewards from the court that brought great honor to their families or even to the whole lineage. The Sheng family women, too, donated for the purpose of winning rewards and honor with the help of male kinsmen. The final instructions of Lady Dong, Sheng Xuanhuai's first wife, ordered her sons to donate money on her behalf whenever disaster struck anywhere in the country. Thus in 1890 her sons donated fifteen hundred taels of silver for disaster relief in Shandong.[57]

Starting in the 1870s, when Shanxi suffered its greatest famine in history, newspapers became a new means to mobilize support for disaster relief and public projects. In order to overcome the insufficiency of official donations, the Zhejiang and Jiangsu male gentry formed a large-scale disaster relief organization. They called for charitable donations, reported relief processes, and publicized the financial details in the newspaper. The efficiency of the philanthropic community deeply affected late Qing society.[58] But the pattern of women's charitable activities did not change as greatly as men's in the 1880s and early 1890s.

Beginning with the 1898 reform, however, leisured ladies learned from male activists to organize public activities on their own by writing letters to each other and publicizing their projects in the newspapers. During the process of establishing China's first girls' school (mentioned earlier), the reformist leaders Liang Qichao and Jing Yuanshan published every detail of the process in the press, mainly in *Shanghai News* and the *News Journal*, including letters and responses from female supporters. Afterward, women's poems appeared frequently in the press as part of the broader support for women's education that the press was promoting. Later, the *News Journal* encouraged more women from respectable families to participate in the preparatory organizational meeting and reported the impressive success of the meeting. The pictorial press *Dianshizhai Pictorial* (Dianshizhai huabao) reported on the occasion, calling it "a grand meeting of both Chinese and foreign ladies." In this meeting, many renowned gentry women in Shanghai were invited to participate and socialize in the public space. The *News Journal* listed the names of the attending ladies on December 9, 1897. The list included Sheng Xuanhuai's successor wife Lady Zhuang, the Sheng daughters, and the eldest daughter-in-law. Others included the wife of the former Circuit Intendant (*daotai*) of Shanghai; the wife, daughters, and daughter-in-law of Jing Yuanshan; the wives of some well-known merchants, and the wife of Liang Qichao.[59] Although Jing Yuanshan initiated the meeting, women were not merely passively involved in these public events.

After the meeting, women collectively published the first *Women's Education Journal* (Nüxue bao) in 1898 to serve as the major propaganda arm of the women's education movement. The women listed in that publication became model activists who inspired others. Other women attempting to initiate public projects would solicit donations from among that list of names, and those donors in turn would greatly enhance the reputation of the organizers as well as the projects' prospects for success. In responding to Pan Yunfang, the female initiator of the Jiangsu disaster relief campaign in 1907, Lady Zhuang publicly echoed Pan's concern about the calamity-stricken people. She noted that even the lowliest women, courtesans, had also collected money for the campaign. She then praised several female charitable organizations, such as the Female Compatriots Charitable Donation Group (Nüzi Guomin Yijuanhui), Beijing Chinese Women's Organization (Beijing Zhongguo Furenhui), and the Puren Charitable Organization (Puren Cishan Hui).[60] At almost the same time, in the 1906–7 disaster relief campaign to relieve flood victims in Jiangsu, Lady Zhuang replied actively to Lady Li, whose husband was a first-rank official. They listed their names together at the top of the announcement and listed the names of another eight genteel ladies below theirs, issuing a public declaration on their behalf welcoming women all over the empire to actively participate in the campaign.[61] In other words, Lady Zhuang understood the importance of newspapers, and she knew how to put them to good use.

In her enthusiasm for charitable activities, however, Lady Zhuang exhibited a native-place preference. As a Jiangsu native, she actively endorsed the disaster relief sent to her native province, but was much less enthusiastic in responding to calls from other provinces. Right after the Jiangsu disaster relief, she received another request, from Wu Zhiying (1868–1934), a friend of the famous female revolutionary Qiu Jin (1875–1907), asking for donations to support the flood victims of Anhui. This time, however, Lady Zhuang demurred. In her response, she indicated that she had heard that Anhui had had a good harvest that year. She asked which areas were actually affected by the flood. Moreover, since she had just lent out 40,000 *yuan* and, at the same time, donated a large amount of money to the Jiangsu relief, she wondered aloud how she could afford another disaster relief campaign. Her reservations aside, however, she responded carefully to Wu Zhiying and praised her for organizing the campaign to support the Anhui people.[62] Similarly, in 1908, when the Beiyang Girls' Normal School was about to open, its president, Jiang Jiafang, asked Lady Zhuang to donate to the school, promising that she would list Lady Zhuang's name in the press as a benefactor. Lady Zhuang agreed to contribute a little portion, but she declined with thanks the offer to have her name listed, probably because her portion was too little.[63]

CONCLUSION

To return to the question raised at the beginning of this chapter, what happened to genteel ladies (*guixiu*) in the last years of the Qing? How did they adapt to the transitional period? Did they embrace the new world enthusiastically? Lady Zhuang's example cannot be applied to every woman, but her case undoubtedly provides a good illustration of how genteel ladies who accompanied their families from the countryside to the city after the Taiping Rebellion experienced the transformation from the culture of late-imperial genteel ladies to the cosmopolitan commercial world of the last years of the Qing.[64]

In Shanghai, erstwhile genteel ladies extended their power to the modern market: even if their investments were not always well planned or farsighted, they helped connect women closely to global commercialization. Women could and did employ the most advanced technology to organize modern networks, which helped them enjoy various modern services in the Republican era. In addition, women organized public activities on their own, which in the long run developed their ability to participate in public issues in the Republican era. Indeed, although the exalted world of "Confucian high culture" and the value of talented women were rejected by reform elites, genteel ladies as a group did not disappear.[65] Women's new economic and cultural authority came not only from their inheritance of the traditional managerial role in the family and their effective family networks but also from their quick accommodation to the modern world and their recognition of the value of "public." Their new roles were largely inherited by Republican-era bourgeois ladies, though in a different setting, as they became effective managers and consumers for their small families as well as for the nation as a whole.

NOTES

1 See "Xingsun gong xingshu" (Sheng Xuanhuai's biography), in *Longxi Shengshi zongpu*, 20.14; Xia, *Sheng Xuanhuai zhuan*, 1–5. Also see Feuerwerker, *China's Early Industrialization*, 83–95.

2 Elman, *Classicism, Politics and Kinship.*

3 Mann, *The Talented Women*, 120.

4 Hucker, *A Dictionary of Official Titles*, 313.

5 *Piling Zhuangshi zupu* (Piling Zhuang family genealogy), 2.26. This text was compiled in 1887 and published in 1935.

6 In addition to the women discussed by Judge in chapter 6 of this volume, "New women" who were intellectually and politically active, such as Kang Aide, Lü Bicheng, Qiu Jin, and Xue Shaohui, were valorized by late Qing intellectuals and have been well studied in recent scholarship. See Ying Hu, "Naming the First 'New Woman' "; Nanxiu Qian, "Revitalizing the *Xianyuan* (Worthy Ladies) Tradition"; Fong, "Alternative Modernities," among others.

7 Such discourse evolved over time in the late Qing era. It originated with Liang Qichao, who criticized wealthy ladies' lack of useful learning. Another reformer, Jing Yuanshan, echoed Liang's views and emphasized the dependent position of the wealthy ladies. In the writings of Jin Tianhe, wealthy women were depicted solely as consumers. See Wang, *Idle Consumers or Productive Workers*, chap. 3.

8 Skinner, *The City in Late Imperial China*, 248.

9 Xiong, *Shanghai tong shi*, 3:3.

10 Ibid., 1.17–22.

11 In fact, principal wives played a crucial role in effectively managing family wealth and affairs. Joseph McDermott has drawn attention to such contributions: see "The Chinese Domestic Bursar." Zeng Jifen's mother-in-law was capable enough to get the family through difficulties and improve the family finances by investing in land. McDermott's discovery has added a feminist perspective on the male-centered Chinese society, in which a focus on "examinations, government, trade, literati asso-

ciations," and merchant associations had come to dominate our understanding of Chinese patterns of upward social mobility and family strategy.

12 Sheng Xuanhuai Dang'an, No. 117550–3, June 19, 1878.

13 Sheng Peiyu, *Shengshi jiazu*, 15. All translations are mine.

14 Sheng Xuanhuai Dang'an, No. 036124, June 1897. The letter has no specific date.

15 Sheng Xuanhuai Dang'an, No. 034905, "Ge chaiguan ji nannü jiaren xingongdan" (Monthly payment to all domestic servants). The document covers the period between 1902 and 1903.

16 Sheng Xuanhuai Dang'an, No. 075421, November 1, 1907; No. 002462, November 24, 1899.

17 Sheng Xuanhuai Dang'an, No. 069294, in 1904. Lady Zhuang would telegraph her husband or relatives, conveying information about the delivery of goods.

18 Sheng Xuanhuai Dang'an, No. 036122, June 1897. Also see No. 036835, November 10, 1907.

19 Sheng Xuanhuai Dang'an, No. 002462, November 24, 1899. Lady Zhuang returned the ginseng she had borrowed from a female relative. Another female relative, however, requested some from her purchase, leaving her only a small portion of the expensive medicine.

20 Sheng Xuanhuai Dang'an, No. 036122, June 1897.

21 Sheng Xuanhuai Dang'an, No. 103750–3, in 1911.

22 Xia, *Sheng Xuanhuai nianpu changbian*, 34–35.

23 Lingmu, "Shanghai jiqi zhibuju de chuangshe guocheng," 298.

24 Sheng Xuanhuai Dang'an, No. 106045–3, January 13, 1899. This could be the truth, because Sheng Changyi's daughter recalled that her father was not satisfied with marrying six concubines. He lived a licentious life and died young. See Sheng, *Shengshi jiazu*, 2.

25 Sheng Xuanhuai Dang'an, No. 002466, December 10, 1899. This sum was substantial, considering the contemporary living standard: an average servant's monthly income reached merely 3 to 9 *yuan*, which varied according to his or her work. See Sheng Xuanhuai Dang'an, No. 034905, which lists the monthly payment to servants.

26 Sheng, "Zhi qi Zhuangshi jiashu" (Letter to wife Lady Zhuang), in *Sheng Xuanhuai weikan xingao*, 272–73, 284.

27 Sheng Xuanhuai Dang'an, No. 036716. This probably dates to the late winter of 1899.

28 Sheng, *Sheng Xuanhuai weikan xingao*, 287.

29 Ibid., 272. Sheng Xuanhuai kept reminding Lady Zhuang of the certainty of loans, and compared it with the uncertainty of the market. However, Lady Zhuang's letters reveal no responses to Sheng's reminders.

30 Sheng Xuanhuai Dang'an, No. 106045–3, January 13, 1899.

31 Sheng Xuanhuai Dang'an, No. 106043, December 29, 1898.

32 Sheng Xuanhuai Dang'an, No. 074379, April 23, 1900.

33 Kennedy, *Testimony of a Confucian Woman*, 44. Also see Zeng, *Chongde laoren*, 23.

34 Sheng, *Sheng Xuanhuai weikan xingao*, 287.

35 Ibid., 285.

36 Sheng Xuanhuai Dang'an, No. 002463, October 26, 1899.

37 Sheng Xuanhuai Dang'an, No. 041907, September 23, 1899. Lady Zhuang's eldest stepdaughter-in-law told her about the family speculation activities and the recent prices.

38 Sheng Xuanhuai Dang'an, No. 036716 and No. 036714. These probably date to late winter of 1899.

39 McDermott, "The Chinese Domestic Bursar," 26 and 27.

40 Ko, *Teachers of the Inner Chambers*, 50–51.

41 A similar method of soliciting funding for schools was employed in the early twentieth century: see chapter 6 in this volume.

42 Jing, *Jing Yuanshan ji*, 206, "Nüxuetang neidongshi jie Guilin Wei Gongren shu (The inner director of China Girls' School receives a letter from honorable Lady Wei of Guilin)."

43 "Nüxuetang jie youren shu bing guixiu shi," *Xinwen bao*, January 29, 1898.

44 Sheng Xuanhuai Dang'an, No. 036657. No specific date, but it was likely written around September 1899.

45 Sheng Xuanhuai Dang'an, No. 036122, June 1897. Lady Zhuang pointed out that she learned of her stepsons' activities from *Subao* (Jiangsu journal) and *Zhinan bao* (Guidance news).

46 Sheng Xuanhuai Dang'an, No. 036718. No specific date, but probably the early 1900s.

47 Sheng Xuanhuai Dang'an, No. 072906, No. 072906-1, and No. 072906-2. All were written in November 1911.

48 Sheng Xuanhuai Dang'an, No. 072906-1, November 17, 1911.

49 Sheng Xuanhuai Dang'an, No. 077005, October 23, 1899. Also see No. 035353, probably written in October 1899.

50 Sheng Xuanhuai Dang'an, No. 069282 and No. 069283, April 14 and 16, 1904, respectively.

51 Sheng Xuanhuai Dang'an, No. 069277, April 29, 1904.

52 Sheng Xuanhuai Dang'an, No. 077005, October 23, 1899; No. 002463, October 26, 1899.

53 Feuerwerker, *China's Early Industrialization*, 100.

54 Ibid., 105, 107.

55 Sheng Xuanhuai Dang'an, No. 002466, December 10, 1899.

56 Sheng Xuanhuai Dang'an, No. 060056, No. 069294, No. 075421, and so on. These cover the period from the 1890s to the early 1900s. The ships included *Xinyu*, *Taishun*, *Jiangfu*, and *Feijing*.

57 Sheng Xuanhuai Dang'an, No. 009786, "Sheng Dongshi juanzhu dongzhen qingyu jianfang zhe (Petition for Establishing a Memorial to Commemorate Lady Dong's Charitable Donation to Shandong)," Spring 1890.

58 Jing Yuanshan was then a disaster relief activist. He knew very well how to use the media to call for public activities. His skill thus influenced the 1890s reform. See Rankin, *Elite Activism and Political Transformation*, 140, 144–47. Also see Jing Yuanshan, *Jing Yuanshan ji*.

59 "Nüxuetang zhongxi dahui ji" *Xinwen bao*, December 9, 1897. Also see Xia, *Wanqing nüxing yu jindai shenghuo*, 33.

60   Sheng Xuanhuai Dang'an, No. 042244–1, "Sheng Zhuang Dehua fu Pan Yunfang han" (Sheng Zhuang Dehua's reply to Pan Yunfang), May 10, 1907.

61   Sheng Xuanhuai Dang'an, No. 043703, "Guangmu Zhongguo nüjie juanzhu zaiqu liangshi gongqi" (Public solicitation of Chinese women to donate for the area of disaster), 1906.

62   Sheng Xuanhuai Dang'an, No. 050543–2, "Zhuang Dehua fu Wu Zhiying Shen Zhanglan han" (Zhuang Dehua's reply to Wu Zhiying and Shen Zhanglan), June 16, 1907. Wu Zhiying came from Anhui, which made her sensitive to disasters in Anhui. But Lady Zhuang was a Jiangsu person. She paid less attention to Anhui issues.

63   Sheng Xuanhuai Dang'an, No. 073797, "Zhuang Dehua zhi Jiang Jiafang han" (Letter from Zhuang Dehua to Jiang Jiafang), February 1908.

64   In striking contrast to Lady Zhuang, the Muslim princess Shah Jahan finally decided to practice purdah in colonial Bhopal in order to maintain her cultural respectability. Perhaps influenced by her "self-made" husband, the princess believed that purdah promised decency for a woman who operated publicly. Metcalf, "Islam and Power in Colonial India," 19.

65   Mann, *Precious Records*, 226.

PART THREE

Radicalism and Ruptures

CHAPTER EIGHT

THE LIFE OF A SLOGAN

Emily Honig

"THE times have changed; men and women are the same. Anything male comrades can do, female comrades can do too" (时代不同了，男女都一样。男同志能办到的事，女同志也能办得到). In scholarly analyses, memoirs, and personal recollections, this famed quotation from Mao Zedong is treated as epitomizing the Cultural Revolution (1966–76) message to women. It is invoked as the title of historian Jiang Jin's account of growing up in Maoist China; Naihua Zhang cites this "popular slogan" of the Cultural Revolution as critical to the construction of her gender identity and "sense of femininity."[1] Women interviewed about their Cultural Revolution experiences invariably punctuate their accounts with a recitation of "The times have changed." Attempts to justify the gendered divisions of labor during the post-Mao economic reforms almost religiously cite the propagation of "gender sameness" as representing the harmful practices of the Cultural Revolution that must be rejected. Post-Mao academic analyses, too, describe the slogan as emblematic of the Cultural Revolution.[2] "During the Cultural Revolution," as one scholar asserts, "the lopsided idea that 'the times have changed; men and women are the same' . . . caused the struggle for women's liberation to regress."[3] And even in the 1980s United States, the Maoist slogan insisting that "anything male comrades can do, female comrades can do too" (along with the slogan "Women hold up half the sky") was appropriated by feminists who believed the presumed liberation of Chinese women was worthy of emulation.

This slogan can by analyzed in a number of ways. Most obviously it can be examined as the state's version of feminism, one that conveyed, as Jiang Jin puts it, "a powerful message to millions of Chinese women that in this new era men and women were equal."[4] And it might be problematized as embracing a vision of gender equality in which women strive to become like men (after all, Mao never instructed that "anything female comrades can do, male comrades can do too"). One might also consider its impact on the lives of women growing up during the Cultural Revolution. This is one of the prominent themes of the accounts in *Some of Us: Chinese Women Growing Up in the Mao Era*: how the slogan, as Naihua Zhang puts it, "inspired girls and women to take unconventional roles and to enter male domains" and to wear "baggy gray or blue outfits."[5] (Or how it inspired Ma Xiaodong to try and "prove it was possible to eliminate physical differences between men and women" by keeping her menstrual period completely secret.)[6] We can see, too, the ways this slogan provided language that could be invoked to challenge "traditional" norms.[7] Finally, one could explore the ways in which this slogan appears and is deployed in Cultural Revolution memoirs, often as a marker of nostalgia for a time long gone.

Instead, our focus here is on the slogan itself, not simply to scrutinize its meanings, but to treat it as a historical subject with a life (including a birth, prime, and death) of its own that might be reconstructed. When, and under what circumstances, was this slogan first articulated? On what traditions did it draw? When (how, why, and by whom) did it become popularized, and what meanings were attached to it? What other messages did it engage, challenge, or contest? What can we learn by disentangling the slogan from the overwhelming assumption that it permeated, dominated, and even represented the Cultural Revolution vision of women?

A WATERY BIRTH

Given the extent to which the slogan "The times have changed . . . Anything male comrades can do, female comrades can do too" is treated as emblematic of the Cultural Revolution, it might seem surprising that it was first articulated before the Cultural Revolution began and did not become popularized until the early 1970s, when the Cultural Revolution was half over. And given

Emily Honig

the slogan's eventual prominence in informing gender roles, it might seem peculiar that it was first articulated in what can only be described as a truly obscure context.

The "times have changed" slogan was first recorded in a *People's Daily* article in May 1965. From this article, we learn that Mao had actually uttered these words a year earlier, in mid-June 1964. (In other words, this famous slogan was not even deemed worthy of recording or reporting when it was first articulated.) The slogan is at best peripheral to the story "Chairmen Mao and Liu [Shaoqi] Swimming at the Thirteen Tombs Reservoir," which focuses on the myriad details of this event. At approximately three o'clock in the afternoon, we learn, two cars arrived at the west end of the reservoir from which two "lofty figures" emerged, who then walked toward the water. At that very moment, students from a high-level school, along with some PLA soldiers, were swimming. Noticing the two luminaries, they all shouted, "Chairman Mao, come and swim! Chairman Liu, come and swim!" Which they did.

The article proceeds to recount in some detail the ensuing conversation between Mao and the young swimmers. Have they swum in high waves, strong currents, and intense wind? he asks. When they admitted that they had not, Mao encouraged them to swim in harsh conditions, as "swimming is a natural form of struggle." We then learn that Mao declined to rest on the island in the middle of the reservoir, thereby inspiring the young people to swim even more vigorously. As the sun dropped lower, it was reported to Mao that some PLA units had learned to swim fully armed. "This is very good," Mao stated. "The armed forces must learn to swim." Mao and the young people then "bathed in the sun together." As they swam back to shore, it became windy and large waves broke. Mao asked if the young swimmers were afraid, to which they replied, "We are not afraid!"

After describing in even more detail the remainder of the swim, the article suddenly reports the presence of several young women swimmers. Sighting them, Chairman Mao, "very mildly and smiling, said: 'The times have changed, men and women are the same. Anything male comrades can do, female comrades can do too.'" Rather than responding with the serious reverence one might expect (particularly given the later import of these words), the report conveys that "hearing Mao's praise, the young women all laughed." This is followed by a concluding paragraph stating that when Mao and Liu returned to shore it was after five o'clock. And so ends this first report of the famed Mao slogan.[8]

The underwhelming impact of this first report of Mao's soon-to-be-famous slogan is reflected in its complete absence from the article in the English-language edition of *Women of China* (Zhongguo funü) describing the same event. In "Millions Go Swimming," we are told about the summer day in 1964 when Mao and Liu "enjoyed swimming with some young people in the Ming Tombs Reservoir." Although the article praises the range of participants—"workers, peasants, office personnel, members of the People's Liberation Army, and students"—it makes no reference to female swimmers. And the only quoted statement of Mao's from that 1964 event is: "Swimming is a sport in which you struggle against nature. You should make yourselves strong by swimming in the big rivers and the sea."[9] Meanwhile, the Chinese edition of *Women of China* did not even report the event.

A year later, in July 1966, the slogan appeared in the *People's Daily* a second time, again in the context of a swimming event, and again with no fanfare about the slogan itself. This time the event in question took place in Wuhan, where, ever since Mao's famed swim across the Yangzi in 1956, an annual swimming competition had been held. This report describes the five thousand men and women swimmers traversing the Yangzi in 1966. In the middle of the article, with no pause or even acknowledgement of a change in subject, the report suddenly refers to the fact that in 1965 a large group of female militia members had swum across the river, implementing Mao's slogan of 1964: "The times have changed; . . . anything male comrades can too female comrades can do too." (Given that the slogan was not even reported until 1965, and even then in a fairly obscure context, it is not clear how these 1965 swimmers across the Yangzi were "implementing" Mao's slogan.) The article immediately shifts back to the Wuhan event of 1966, listing the dignitaries present, describing the weather conditions, the red flags carried by some swimmers, and the commemorative badges they were awarded.[10]

On this occasion, the Chinese women's magazine *Zhongguo funü* (Women of China) did report the Wuhan swimming event, with enormous bold print on the first page announcing, "Mao Swims across the Yangzi River." Forging through the waves, the ensuing report informs readers, "Mao chatted with nearby comrades. When one young woman boasted to Mao that this was her second time swimming across the Yangzi, Mao smiled and replied, "The Yangzi is deep and wide. It is indeed a good place to swim." When Mao then noticed another young woman able to swim with only one kind of stroke, he showed her the backstroke and gently encouraged her: "The Yangzi water is deep and fast. It is good for training the body and you can also temper your determination." Although this report goes on to praise the increase in the number of women swimmers (from twenty in 1956 to a thousand at this 1966 event), it makes no reference whatsoever to Mao's slogan.[11]

This is in many ways a strange "origin story" for a dictum that eventually became so prominent and influential. The words that later achieved slogan status seem almost random, if not peripheral to the events being reported. One has to wonder whether Mao even said these words (after all, who among the swimmers would have recorded and then reported Mao's statement?), or whether it was an embellishment or rhetorical flourish inserted by whichever journalist composed the story.[12]

Let's assume, however, that "The times have changed" represents something Mao actually said. Then, as far as we can determine, the slogan was first uttered in 1964, and reported in 1965 and again in 1966—in each case referring to swimming competitions. The context of swimming may not be entirely surprising or strange, given the extent to which Mao had highlighted the relationship of swimming to revolutionary struggle ever since his youth. One of his earliest surviving poems is titled "In Praise of Swimming";[13] as an adolescent he frequently advocated swimming as a way of strengthening the bodies of Chinese citizens for revolution. In 1956, after swimming across the Yangzi for the first time, he composed another poem, "Swimming," in which he exclaimed, "I am swimming across the great Yangzi. . . . Let the wind blow and waves beat. Better far than idly strolling in a courtyard." In addition to the poem, Mao issued the statement that inspired thousands of youth, over the course of the next decade, to participate in swimming competitions: "Swimming is a sport in which the swimmers battle against Nature; you should go into the big rivers and seas to temper yourselves."[14] His swim across the Yangzi in Wuhan in July 1966, commemorating the ten-year anniversary of his first Yangzi swim, in part signaled the beginning of the Cultural Revolution. And clearly swimming was on his mind in 1964; for only a month after the Ming Tombs swim, he interrogated his nephew, Mao Yuanxin, about his swimming abilities, advising him to swim in great winds and waves, to practice it resolutely every day. His nephew, perhaps trying to persuade Mao of his swimming abilities, recounted a time when he had found it warmer in the water than in the cold air and therefore continued swimming. "In fact," Mao retorted, "staring angrily" at Yuanxin, "you like comfort and fear difficulties!"[15]

So, at the beginning of the Cultural Revolution, the slogan was scarcely known, barely publicized, and not invoked in relation to work (the context in which it later became most commonly understood). What was Mao thinking when he made the statement? Was this idea of male and female sameness something that suddenly popped into his head? Was he simply paraphrasing rhetoric that had become popular at the time? Or was he articulating an entirely new vision of women's liberation in the context of China's socialist revolution?

"WOMEN CAN OUTDO THE MEN"

Even if no references to Mao's "The times have changed" slogan can be found in the 1950s or early 1960s, it nonetheless clearly echoes or perhaps derives from popular rhetoric about women's work ability during the Great Leap Forward. During this period, a time when both rural and urban women were forming "shock brigades" (as well as groups with names such as "Nine Lily Magnolias," "One Hundred Blossoms," or "Seventy-Two Women Generals"),[16] countless reports praised women's strength as equivalent to that of men, as reflected in the phrase "What men can do, women can do" (男人能干妇女一样能干),[17] which began to appear in the media. Sometimes the phrase was more specific, as in: "If men can smelt iron, women can smelt iron too."[18] In a number of cases, the point was not simply that women could do the same things as men but that they could outdo them as well. For example, the slogan of a women's shock brigade in Jiangning county, Jiangsu, was: "Whatever men can do, we can do too; whatever men cannot do, we can do. Go, go, go. We can outdo the men!"[19]

As we already know, these pithy declarations were less about women performing jobs equivalent to those of men than about mobilizing women to take over the agricultural jobs formerly—but no longer—performed by male laborers, who had been recruited to work on major construction projects of the communes. These slogans reflected (and contributed to) a transformed labor market that required a new division of labor—one in which male workers continued to dominate the more highly skilled and highly remunerated jobs.[20]

It was in this same context of the late 1950s labor transformations that the other slogan commonly associated with the Cultural Revolution "line" regarding women—"Women hold up half the sky"—has its origins. Appearing in a 1958 *People's Daily* article titled "The Production Army That Should Not Be Overlooked," women engaged in iron smelting were praised for "holding up half the sky," a phrase apparently derived from a popular saying in Hunan villages: "Women are half the sky."[21] In spite of its later association with women's participation in the labor force, this phrase was first reported in a 1956 *People's Daily* article with the unlikely title "Protect the Health of Rural Women and Children." Commending the increasing numbers of women participating in agricultural labor, the article warns of local officials who—while shouting slogans such as "Labor is glorious!" "To depend on men for a living is despicable!" and "If women want to be liberated, they must engage in production the same as men!"—were overlooking women's responsibilities for household chores and child care. "It's one thing to invoke these slogans to encourage women with backwards thinking," the author explains, "but to blindly shout these slogans will eventually cause harm to the health of women and children." Moreover, the author points out, "taking good care of housework and children, thereby enabling men to work without worries—is that not a significant contribution to agricultural production?" It is in this context that, at the end of the article, after repeating the necessity of advocating that women also perform their jobs in the home, the author finally says, "There is a folk saying in Hunan villages: 'Women are half the sky' [*Funü shi ban bian tian*]. In the high tide of building socialism, is it possible to ignore the protection of health and safety of women and children?"[22] Even in 1964, when the phrase had evolved to "Women hold up half the sky" (*Funü neng ding ban bian tian*), it was invoked often in the context of charges to attend to the well-being of women being drawn into production.[23] By the 1970s, when the slogan "Women hold up half the sky" finally became far more widely propagated (sometimes in conjunction with "The times have changed"), it was most likely long forgotten that the original meaning had to do with recognizing the importance of women's responsibilities for the household.

A concern with gender difference, and more specifically with guarding women's health, became even more prominent in the years following the Great Leap Forward, and this is worth noting in our effort to trace the history of Mao's "The times have changed" slogan. Between the Great Leap Forward's propagation of slogans about gender "sameness" and 1964, when Mao allegedly reworked these into his "The times have changed" statement, an entirely different message about women's work emerged, one informed by beliefs about gender difference. Beginning in 1960, numerous Women's Federation reports raised concern about the extent to which women's health had been neglected in assigning jobs. In Jiangsu, for example, a large number of rural women suffered from headaches, dizziness, and a curtailment of their menstrual periods. (In several counties, some 65 percent of women had "lost" their periods. In one county it was up to 82 percent.) The rate of miscarriages also increased. "You must take care not to have women do work that is too heavy," many reports instructed. Others more specifically cautioned against assigning women to do "men's work," while cadres who failed to consider women's "biology" or "special conditions" in assigning jobs were criticized.[24] And whatever work women did, accommodations were to be made for their "four periods" (menstruation, pregnancy, childbirth, and nursing).[25]

These concerns were not confined to rural women, nor to reports by provincial Women's Federations. In 1961, for example, the *People's Daily* reported that the Hangzhou No. 1 Cotton Spinning, Weaving, and Dying Factory was "strengthening its efforts to protect women workers" by "making work assignments based on the special characteristics of women workers." In addition, the factory was implementing a system for registering women's periods, establishing a washroom for women workers in every workshop, providing medical examinations for pregnant women, ensuring that women in late pregnancy be assigned light work, and providing pregnant women with nourishing food in the cafeteria.[26] A report on factories in Jiangsu lamented that accommodations for women's menstruation had been sorely neglected: facing a lack of paper or cloth to use, many women resorted to snatching any scraps of material they could find, some of which were not sanitary, and women were often bleeding onto their shoes and the workshop floor; although women were entitled to rest when they had their periods, there were no appropriate places in the factories for them to do so.[27]

There are a number of ways to interpret these concerns. One is to take them literally, as a reflection of ongoing and unresolved problems. Given what we know about the early 1960s (for example, the famine of the "three hard years"), it is also possible that expressing concern about women's health was an indirect—but safe—way of articulating objection to the Great Leap Forward.

Nevertheless, at the time Mao first uttered, "The times have changed," in 1964, the most salient rhetoric about gender emphasized the physiological differences between men and women and the importance of attending to women's "special characteristics." Men and women were *not* the same: women were *not* to demonstrate (or be asked to demonstrate) that they could do the same things as men or even outperform men at certain jobs. In stating that "men and women are the same," that "anything male comrades can do, female comrades can do too," Mao was not only contradicting current beliefs about the sexual division of labor but also referencing rhetoric of the Great Leap Forward that had since been rejected.

And then there is the fact that the first time that "The times have changed" slogan was spoken was not in the context of work (the context that the Great Leap Forward rhetoric referred to) but rather was an enthusiastic reaction to the sight of female swimmers. And so it was for the reports alluding to this slogan for the subsequent three years.

One other aspect of the dictum, as it was reported in 1964, is worth noting. While the phrase "anything male comrades can do, female comrades can do too" differs only slightly from the Great Leap Forward declarations that "what men can do, women can do," Mao's version adds the prefatory phrase "The times have changed; men and women are the same," thereby suggesting that this was not merely a future vision but something that had already been accomplished. Such subtle shifts, however, were probably not noticed in 1964–65, when these statements were at best buried deep in news reports that were few and far between.

INTO THE PUBLIC

When the Cultural Revolution began in 1966, young urban female Red Guards donned male clothing, cut their hair short like men, and in many cases engaged in acts of violence similar to those of their male counterparts. One might imagine they had been inspired by Mao's "The times have changed" slogan. In fact, though, the slogan had almost no public life during the first years of the Cultural Revolution. To the extent that Maoist slogans inspired female Red Guard fashion and behavior, it is far more likely that they were influenced by lines he wrote in 1961: "How remarkable the spirit of Chinese women: they love martial dress, not dressing up."[28] Meanwhile, the only Maoist slogan about women that was publicized in the early Cultural Revolution was his declaration that "the day that the women of China rise up is the day that the Chinese revolution will be victorious."[29]

It was not until the early 1970s that the slogan "The times have changed" began to appear with frequency in the media, earning a place among Mao's published quotations in 1972.[30] No longer relegated to stories about swimming competitions, it now appeared as a crucial element of reports praising women who assumed jobs conventionally performed by men. For example, a group of women telephone operators, when confronted by a broken phone line, initially hesitated, believing that "climbing poles is not suitable work for women." But then, the news report informs us, "one of their leaders gathered them around the bottom of the telephone pole and together they studied Chairman Mao's teaching, 'The times have changed, men and women are the same. Anything men comrades can do, female comrades can do too.' They then had the confidence to scale the poles."[31]

Over the next several years, an increasing number of accounts praised women for performing "men's work"—for example, for engaging in live-wire electric work, forming well-drilling teams, handling explosives, working in mines, and so on. In every case, these reports emphasized women's initial hesitation, the formation of study groups to focus on Mao's teachings, and how women were then motivated to take on these jobs as a result of studying Mao's now famed slogan "Anything male comrades can do, female comrades can do too."

One might be tempted, at this point, to launch into an analysis of the content of these articles, exploring the range of jobs women assumed, the challenges they faced, and how they invoked Mao Zedong's thought to overcome these challenges. Of greater relevance here, though, is the changing amplitude of the slogan. Jin Yihong, in an analysis of the Iron Girls (young rural women who, in the early 1960s, were famed for performing the most arduous jobs), observes that the slogan "The times have changed" was most intensely publicized from 1970 to 1973, when "this quotation was used so frequently that people sometimes felt that it appeared everywhere."[32] During these three years, she explains, "China was engaged in agricultural infrastructure development on a massive scale." While men were drawn to work on these new projects, women were mobilized to assume the jobs related to agricultural production. The popularization of the slogan, according to her analysis, must be understood in the context of the feminization of agriculture that she observes took place in the early 1970s.[33]

The transformation of the division of labor noted by Jin Yihong is clearly part of the story, as attested to by a number of reports on sent-down youth. For example, a 1974 investigation of health problems of female sent-down youth at the Dongfeng State Farm pointed out that while women represented 54 percent of the laborers on the state farm, they did 70 percent of the field work, because "male comrades went to operate tractors or engage in the mechanization of agriculture."[34] Women interviewed about their work histories often unwittingly provided anecdotal evidence that corroborates changes in the gendered division of labor taking place in the early 1970s. For example, a woman from southern Jiangsu described how her production brigade began to double-crop rice in 1971–72. Before that time, she explained, transplanting seedlings had been done entirely by men. Citing Mao's slogan "The times have changed; . . . anything male comrades can do, female comrades can do too," she described how women took over those jobs. Later in the interview, when asked what men were doing after women took over the transplanting of rice, she replied that they had taken jobs in commune or brigade enterprises "that only wanted male workers and refused to accept women workers."[35]

Although it seems logical to link the propagation of this slogan to a transformation of the labor market, much more needs to be known about the economic shifts taking place at that time. From the time of the Great Leap Forward, rural men were periodically drawn away from field work to commune enterprises. Was there something new and different about the early 1970s that required an intensification of women's agricultural work?[36] We know even less about urban China at this time. On the one hand, numerous reports invoking the slogan "The times have changed" describe urban factory workers. And yet, given the vast number of urban, educated youth sent to the countryside during these years, we can surmise that if anything, there was a surplus of employable workers in the cities. Why, then, would women need to be instructed to take on jobs formerly performed by male workers?

As it turns out, the early 1970s was not necessarily the height of the slogan's propagation. A closer scrutiny of the *People's Daily* reveals a somewhat different chronology. While the number of articles invoking the slogan gradually increased in the early 1970s (from eight in 1970 to eighteen in 1972), the most dramatic publicizing of the slogan occurred between 1973 and 1975: forty-two times in 1973, ninety-six times in 1974, and forty-two times in 1975.[37] In other words, if there was a moment when the slogan was at its most widespread, it was most clearly in 1974. And the slogan "Women hold up half the sky" also seems to have reached its climax of media popularity in 1974. This is attested to by, among other things, a booklet published in Jiangsu that describes the melody and movements of the "women hold up half the sky dance," along with detailed drawings and directions for making the appropriate props.[38]

Does the fact that the slogan was actually at its peak of media popularity in 1973–75 change our understanding of its meaning? At minimum, it seems imperative to consider several political developments of those years. Most obvious, perhaps, is the Campaign to Criticize Lin Biao and Confucius, which, on the surface at least, confronted women's subordinate status and took place at precisely the same time.[39] During these years, news reports declaring the successful engagement of women in occupations previously dominated by men not only cited the slogan "The times have changed" but also frequently linked it to the phrase "Women hold up half the sky." And these accounts are invariably peppered with references to the Campaign to Criticize Lin Biao and Confucius and its struggle to combat discrimination against women. For example, a *People's Daily* report of 1974 titled "Holding Up Half the Sky: Become Masters of the New Era; Recall the Tianjin Cultural Revolution Women Brickyard Workers' Small Group" recounts how the Party Committee organized women to diligently study Chairman Mao's slogan "The times have changed; men and women are the same" as well as to criticize the feudal idea of "respecting men and looking down on women."[40] Likewise, another report on women workers, after citing the slogan "The times have changed" immediately states that "in our current political campaign to criticize Lin Biao and Confucius we must resolutely promote women holding up half the sky."[41] Finally, a poem published on the occasion of Women's Day in 1975, bearing the title "We Can Hold Up Half the Sky," included criticisms of Lin Biao and Confucius while expressing gratitude to Chairman Mao, who "believes in us," by stating, "The times have changed; men and women are the same. Anything male comrades can do, female comrades can do too."[42] Such reports were not confined to *People's Daily* but were in *Red Flag* (Hong qi) as well as provincial newspapers such as the *Heilongjiang Daily* (Heilongjian ribao) and the *Enlightenment Daily* (Guangming ribao).[43]

In the context of the campaign, reporters occasionally referred to Mao's slogan as if it had been popular throughout the Cultural Revolution. For example, an article titled "Destroy Old Beliefs, Hold Up Half the Sky," after enumerating the multitude of teachings of Confucius that were oppressive to women, highlighted the formation of a women's herding team: "At the time of National Day in 1969, ten of us sisters, not yet nineteen years old, took the initiative to organize the first women's herding team. At first, some people looked down at us, saying things like: 'Women really think they can herd horses? What a joke!' But we diligently studied Chairman Mao's teaching 'The times have changed; men and women are the same. Anything male comrades can do, female comrades can do too.' And that gave us inspiration to challenge old beliefs."[44]

Likewise, the head of a production brigade in Heilongjiang, in a 1973 account, described how women began to really "hold up half the sky" in

1969 when they "repeatedly studied Chairman Mao's great teaching, 'The times have changed; men and women are the same. Anything male comrades can do, female comrades can do too.'"[45] While it is remotely possible that women, in 1969, were studying this particular teaching of Mao, it is far more likely that the teaching was retrospectively inserted into stories written in 1973–74, a time when the slogan was being widely propagated.

The role of Jiang Qing, who was presumed to have instigated this campaign, is also worth considering, particularly given the prominent role she played in orchestrating state propaganda at this time. The year 1974, according to one of her biographers, Ross Terrill, was a time when she enjoyed a far more prominent public role than she had since her marriage to Mao in the 1940s: a major celebration of the tenth anniversary of her 1964 opera reform was held; Jiang Qing continually issued "instructions," received visiting foreign leaders, and was featured in both newspaper and television reporting.

Several specific aspects of her activities at this time may be relevant to the propagation of the slogan. What stands out most clearly is her quest to succeed Mao in ruling China. The Campaign to Criticize Lin Biao and Confucius itself is commonly understood as a thinly veiled effort by Jiang Qing to discredit Zhou Enlai (whom she perceived as a competitor for power) while, at the same time—through attacks on Confucian beliefs of "respecting men and looking down on women"—arguing that women were as capable as men of governing. In conjunction with the campaign, Jiang Qing orchestrated a media effort to promote the accomplishments of the Tang-dynasty empress Wu Zetian (usually described in the historical record as a "lustful, power-hungry shrew").[46]

Meanwhile, and perhaps in this context, Jiang Qing's public speeches relentlessly denounced the subordinate status assigned to women. Addressing an audience of more than a thousand women in Tianjin in June 1974, she claimed that "women in the Han dynasty were relatively free, as evidenced by the fact that they could have a 'male concubine.'" Those in her audience could do the same, she insisted. Several days later she went to the town of Xiaoxinzhuang (her model village of implementation of the Campaign to Criticize Lin Biao and Confucius). At a gathering to promote this campaign, the first person to speak was a male party member, whom Jiang repeatedly interrupted by talking about the need to criticize the Confucian belief of "respecting men and looking down on women." As soon as he finished speaking, Jiang Qing shouted that she wanted "half the sky" to speak. When a woman rose up to speak, Jiang Qing criticized her for having permitted a man to speak first. "Next time you must be more courageous and not let men speak first," she instructed. Later, when Jiang Qing herself spoke, she explained, "Marx said that productive forces are the most important factor. But who produces the productive forces? They are produced by women."[47]

By the time she returned to Xiaoxinzhuang in August 1976, Jiang Qing more explicitly linked her passion for women's equality with her aspirations for political power. "I'll say a few words for women," she began.

> Isn't it that women give birth to both men and women? Men are simple. All they have are spermatozoa. When I talked this way at the Politburo, they laughed at me. The Politburo members are influenced by Deng Xiaoping's male chauvinism. . . . Men cannot do whatever they like just because they are physically strong. Men should give way to women and let women run things. In tribal society it was women who controlled the power, and with the development of productive power, the country will eventually be administered by women. Women can also become emperors, even in the Communist society.[48]

"I am a female chauvinist!" she declared several days later. And the following month, with Mao on the verge of death, she raged at the group of male commune members who greeted her at Dazhai. "Why are all of you men?" she fumed. "Aren't there any women? Go and find some for me. . . . Women will control the power!"[49]

On some occasions, she punctuated her comments about women with the slogans "The times have changed" and "Women hold up half the sky." For example, while visiting an offshore oil-drilling enterprise near the Tianjin port, she was dismayed to discover that all the workers on the rig were male. "Why are there no women workers?" Jiang Qing demanded of the chairman of the Revolutionary Committee. "Have you forgotten Chairman Mao's saying that women hold up half the sky. . . . Anything men can do, women can also do?"[50] The obvious implication of this slogan, in conjunction with all her other statements about women, is that whatever Mao could do (such as being chairman of the People's Republic), Jiang Qing could do too.[51]

Besides Jiang Qing and the Campaign to Criticize Lin Biao and Confucius, the Women's Federation, too, is important to consider in any attempt to explain the timing of the propagation of the slogan. Although it is often assumed that the federation was disbanded throughout the Cultural Revolution and not revived until 1977, in fact the local and provincial "chapters"

Emily Honig

were reestablished in 1973 and, as archival research indicates, were actively engaged in confronting issues of women in the context of work. Whether the federation played a role in advancing slogans about gender sameness, however, is difficult to determine.[52] It becomes even more challenging when we recognize other messages about women being propagated at this time. For example, during the very same years that the slogan "The times have changed" was most intensely publicized, other voices were amplifying concern about the neglect of women's health, particularly their "four periods," attendant on the pursuit of gender "sameness." According to a report from a production brigade in Hunan, women's "biological characteristics" needed to be considered in the assignment of agricultural work: during menstruation, women should be transferred from "wet work" to "dry work"; when nursing, women should be transferred from distant jobs to nearby ones; and during pregnancy, women should be transferred from heavy to light work.[53] In 1974, the Shanghai Agricultural Bureau issued a report deploring the "deteriorating condition of the physical health of female sent-down youth working on state farms" and calling on local officials to "protect the four periods of female comrades."[54] Women should not, the report instructed, be walking barefoot or squatting in wet rice paddies during their menstrual periods. Likewise, the Shanghai Municipal Bureau, in 1974, issued a number of reports expressing concern about the need to provide protection for women workers during their "four periods."[55]

At minimum, this simultaneous propagation of the slogan declaring gender sameness and injunctions to attend to gender difference suggests more of a conversation, if not conflict, than we usually recognize. Here, Wang Zheng's scholarship on the Women's Federation may be instructive, since it forces us to consider the ways in which the production of a slogan might well not be the product of a seamless and monolithic state and, instead, might reflect fissures, divisions, and contestations. "How do we tease out possible hidden feminist interventions from apparent reiteration of statist production?" she asks in analyzing the Women's Federation. "How do we conceptualize a feminist contestation that both subverts patriarchal dominance and reproduces masculinist language and subjectivity?"[56] If the birth and rise to fame of this slogan involves any kind of feminist intervention, we are still left wondering: what was a stake, what was being contested, whose interests were being represented, and for what ends? Nor can we know, without further research, which position the newly revived local and provincial Women's Federation chapters took: an insistence that women were the same as men and therefore could perform jobs previously dominated by men, or an insistence that women were physically and biologically different from men and that women's health required protection.[57]

THE AFTERLIFE OF A SLOGAN

The Cultural Revolution had barely ended when the state, no longer a Maoist one, invoked the slogan "The times have changed" for an entirely new purpose. In economic planning, the notion that "men and women are the same" was being replaced by an emphasis on gender difference. But the simultaneously promoted family-planning campaign harnessed the slogan as part of its effort to persuade citizens that one child—whether a daughter or a son—was enough, as "men and women are the same." In 1977, for example, a county in Jiangsu reported on its efforts to encourage family planning. One major part of its campaign was to propagate the "new thinking" that "the times have changed; men and women are the same." A popular poster of the late 1970s reinforced the message: bold letters state, "The times have changed; men and women are the same," accompanied by a picture depicting a couple happily holding their baby daughter. Another poster, after declaring, "The times have changed; men and women are the same," instructs viewers to "criticize 'respecting men while looking down on women'; do a good job of family planning."

In the context of the family-planning campaign, groups of women also invoked the slogan in their complaints about problems resulting from the policy. In one instance, a group of fifteen rural women in Anhui wrote a letter to the editor of *People's Daily*, titled "We Demand a Second Liberation." Identifying themselves as "mothers of daughters," they wrote, "Our hearts have been heavy with sadness ever since the beginning of the propagation of the family-planning campaign." Each of them, after giving birth to a girl, repeatedly tried to produce a son, and all ended up with multiple daughters. "This has destroyed our health," they complained, "and the discrimination we face is even worse. . . . Why have we done something so injurious to both our country and to ourselves? Because here, where we live, a woman who has not produced a son is the object of discrimination and abuse." (They then describe the gifts bestowed on mothers who give birth to a boy, and the despicable treatment of women who give birth to a girl.) "We cannot understand it," their letter concludes. "Thirty years after Liberation, how can it be that we are still oppressed by such backward and feudal thinking? Chairman

Emily Honig

Mao said, 'The times have changed; men and women are the same.' However, even today, they are *not* the same!"[58]

The All-China Women's Federation issued a public response to the letter, acknowledging that it had received similar complaints about women being abused, and in some cases even beaten to death, for giving birth to a daughter. Federation officials pleaded for widespread propaganda to spread the idea that "men and women are the same."[59] In the context of the family planning campaign, then, state agencies and individual citizens invoked the slogan as part of an effort to persuade people that baby girls were as valuable as baby boys. If anything, the slogan was wielded as a reminder: men and women are now the same.

Over subsequent decades, the slogan was more frequently invoked by a range of individuals to critique the impact of the economic reforms on women's status. In this context, it came to represent something that was regrettably no longer true. For example, a young woman who graduated from the Beijing Institute of Commerce (Shangxueyuan) in 1987, the first member of a workers' family to attend college, had studied diligently and looked forward to enjoying the fruits of her hard work. Instead, she complained, she suffered grave disappointment. "Just because I am a female student, I have been rejected by various work units. . . . People often say, 'Men and women are the same,'" she wrote. "Is it possible that this is nothing but an empty slogan?"[60] In the early 1990s, an article titled "The Times Have Changed; Men and Women Are Still Not the Same" (Shidai butongle; nannü haishi buyiyang) complained about the disproportionate number of women being laid off their jobs. In the past, the author suggested, the ideal that "men and women are the same" prevented this kind of discrimination.[61] And in 2010, several articles began by asking, "The times have changed; are men and women the same?" The answer was invariably negative, as the articles detailed the ways in which women had not been treated equally in the reform era.[62] "The Chinese constitution clearly states that men and women are equal," noted one article, "but in fact the status of women is much lower." This was evidenced in female feticide and infanticide, the lower incomes of women, and the high suicide rate of women in China.[63]

While these iterations of the slogan attest to its afterlife, they were relatively few and far between. There was, however, one moment in the post-Mao era when the slogan regained more widespread popularity, albeit in a context very different from that of women's status in the workforce: the 2008 rap song "The Times Have Changed; Men and Women Are the Same." Addressing the difficulties of finding romance, the rapper complains about going to bars only to find that the patrons are gay or engaged in cross-dressing or both. Referring to graffiti on the wall of a bathroom, the song is punctuated by the refrain "The times have changed; men and women *are* the same!"

CONCLUSION

The point here is not simply to determine that Mao actually articulated message "The times have changed" well before the Cultural Revolution began (although it is intriguing to realize that this slogan that became so renowned was barely noticed when it was first spoken). More important is that the slogan was scarcely known during the first half of the Cultural Revolution and reached its zenith of media popularity only in 1974, and that it seems to have been closely linked to the Campaign to Criticize Lin Biao and Confucius. Here we see that even a slogan treated, particularly in retrospective accounts, as emblematic of—if not synonymous with—the Cultural Revolution has a far more specific history, reminding us that the Cultural Revolution was not a single, unified event.

This examination of Mao's slogan also suggests the ways in which the boundary between the Cultural Revolution and subsequent post-Mao economic reforms is not as absolute as is often assumed. While the slogan implies a kind of gender sameness, we see, too, that the slogan was accompanied by a simultaneous discussion of gender specificity, as evident from the articles and reports instructing officials to attend to women's physiological characteristics and needs that differed from those of men. In other words, even in the context of state rhetoric and propaganda, the Cultural Revolution was not simply about making women and men the same; it also embraced a recognition of difference.

The seemingly widespread discussion of the need to recognize women's "four periods" when assigning jobs in the early 1970s also makes us reassess the common assumption that the implementation of measures to protect the health of women workers was new to the post-Mao reforms. For example, writing about Chinese women workers during the economic reforms, Margaret Woo observes, "For urban women workers, China has turned to 'protective' legislation which focuses on the biological differences between women and men. . . . These laws constitute a marked departure from the prior policies of the Cultural Revolution, which emphasized the belief that 'women are the same as men.'"[64] As we have seen, attention to women's "four periods" was emphasized in the years following the Great Leap Forward (when it was most likely a reaction to injuries sustained by some women as a result of the emphasis on women taking on jobs formerly performed by men). It was also emphasized during the Cultural Revolution, when—even if it was not a reaction to the slogan "Anything male comrades can do, female comrades can do too"—it was nonetheless promoted simultaneously. The rhetoric regarding women's physiological specificity, and the mandate for protecting the health of women workers, long predated the economic reforms.

This attempt to construct the life of a slogan ultimately raises more questions than it answers. First, how are we to understand the transformation of seemingly random statements by Mao into popular slogans, honored quotations, or "supreme instructions"? In this case, we see Mao in 1964 donning a bathing suit, swimming with Liu Shaoqi in a reservoir near Beijing, and commenting on everything from the nature of swimming as a form of struggle to the sight of several female swimmers. Only years later does this statement get picked up and circulated; and only years after that does it become one of the emblematic Mao quotations on women's liberation. His comment about women's ability to do whatever men can do is clearly referencing rhetoric of the Great Leap Forward, but was Mao conscious of this when he made the statement? Was his intention to be descriptive, derivative, or prescriptive?

A second set of questions concerns the deployment of the slogan. Who was orchestrating the reporting and eventual propagation of the slogan? Was it Jiang Qing? Was it Jiang Qing in collaboration with the organizers of the Campaign to Criticize Lin Biao and Confucius? Was it the Women's Federation? And how did this slogan, which never made it into Mao's "Little Red Book," become deployed in such a way that it nonetheless became emblematic of the Cultural Revolution's (if not Mao's) approach to women's liberation?

Given everything we have seen about the life of this slogan, it is impossible not to wonder whether it was only after the Cultural Revolution that it gained such prominent status. After all, although it was often invoked in the press, not until 1977 did it appear in bold letters on the front page of that year's International Women's Day edition of *Renmin ribao* (followed by an article about the formation of an all-women's oil-drilling brigade at Daqing).[65]

Perhaps the fact that the slogan (along with the phrase "Women hold up half the sky) was yoked to a campaign waged by Jiang Qing helps account for its merciless condemnation in the years after the arrest of the Gang of

Four. And perhaps the subsequent economic reforms required a distorted representation of the Cultural Revolution—a lifting out of the slogan as if it represented a perverted form of social reality during the pre-reform era, one that needed to be put to its death.

NOTES

1 Jin, "Times Have Changed; Men and Women Are the Same," 100. Zhang, "In a World Together Yet Apart," 12–15.

2 See, for example, Huang, " 'Wenge' nüxing," 40–41. Although Huang attributes the slogan's articulation to a 1965 report, and also implies that it did not receive substantial press coverage until 1970, she nonetheless describes the slogan as emblematic of the "ultraleft" attitude toward women during the entire period of the Cultural Revolution. Also see Evans, "Comrade Sisters."

3 Huang, " 'Wenge' nüxing," 40. All translations are mine.

4 Jin, "Times Have Changed; Men and Women Are the Same," 100.

5 Zhang, "In a World Together Yet Apart," 14–15.

6 Ye with Ma, Growing Up in the People's Republic, 104.

7 For a discussion of this, see Honig, "Iron Girls Revisited," 97–110.

8 Renmin ribao, May 27, 1965.

9 Ho, "Millions Go Swimming," 20–21.

10 Renmin ribao, July 19, 1966.

11 Zhongguo funü, 8 (1966): 9–12.

12 Little has been written about the process through which utterances of Mao's became political slogans. One of the few accounts concerns his 1957 statement "The people's commune is great," picked up by a journalist standing nearby. See Li, The Private Life of Chairman Mao, 269. Thanks to Gail Hershatter for calling this to my attention.

13 Schram, Mao's Road to Power, 1:159.

14 "Chairman Mao Swims in the Yangtse," Beijing Review, no. 31 (July 29, 1966), 5.

15 Schram, Chairman Mao Talks to the People.

16 See "Jiji canjia jishu geming yundong nuli zheng zu jinnian nongye de fengshou,"1–2; Tang, "Qixiannü chayang shensu rufei," 3–4.

17 See, for example, Xu, "Nanren neng gan funü yiyang neng gan."

18 Jiang, "Xiang gangtie jinjun de nü zhanshi," 1. A similar phrase that appeared in the late 1950s was: "Nanren gandeliao, nüren ye gandeliao." See Zhongguo funü, July 1958.

19 Nanjingshi Fulian, Yuejin zhong de Nanjing funü, 12. The phrase "women overtaking men" (saiguo nanzi han) also appears in Jiangsu Sheng Fulian, "Jiangsu sheng di'er jie nü daibiao dahui daibiao fayan."

20 See Honig, "Tiaoyue xingbie fenjie."

21 Geng, "Guanyu 'tieguniang zai sikao,' " 70.

22 Renmin ribao, May 16, 1956.

23 *Renmin ribao*, July 10, 1964.

24 See Jiangsu Sheng Funü Lianhehui Bangongshi, "Jiangsu sheng funü lianhe-hui guanyu," 1962.2.16. Jiangsu Sheng Funü Lianhehui, "Sheng fulian gongzuo baogao," 1961.4–1961.8; Jiangsu Sheng Zonggonghui Nügong Bu, "Sheng zonggon-ghui guanyu zhaokai nügong jiawu gongzuo huiyi de wenjian," 1962.10.8; Jiangsu Sheng Funü Lianhehui, "Nongcun funü laodong baohu de qingkuang he yijian," 1962.2.16.

25 Also see Shaanxi Sheng Funü Lianhehui, *Shaanxi funü yundong 40 nian da shiji, 1949–1989*, 35. According to Kimberley Manning, efforts to protect rural women during the "four periods" were undertaken by the All China Women's Federation in the early 1950s and intensified during the Great Leap Forward. See "The Gendered Politics," 359.

26 *Renmin ribao*, June 22, 1961.

27 Jiangsu Sheng Zonggonghui Nügong Bu, "Sheng zonggonghui guanyu zhaokai nügong jiawu gongzuo huiyi de wenjian." Also see Shanghai Shehui Kexueyuan, *Shanghai laodong zhi*, 409, for discussion of urban agencies that, in 1960, instructed all work units in Shanghai to pay attention to women's "special characteristics." Also see Shaanxi Sheng Funü Lianhehui, *Shaanxi funü yundong 40 nian da shiji*, 35.

28 The poem is published in Mao Zedong, *Mao Zhuxi shici*.

29 *Zhongguo funü*, August 20, 1966, 14–15.

30 *Renmin ribao*, March 8, 1972. Quite possibly, the slogan appeared a year earlier as a Mao quotation. See, for example, the prefatory page to *Chinese Literature*, September 1971. which states that the phrase "the times have changed, and today men and women are equal" is a "quotation from Chairman Mao Tsetung."

31 *Renmin ribao*, March 7, 1970.

32 Jin et al., "Rethinking the 'Iron Girls,'" 617. Her analysis of the slogan's propagation is based on a survey of *Renmin ribao*.

33 Ibid., 618–19.

34 Shanghaishi Laodongju, Laodong Baohuchu, "Nongchang nüzhishi qingnian tizhi."

35 Ying Guizhen, Women's Federation of the Yu Huatai district of Nanjing, interview by author, May 6, 1997.

36 It is possible that the expansion of collective sidelines and small-scale industry resulted in a need for more female labor in agriculture. See Johnson, *Women, the Family, and Peasant Revolution*, 184.

37 This is based on *Renmin ribao dianzi ban* (1946–2005). Available at http://prl5.sdsc.edu.oca.ucsc.edu/WEB/INDEX.html. This is admittedly a preliminary calculation; a more accurate estimate of the slogan's popularity will require a survey of other publications of the time.

38 See Dongtai Xian Wenyituan Jiti, *Funü neng ding banbiantian (wudao)*.

39 Some articles in *Renmin ribao* explicitly link the slogan to the Campaign to Criti-cize Lin Biao and Confucius. See, for example, *Renmin ribao*, March 8, 1974; March 13, 1974; March 17, 1974; November 14, 1974; January 6, 1975; February 6, 1975; March 8, 1975; February 11, 1975.

40 *Renmin ribao*, April 18, 1974.

41 *Renmin ribao*, March 8, 1974. Also see "Destroy Old Thinking: Hold Up 'Half the Sky,' " in *Renmin ribao*, March 12, 1974.

42 *Renmin ribao*, March 8, 1975.

43 Many of these are collected in *Zhandou zai nonglin zhanxianshang de funü*.

44 *Renmin ribao*, March 12, 1974.

45 *Zhandou zai nong lin zhanxian shang de funü*, 75.

46 Terrill, *Madame Mao*, 311.

47 "Jiangqing liangci laidao Xiaoxinzhuang," *Guangmin ribao*, April 27, 2005, available at www.gmw.cn/content/2005–04/27/content_227138.htm.

48 Yan and Gao, *Turbulent Decade*, 517.

49 Ibid., 518.

50 Terrill, *Madame Mao*, 333–34. Four women were immediately recruited to work on the rig. This triggered a problem around toilets. When there was an all-male workforce, there had been no toilets at all; Jiang Qing insisted that a toilet for women be constructed. Then, because there was a toilet for women, one had to be constructed for men as well.

51 The main, other thing we know about Jiang Qing at this time is that she commissioned the infamous Jiang Qing dress in 1974: a floor-length skirt with "plum blossoms and hundreds of pleats," which represented a synthesis of styles from the Tang, Song, and Yuan dynasties. Although she had hopes it would become a national dress for women, it never really took off. However, she wore it herself, as did Chinese delegates traveling abroad (such as the sportswomen traveling to Iran for the Asian Games, who were issued the dress). For accounts of the Jiang Qing dress, see Terrill, *Madam Mao*, 334; Yan and Gao, *Turbulent Decade*, 444–45; and Finnane, *Changing Clothes*, 248–50. Jiang Qing also reportedly appeared on television in summer 1974 with her hair permed, greeting foreign guests. Terrill, *Madam Mao*, 334.

52 In Jiangsu, at least, the provincial Women's Federation had published booklets during the Great Leap Forward supporting the idea that "whatever male comrades can do, female comrades can do too"; during the early 1960s, however, the same federation issued reports expressing concern about the injurious consequences of this for women's health.

53 "Guanxin nü sheyuan shenghuo," *Renmin ribao*, August 19, 1972.

54 Zhonggong Shanghaishi Nongyeju Weiyuanhui, "Report of June 15, 1974," Shanghai Municipal Archives.

55 Shanghaishi Laodongju, Laodong Baohuchu, "Nongchang nüzhishi qingnian tizhi."

56 Wang, "State Feminism?" 522, 542. Also see Wang, "Dilemmas of Inside Agitators." Michael Schoenhals's *Doing Things with Words* is also suggestive on this point.

57 Kimberley Manning's research on the Great Leap Forward suggests one possible answer: she argues that grassroots women leaders "neglected the health of women and children because they were recruited and trained in grassroots Party organizations. Whereas the leadership of the Chinese Communist Party (CCP) and the All China Women's Federation (ACWF) sought to implement a Marxist maternalist conception of sexual equality that stressed physiological difference, grassroots Party organizations operated on the basis of a revolutionary Maoist ethic according

to which all were expected to struggle equally. Trained by the local Party organizations, a number of rural women leaders identified with interpretations of sexual equality put forth by the local Party, not by the Party and ACWF leadership." See "The Gendered Politics," 350–51.

58   *Renmin ribao*, February 23, 1983, 3.

59   *Renmin ribao*, March 3, 1983, 3.

60   *Renmin ribao*, December 26, 1987, 5.

61   Pan, "Shidai butongle," 45.

62   "Daxuesheng zhao gongzuo: Nansheng geng you youli," in *Xinwen zhongxin*, March 2, 2010, www.sina.com.cn.

63   Wang, "Shidai butongle."

64   Woo, "Chinese Women Workers," 279. Also see Shanghai Shehui Kexueyuan, *Shanghai laodong zhi*, 409. This account recognizes the emphasis on protecting women's health during the early 1960s, but then asserts, "During the Cultural Revolution, the work of protecting women workers stopped" and only resumed in 1978.

65   *Renmin ribao,* March 8, 1977, 1. Described in *Renmin ribao*, March 8, 2010, 4.

CHAPTER NINE

BAD TRANSMISSION

Gail Hershatter

Across generations, different sets of memories, frequently in the shape of implicit background narratives, will encounter each other; so that, although physically present to one another in a particular setting, the different generations may remain mentally and emotionally insulated, the memories of one generation locked irretrievably, as it were, in the brains and bodies of that generation.

Paul Connerton, *How Societies Remember*

W HAT remains of the massive midcentury state project to build socialism in China's countryside? What sense do people make of a society that has been dismantled and rearranged, leaving little material trace? During the collective years, women were mobilized in gender-specific ways to contribute to socialist construction. As we enter the fourth decade of post-Mao economic reform, what stories do older women tell about who they were, how they spent their working lives, and why their actions mattered? And when these women speak, what do their daughters hear?

This chapter is an extended afterthought about the women whose lives I explored in *The Gender of Memory*, a book about China's collective past with particular attention to the first decade of the People's Republic.[1] For that book I worked with Chinese researcher Gao Xiaoxian collecting the life histories of older rural Shaanxi women and a smaller number of surviving men.[2] They gave us rich accounts of agricultural labor, domestic work, and shared notions of virtue. The chapter begins with an abbreviated account of what we learned.

The afterthought is about how women born before 1949 transmit their memories of the 1950s to their daughters and what the daughters are able to hear and understand. At first this looks like a case of bad transmission, a case of intergenerational messages misconstrued or gone awry. But a closer examination suggests a complex process, in which notions of virtue recirculate and are repurposed for new historical circumstances.

WOMEN AND RURAL COLLECTIVIZATION

Life changed repeatedly and unimaginably for rural women born in chaotic, bandit-infested, famine-riven, war-torn Shaanxi in the first four decades of the twentieth century.[3] These women came of age in the 1950s, spent their adult years in collective agriculture, and are passing through old age in an era of accelerated privatization. The memories we heard from village women and men were indelibly marked by gender. A gendered division of labor was a constant feature of village life across the collective period, even as the content of normative tasks for men and women changed.

In the 1950s and 1960s, as is well known, the party-state of the People's Republic of China initiated a land reform and then, in short order, collectivized Chinese agriculture and launched it into the disastrous Great Leap Forward of 1958–61. At each stage of this process, party cadres and newly cultivated local officials put enormous effort into mobilizing women, first for political struggle against landlords and subsequently for collective work in the fields. The party-state undertook initiatives to reform some rural marriage practices while leaving patrilocal marriage intact; to teach rural women to read, with limited success; and to introduce scientific and sterile childbirth procedures into village households. Central to these efforts was the creation of an active state presence at the village level, which included the recruitment of at least one woman on each production team responsible for mobilizing others. Cadres from the Women's Federation spent long periods living in villages staffing these initiatives. They worked as well on the development and publicizing of women labor models who could transmit new

　　　　　　　　　Gail Hershatter

agricultural techniques and introduce new forms of political behavior for the edification of ordinary village women.

In at least one sense, all of this mobilization was successful. The move of women into basic-level agriculture freed rural male labor for infrastructure construction, small-scale industrial development, and entry into a flexible reserve army of contract labor for urban factories. Beginning with the Great Leap Forward, long before the onset of the 1980s economic reforms and the 1990s departure of many rural women for factories in coastal regions, rural women's agricultural labor undergirded what some Chinese scholars have called "socialist accumulation." The groundwork for China's current economic boom was laid during the collective years, and women's labor played a crucial part.

At the same time, another aspect of rural women's labor—the domestic work of producing clothing and shoes for growing numbers of surviving children—was rendered invisible in official state discourse. No labor model was ever celebrated for doing her needlework by oil-lamp light late into the night, though many models and ordinary women did so. Domestic labor was supposed to be socialized in an endlessly deferred future, as a by-product of socialist transformation. The domestic realm, understood as dependent on changes in the organization of production, was not much theorized or even mapped. It no longer occupied the status it had enjoyed in late imperial discourse as the foundation of social stability, or in the early twentieth century as the site of passionate critiques. It remained a site of unceasing but largely occluded labor, performed in moments snatched from the collective fields. Women's Federation cadres worried periodically in their internal reports about the "special burdens" on women and the strains caused by what we would now call the double day or extra shift. After the Great Leap Forward failed, however, the socialization of housework never again became a policy issue, and women's relentless daily domestic burden continued unremarked. Married women with children spent much of the collective period in a state of low-level exhaustion.

When women learned in the 1950s to "speak bitterness," articulating the often horrific privations of their early years, they frequently invoked standard descriptions of women's normative conduct that did not correspond to their own personal circumstances. They spoke about the bitterness of having been confined to the family courtyard before 1949, for instance, even when the details of their stories were all about their work out in the opium fields, their time on the road fleeing famine or bandits, or their trips to sell cloth and thread at periodic markets. We have come to expect such hollowing out of everyday lived experience in state discourse and formulaic speak-bitterness tales. But what about more intimate transmissions of experience—the stories told or alluded to in daily family interactions between mothers and daughters?

In the 1990s and the first few years of the twenty-first century, as women wove reflective stories in their old age, their stories of the past were suffused with pride in their previous capabilities, now diminished. Their narratives of the 1950s remonstrated with family members and a wider society who had depended on, expected, and yet generally failed to recognize much of their labor, and who now had begun to regard aging women as a burden. They deployed their memories in this new and often neglectful environment, talking back to the present, making a case for their own contributions and continued worth. In their personal narratives, they emphasized their own constancy of character in the face of lifelong challenges. They seldom referred to virtue per se, but they cited their own virtuous behavior: industriousness under conditions of collective poverty, willingness to work hard, thriftiness, and dedication to raising their children. They also attached high value to their filial performance of the role of daughter-in-law, including their willingness to care for the older generation—a value that has not been universally adopted by their own numerous grown children and daughters-in-law.

What follows is a rumination about transmission, based upon separate conversations with Wang Xiqin and her daughter Wang Nilan.[4] Nilan has lived her entire life in close proximity to her mother; her marital home is a short bicycle ride away. The two are in frequent conversation, sharing a family history and the memory of at least one searing family trauma. The sense that Nilan makes of her mother Xiqin's life, however, is shaped by additional factors beyond lifelong familiarity. Living in close proximity and with overlapping personal histories, each woman brings a generationally inflected frame of reference to bear on the stories she tells and hears. Within each woman's frame of reference, cultural remnants of an older, familiar language of virtue circulate and recombine in surprising, nonlinear ways. Transmission is a historical process as well as a personal one.

WANG XIQIN: THE MOTHER'S STORY

Wang Xiqin was born in 1932, the year of the monkey, in Shuangwang village, Weinan county, several hours' journey from Xi'an. She was the only daughter among ten children. Before she turned ten, Xiqin learned to spin from her mother, an industrious woman who could spin a *jin* (half a kilo) of thread in a day and a night. Two years later, at the age of twelve, Xiqin became engaged. At the same time, she went to work removing seeds from cotton (*dahua*) in a small factory in the Weinan county seat. In 1948, the year before the People's Republic was established, she married, at the age of sixteen, into Village B, five or six *li* away.[5] The marriage took place earlier than planned, because her natal family needed the bride-price money (16,000 *yuan*) to ransom her father out of the army.

Xiqin's new husband did not live at home for most of the first decade of their marriage. He had left, seeking employment, when he was fourteen, working first in a shop in Weinan, then after 1949 in a cotton company north of the river, and finally in the provincial cotton company in Xi'an. His mother was dead and his father, too, had been conscripted into the Nationalist army. (Xiqin believes that her mother-in-law died of fright and anxiety when Xiqin's father-in-law was conscripted.) With no resident husband and no mother-in-law, Xiqin's new family consisted of three of her new husband's younger siblings; her husband's disabled uncle; the uncle's wife, Tang Shulian; and five of their twelve children. Tang Shulian, Xiqin's aunt-in-law (or, in local terms, her aunt), was the virtual head of household. The village's only midwife, Shulian also worked in the fields and spun and wove. Her weaving, sold at market, was crucial to the family's survival. In her new home, Xiqin learned to weave from Shulian and also began to work in the family's fields, since there were no able-bodied men at home (or, as she and many of the other local women phrased it, "nobody was at home").[6] Xiqin's conscripted father-in-law returned home just before Liberation in 1949.

During the land reform of the early 1950s, Wang Xiqin's marital family were labeled poor peasants. She remembers the early years of the People's Republic as a time of hard work but also easy talk and laughter among young women who, ten years earlier, would have been isolated in the homes of their in-laws. After 1949, Xiqin's aunt Tang Shulian continued to deliver babies. For a year or two, Shulian also entered the labor exchange group organized by her neighbor, the widow Cao Zhuxiang, in which a group of women wove cloth for sale. (Cao Zhuxiang later became a local leader and regional labor model.) Still a teenager, Xiqin sometimes joined the group of older women in spinning thread. Then she became the head of a labor exchange group that during the winter months hoed the land of families who did not have able-bodied laborers. When the growing season began, with other women she hoed cotton, cut seedlings, and weeded. With each stage of collectivization—mutual aid groups, lower cooperatives, higher cooperatives—Xiqin was always one of the first to join: *When I stayed at home I felt unhappy. I felt comfortable when I was in the field. I talked and you laughed. We sang songs we learned in the adult school. It was so much fun.*

Life in her husband's home, however, was full of tension. Wang Xiqin's first three pregnancies ended in miscarriages and stillbirths, at eight, nine, and seven months. She attributes these losses to stress from ongoing strife with another of her husband's aunts, whom she refers to as Sanma (Third Mother). Sanma beat and quarreled with her, badly scratched her face, and pressured her to establish a household separate from that of her beloved other aunt-in-law, Shulian. Sanma also opposed Xiqin's work with the labor exchange group, implying that she was promiscuous and denouncing her to her newly returned father-in-law. Xiqin was angry enough that she returned to her natal home in Shuangwang and talked to her father about a divorce, even though she had no objections to her husband, only to some of his relatives. Her father vetoed the idea. No one in the Wang family had ever divorced, he told her, adding that she should *just muddle through. If you can't make a go of it, let your father-in-law live by himself and you live with your aunt [Shulian].* Ultimately, Xiqin says, *I was afraid to make the adults angry. So I said not to divorce. That's how we muddled our way along.*

Xiqin's relationship with her husband's aunt Tang Shulian was a close one. Drawing on her skills as a midwife, Shulian tried to prevent at least one of Xiqin's stillbirths by brewing a bit of gold in water for her to drink and then sprinkling salt on the baby's arm (which had emerged first) to force it back into the birth canal, but these measures failed. Shulian was in favor of the government-sponsored new scientific midwifery, and when Xiqin became pregnant for a fourth time, the older woman urged her to go to the hospital in the county seat and stay there until she had the baby. Xiqin's husband, then working in Xi'an, obtained some donkey meat for her to eat to help her maintain the pregnancy. Eventually Xiqin had four children: a son delivered in the Weinan hospital in 1953; a daughter, Nilan, born in a hospital in Xi'an in 1957; a son delivered by Shulian at home in about 1962; and a youngest daughter, Xiaoqin, also born at home, in 1963.

Xiqin's child-care needs were less acute then those of her neighbors, because in the early years of the collective, Shulian's disabled husband helped to care for Xiqin's toddlers while she worked in the fields. In the winter of 1957 Xiqin's husband, who had continued to work away from home, finally returned to the village to "join the agricultural frontline." He found work tending the livestock and eventually served as team accountant. One of the factors in the return of Xiqin's husband was that he did not want to be away from his daughter Nilan.

The following year the Great Leap Forward began, and for several months women took their grain-sifting baskets and went to the riverbank, about ten *li* away, to pan the riverbank sand for iron ore. People with children were not supposed to bring them to the riverbank, but Xiqin brought the baby, Nilan, then a year and a half old, carrying steamed bread to feed her: *I went myself, taking my child. No matter what, I wouldn't give my child to anyone.* Xiqin remembers vividly the day her husband obeyed the order to smash up their kitchen pots to be smelted: *The children's father [wa ta ba] first took my pot, a number three pot, with a very thin bottom, very well cast. I ran over and said I wanted it back, but they put it down there, and he took a steelyard and smashed it. It made me so angry that I cursed and cried. I said, my father bought me such a good pot.*

As the Great Leap began to collapse, people grew more dissatisfied with the diminishing food supplies. Xiqin's husband, no longer able to afford tobacco, gave up smoking. Xiqin herself was subjected to public criticism in the meeting square, accused of saying that the dining halls should be disbanded. Behind the political criticism was a more mundane conflict: people had discovered that she was secretly tending a patch of alfalfa to feed the oxen, and many of them had begun to steal from her alfalfa patch. Xiqin was so upset by this conflict that it made her sick, and she briefly considered jumping into a well, but was unwilling to abandon her children.

After the Great Leap ended, there was a drive to cultivate cotton in the mid-1960s, in which women were mobilized to take responsibility for the cotton crop. By 1964 Xiqin's husband had left the village again, to work for a short period north of the Wei River. In 1965, during the Socialist Education Movement, Xiqin was wrongly accused of taking more than nine hundred *jin* of grain for her family. By that time her brother-in-law was the team leader and her husband was the team accountant, and the accusation appears to have been part of a larger attack on the family. She and her family were forced to pay more than 1,000 *yuan* in restitution, in spite of the lack of proof.

Like many other women, Xiqin made her children's clothes at night. *As soon as it was dark I would spin. I would spin several skeins [suizi], wind several bobbins [louzi], and on the second night I would spin them, and the next day . . . I would weave, and then tonight I could not spin, instead I would weave. . . . At that time, I had a watch and looked at the watch, and at twelve or one I would have done enough to sleep, and I would put down the cloth on the loom. That was how we did it.* Throughout the entire collective period, she wove cloth for her family's use; and even after the reforms began in the 1980s she continued to weave betrothal gifts for the children, stopping only in about 2003.

Xiqin told us that her status in the family began to rise when her husband returned to the village in 1957, replacing his father as the head of household. As his standing in the family rose, so did hers, cemented by her status as a mother. *Now my words count in the family. Even giving gifts to relatives, we give them whatever I decide. I decide it. Did you dare to do so in the early days? When someone in my natal family had a birthday, I steamed several mo [a local term for steamed bread, or mantou]. My father-in-law threw them away and didn't allow me to go out the door.* In spite of her bitter early memories of life in her husband's family, when she talked to us in 1996 she pronounced herself pleased with the current state of relative material abundance. She pointed out that she and her husband had half a dozen quilts, and her daughter-in-law more than ten. She enjoyed being in charge of her own family, deciding how the family's money should be spent.

Xiqin's satisfaction was all the more remarkable because, two years before this interview, she had suffered the loss of her younger daughter. At our first interview, in 1996, she had burst into tears almost as soon as she began talking. Unlike some of our interviewees, she was upset not by bitter memories of the 1940s or 1950s, but by the events of 1994, when her younger daughter, Xiaoqin, had apparently hanged herself over an unhappy marriage. At the time of our visit, this suicide was still a topic of active community conversation. A county Women's Federation cadre told us that Xiaoqin had married her husband when he was very poor. Then he got some more schooling and found a job working for the county-seat branch of the trade union, across the hall from the Women's Federation offices. Like many men moving up the occupational ladder, he apparently had wanted to leave his wife and start over. He asked Xiaoqin for a divorce. She told him if he ever brought it up again she would kill herself, since he hadn't given her any reasons. Xiaoqin then went to the Women's Federation, and one of the county federation cadres moved heaven and earth to get her transferred to a job in the county seat, so that she could cohabit with her husband and decide whether she wanted to agree to a divorce. Before the work transfer came through, however, Xiaoqin was found hanged in her husband's apartment one Sunday afternoon while he slept on the bed. He was awakened only when his classmate entered the room and began to shout. The federation cadre commented to us that Xiaoqin's husband had conducted himself very badly with respect to her. Some in the community suspected that he and the classmate might well have killed Xiaoqin and faked the discovery of a suicide scene. The Women's Federation called for a full police investigation, and Xiaoqin's older sister, Nilan, and her husband supported this. But Wang Xiqin would not pursue it. She did not want her three-year-old grandson to lose both parents.

We did not see Xiqin for a decade after 1996. Her husband died four or five years before our second interview with her, in 2006. At that time she was living with one of her sons, still in a brick-and-daub house, unlike some of the fancier houses built by families who had sons working outside the village. Nevertheless, she expressed satisfaction at having come through tough times, at *the fact that I have lived until now, and know that I have brought in two daughters-in-law for my sons, and know that I have a great-grandson.* She had not forgotten the unreasonable adults who made her early married years miserable, or the unwarranted political accusations that twice disrupted her adult life. But the story she told us was, fundamentally, one in which life got steadily better over time, although the direct role of the revolution in that improvement was tangential.

WANG NILAN: THE DAUGHTER'S STORY

When we first met Xiqin's only surviving daughter, Wang Nilan, in 1996, she was a thirty-nine-year-old chicken farmer. A junior middle-school graduate, Nilan was married to a senior middle-school graduate who, before the reforms, had been a vice head of the production team, an accountant, and then head of the militia. Nilan herself had worked in the fields. By 1996, Nilan and her husband were entrepreneurs. Starting with fifty chickens, they had expanded to a farm with more than a thousand chickens that year, making money from the sale of the eggs. Nilan's husband was the overall business strategist and feed researcher. Nilan (speaking in 2006) described her role in the chicken business as that of the *commander-in-chief, in charge of all daily decisions.*

During our 1996 visit, Nilan invited Gao Xiaoxian and me to accompany her husband and her to one of the open-air dances held almost every night in the economic development zone (*kaifa qu*), attended mostly by area farmers. She appeared at about nine one evening to pick us up, dressed in a black skirt, a white frilly blouse, pearls, and beige cloth pumps, with her hair in a bun trimmed with white lace. Six of us rode two motorcycles to the dance, a sedate ride that was nonetheless terrifying because of the crowded seating and bumpy roads. The open-air clearing was full of men and women farmers dressed to kill and dancing with consummate skill: men with men, smoking while dancing with each other trying to learn steps; women with women; women with men. Nilan and her husband cut quite a figure, with full mastery of ballroom dancing techniques. (She also made some unsuccessful attempts to teach me disco moves, but I stopped as soon as I realized that a dozen people were carefully copying my unskilled thrashing, and probably a hundred more were watching.) Nilan and her husband, I later learned, danced there almost nightly. Struck by the experiential chasm between the stories we were hearing from Nilan's mother, Xiqin, and others all day, and what I had seen that night, I wrote that I wanted to do "a history of this village, one that encompasses Wang Xiqin and Nilan, her daughter, who probably share more than one can tell from appearances; they look to have grown up on different planets."

In 2006, when we next visited Xiqin after a decade and asked to see Nilan, she arrived on a bicycle (no motorcycle this time). I didn't recognize her; she was coarser of face and broader of body, reminding me that all of us were aging as this project extended year after year. But she was still dressed and coiffed impeccably: gray-and-cerise cotton short-sleeved sweater, pearls again, worked-silver earrings, a bracelet of thin beads, tan pants, black pointy pumps, reddish hair pulled back. She had lost her father since we last met, and her husband the dancing chicken farmer had been badly hurt in an auto accident, although she said he had recovered.

Whereas the massive changes of collectivization shaped the adult working life of her mother, Xiqin, Nilan's adult years have been spent dealing with the opportunities and pressures engendered by the economic reforms. Mother and daughter share the experience of life in the speeded-up temporality of state-initiated change, but the specific changes each has weathered differ.

In 2006 we sat down with Wang Nilan and asked her what her mother had told her about life before 1949 and during the early years of the collective. She began her answer with a story about herself, as well as her mother's observation about the younger generation. *Before I was married, when I was a girl, sometimes when it was dark I would go out to watch movies, and she would say, "Look at how accustomed you are to that. Back then, what girl would dare to go out?" As soon as it was dark we would get together in groups and go watch movies, whether it was in Mutong or Baiyang, basically any-where within about 5 li. Unlike in the old society, where you became someone's daughter-in-law and so forth.*

Nilan then moved rapidly to a generalized denunciation of the past, recounted in the heartfelt but impersonal terms culled from the potted history that circulates in rural Shaanxi about the prerevolutionary years. *In the old society they definitely were under the control of feudal thinking, and women were definitely very pitiful [kelian]. After marriage, look, women were so pitiful [xihuang taitai]. Wives [wuli, literally "those within the room"] had to do the three followings and four virtues: you had to respect the elders, respect the sisters[-in-law], older and younger; you had to respect them all—you were in someone's home [as his wife] [ni dao renjia wuli]. Then there were the eight classics [zheng er ba jing], women's traditional virtue [chuantong meide], work hard and take criticism without any complaint, do every kind of work, absorb every kind of anger. As soon as you married it was no good.*

When we asked Nilan to expand on her description of "feudal thinking" and to tell us what her mother had told her about it, her answer combined elements from the prerevolutionary and the collective years. First were standard bromides about pre-Liberation life that may have been recounted to her by her mother, but that we had been hearing for years from so many people that they can be regarded as ambient common sense. *In the old society, my mother told me, if you give birth to a son he will travel the world; if you give birth to a daughter she will go round and round the cooking pot [zhua hao de nanzi zou zhou xian, zhua hao de nüzi guobian zhuan]. It is already determined. No matter how good and capable a girl you are, you are going to be in the household. If you go out, you won't be able to do anything. That boy, no matter how mediocre he is, he will be able to run out and indulge himself. As a girl you can't go out; you can only stay at home. They tie you up in the house, restrain you. A woman at home did not regard herself as a person. For example, if she was sitting in the house, and someone came by outside—"Is there someone here?"—as soon as she saw that a man was not at home, she would answer, "No one is here." The idea was that if the man was not at home, that was the same as no one being there. She did not regard herself as a person. That was the biggest feudal thinking.*

Second, Nilan gave us examples of feudalism whose time provenance was unclear, suggesting that although the era of feudalism was supposed to end with Liberation in 1949, the term and the behaviors it denoted could be flexibly ported into the post-1949 period, when the only officially recognized feudalism was in the form of "feudal remnants." *Men had to give permission. No one listened to what women said. They would follow what men said, but if women said something they would say, "Women know nothing." Sometimes, when men took some friends home, the wives would cook and the husband and his friends could eat and chat. But whenever the women wanted to join the conversation, the husband would object and say women should not talk too much and they should sit elsewhere. These are remnants of the feudal thinking. Another thing was: clothing was inconvenient. At that time women had feudal thinking, and young girls, at that time, to put it crudely [nanting hua], they didn't dare to let this [points to her chest] show. They bound it tight; they all didn't dare to wear a bra; they bound it up because they were afraid someone would look. It looked so weird. That was feudal, they were afraid that someone would see something.*

Finally, Nilan offered instances of feudalism that dated unambiguously from the collective period. *When they went to work during the time of the production team, as soon as three or five people were together, as soon as a man spoke with a woman, the masses all began to discuss it. "Look at that woman." As soon as she talked to a man, it was unbecoming, just as though you were not conforming to female virtue. They would look and say, "That girl is like a crazy person." This was the influence of feudal thinking. Also, with respect to economics, all economic decisions were in the control of the husband. Income, for example. If the wife [wuli] sold a pig, or sold something else, the husband pocketed the money, or if she wanted to sew some shoes for the children, she had to ask the husband for money. This was passed down from the influence of feudal thinking.*

Family dynamics, Nilan implied, continued to bear the marks of feudalism well into her own generation. *When you become a daughter-in-law and go to someone else's house, you have to tolerate things and yield to others. You are in the wrong just because you have come to a new place. When other people criticize you, you dare not say anything. Sometimes the parents-in-law are good; they won't say anything. But sometimes they try to find fault with you. Sometimes the elders complain that you did not do something well, and you talk back. Some husbands would yell at you for talking back. And some would not even yell—they beat you up. The older generation had feudal thinking, and my generation had it handed down. "Beating a daughter-in-law/wife is like kneading dough" [da de xifu rou dao de mian]. That was a saying. They also said, "If you don't beat her for three days she will climb on the roof and take off the tiles" [san tian buda shang fang jiewa], meaning that with that kind of unrestrained daughter-in-law, you needed to suppress daughters-in-law who had a touch of that in their character. That was feudal thinking.*

Even women's mode of speaking had remained subdued well into the collective years, Nilan felt. *When my mother's generation spoke, it was all qiqi chuchu [an onomatopoetic imitation of clucking and tittering]. Now, . . . if you see three married women, it's like watching an opera. Like me, I speak in a loud voice. I laugh out loud. Back then women all spoke in whispers. No one dared to speak loudly. That was the influence of the old society.*

Nilan concluded her rapid-fire recitation of women's subjugation under feudalism with an intriguing statement: *But there are some traditional virtues that are still passed down.* We took note of Nilan's passing reference to traditional virtue for two reasons. First, in spite of her energetic commentary denouncing past feudalism, she seemed to suggest that there was something worth retaining from that past. Second, during the hundreds of hours of interviews we had conducted with older women, in which they often recited examples of their own virtuous behavior in the face of perfidy or indifference, I did not recall ever having heard a an older rural Shaanxi woman use the term that Nilan used, *meide* (virtue or moral excellence). The term did, however, appear in contemporary women's magazines. Nilan had come of age in the late collective years and had become an entrepreneur and a stylish recreational dancer in the reform era. She was a junior middle-school graduate; she might have been a reader of women's magazines. Where was this term "traditional virtue" coming from? When we asked what she meant by it, her answer centered on a disagreeable household task: *After you marry and go to someone else's home, you respect the old and love the young: respect the elders, love the father and mother, respect all the sisters and love them. Traditional virtue is doing hard work and taking criticism without any complaint. For example, when you get up in the morning, you ask the elders if they slept well or not, as it has been transmitted to my generation and is still practiced. When you are a daughter-in-law, in the morning you get up and empty the chamber pot for the elders.*

I married in 1980, on New Year's Day (not the lunar new year; unlike her mother, Nilan refers to time by the solar calendar). Then, when people married, they still emptied people's chamber pots. That was handed down from Chinese tradition. When I was still in my mother's house, my mother said, "Get up early; our daughter has to get up and practice emptying the chamber pot." My personality can be a bit impatient. My father was educated, so he spoiled me. . . . I emptied the chamber pot twice, and knocked it over twice. . . .

I disliked the stink and I took paper and lined it. . . . My father said, "If you tell her to empty the chamber pot [again], I will be so angry I will throw you out." So my mother didn't ask me to empty it.

When I was a daughter-in-law and emptied the chamber pot for the elders, it was so awful I wanted to puke. The smell was so bad that it was like—after I emptied it for several days, the elders said, "Forget it, don't empty it," and gradually I didn't empty it. For three days after you marry, you empty their chamber pots. When it came to my generation, when we brought in a daughter-in-law, I didn't want her to empty it. In Nilan's story, her willingness to perform a nauseating task sets the stage for beneficence: from her own father, then from her in-laws, and finally from herself as a new mother-in-law.

In contrast to her critical description of an archetypal "feudal" household full of nitpicking in-laws, Nilan offered as the contemporary embodiment of traditional virtue the figure of a mother-in-law who mediated conflicts and a daughter-in-law who avoided them: *There were three big things for women. The first is to be a good daughter [xiao gu], the second is to be a good daughter-in-law [xifu], and the third is to be a good mother-in-law. If you want your son to get a wife, you need to be a good mother-in-law. The mother-in-law must mediate quarrels between the young couple. You should not try to find faults only in the daughter-in-law, but rather criticize both. To be a good daughter-in-law, one should avoid conflicts. Whatever the husband's brothers say, you should put up with it. This is traditional virtue.* Perhaps so, but it is one quite possibly inflected by contemporary TV domestic dramas and the advice columns in many women's magazines. A few minutes later, Nilan commented that in contrast to her mother's generation, women her age *will talk back more, take issue with how the elders are doing something if they think they have a better way.* The virtue of conflict avoidance and the valorization of speaking one's mind coexist with no apparent conflict in her account of current family dynamics.

Nilan, like her mother, anchors her account in a conviction that life in the Shaanxi countryside is characterized by progress. In comparison to her mother's generation, she regards herself as lucky: *They say that women hold up half the sky; but as I see it, women hold up most of the sky. The difference is this: women in the 1950s still were more seriously influenced by the feudal thinking transmitted from the old society. Women now—it is much better, in every respect.*

What is entailed in the transmission of a usable past from Xiqin to her daughter, Nilan, born a quarter century, and a revolution, later? In the last half of the twentieth century and the early years of the twenty-first, change became the currency of official public discussion in post-Liberation Shaanxi villages: change away from feudalism and toward a socialist modernity, then away from socialist modernity and toward market socialism. (How people worked out social practices under the sign of these state-initiated projects is a complicated story, one I tackle in *The Gender of Memory*.) When Nilan talks, feudalism and its slow decline are her starting point, and progress is her narrative skein, even if feudal remnants persisted much longer than an earlier generation of village and outside activists had imagined they would. In that respect, she is transmitting a story of progress on which state sources, her mother, Xiqin, and she herself all agree.

When it comes to traditional virtue, however, the sequence is more complicated. State sources are silent on this subject. Xiqin's generation is eloquent on the subject of their own virtue, but they do not seem to use the term itself. For Nilan, however, "virtue" is a live term, one she introduces unprompted. Its content is not about submission and hierarchy, and only partly about hard work and selflessness. Virtue, once a powerful and flinty notion that moved extraordinary women to extraordinary deeds in the imperial era, survived in the collective period in the form of sacrifice for the family and industriousness in the face of scarcity. Now it is apparently having a soft afterlife in the realm of interpersonal relationships and people management skills. What, precisely, is being transmitted here?

It would be easy to conclude—and the conclusion might be warranted—that this is a case of bad transmission, garbled or interrupted in the time of unrelenting and accelerated change that we call "modernity." Eras of large-scale migration, war, revolution, and intensive state-initiated social intervention may well be expected to make each succeeding generation's experience so distinct from the one before it that mutual comprehension is impossible. If we want to ask what daughters know about the lives of their mothers and about the ethical and emotional matrices through which their mothers understood their own lives, we also have to ask: is the inability to draw on one's own experience, in order to understand that of one's mother, a feature of the ceaseless transformation associated with modernity?

And yet, the work of many historians who write about the imperial period suggests that transmission is complicated even when it is not punctuated by a revolution or a moment of time-space compression. A canon of writings about women's virtue accreted slowly over the years, with many byways and variations. It became important for educated women to be familiar with these writings and practices, and for educated men to celebrate their kinswomen for being knowledgeable in the canon of virtue and for practicing it. The imperial past as experienced in the "inner chambers" was almost never placid, and big events impinged with some frequency not only on the careers of the men but also on the responsibilities and commitments of the women. Examples of works on these themes include Beverly Bossler's work on the Song-Yuan cataclysm, Dorothy Ko's on the cult of sentiment (*qing*) in the late Ming, Ellen Widmer's on epistolary practices, and Susan Mann's on the *querelle des femmes* and the world the Taiping tore apart.[7]

The Talented Women of the Zhang Family, an explicitly multigenerational work by Susan Mann, raises issues of accretion, disruption, and context in a particularly pointed fashion. The Zhang daughters may have read the same classics of womanly virtue that their mother, Tang Yaoqing, had read; they also shared with her a familiarity with a dense and allusive world of poetry. But they read and listened and wrote and moved across the landscape in an increasingly tumultuous time, and at least one of the sisters registered in her writings a concern about foreign encroachment. In the next generation, Zhang Wanying's daughter Wang Caipin was an educated woman as well—a teacher—but the very lacunae in our information about her life bespeak a landscape turned upside down by war and by social as well as geographical dislocation. One has to wonder: born in 1826, threatened by the Taiping at twenty-eight *sui*, widowed at thirty *sui*, what did Wang Caipin know about the world of her grandmother, Tang Yaoqing, who died when she was five? Did she read the works that her grandmother had read? Did she listen to her mother and aunts describe her grandmother's life, or did she read anything they wrote about it? If she knew about and admired her grandmother's industriousness and perseverance during the long years of family poverty, did she do so in terms colored by the peripatetic circumstances of her own life? Did she understand herself as a virtuous woman in the same tradition of virtue that her grandmother had practiced? When she read or wrote about virtue (did she?), was it in terms that would have been recognizable to Tang Youqing, or to Caipin's own talented mother and aunts?

These are unanswerable questions, but it is important that we ask them and see where they lead us. Such work incites us all, not just to research the lives of the women who interest us, but also to try to inhabit those lives, imaginatively but responsibly, in order to re-create them as best we can. We need to ask ourselves not only what women read (in the case of literate women) or what they heard directly in didactic form in their families but also what kinds of messages they received from the world beyond the family or even the community (neither of which was in stasis). We need to ask which strains of thought and what stories were oft-told and which ones were dropped, and how women might have made sense of mixed or conflicting signals, about virtue and many other matters.

History writing, of course, presents many other problems of transmission besides the mother-daughter connection. But in thinking about what a woman knew about what came before her, what she might have admired but nonetheless discarded as impracticable, what she might have reconfigured to suit her contemporary needs, we may have to rethink our own attitudes about bad transmission. Perhaps intergenerational communication about the past always entails bad transmission. It is not like an auto transmission, which can be taken to a mechanic when it starts to make a clunking noise. Nor is it like a radio broadcast full of static, where one can twiddle the dial until the signal is clear. In the case of generational transmission and its implications for writing gendered history, the clunking noise and the static are not the problem: they are part of the transmission itself, or else perhaps a diagnostic of how transmission works. Bromides about feudalism and sudden eruptions about the communication skills of mothers-in-law are not a distortion in the transmission of virtue. They are clues to the wider environment in which stories told by an older generation are heard and reencoded in contemporary terms, inflected by contemporary dilemmas. Rather than screening them out as ancillary noise, perhaps we should ask what we can learn if we amplify them and listen carefully.

NOTES

Epigraph: Connerton, *How Societies Remember*, 3.

1   Hershatter, *The Gender of Memory*.

2   Gao Xiaoxian is writing her own books based on this material: a history of Shaanxi women's rural labor over the past half century, and a collection of oral histories.

3   This account is adapted, and borrows some phrasing, from Hershatter, *The Gender of Memory*.

4   Names of the interviewees and their family members have been changed. Wang Xiqin was interviewed in 1996 and 2006. Wang Nilan (not the same surname, but a

homonym) was interviewed separately in 2006. The chapter also draws on my field notes from both visits to Village B. My thanks to Xiaoping Sun for a draft translation of our first interview with Xiqin, and to Yajun Mo for supplementing my translation of our 2006 interview with Nilan. Any errors or interpretative peculiarities are mine.

5   One *li* is approximately one-third of a mile.

6   For further discussion of this phrase, see Hershatter, *The Gender of Memory*, chapter 2.

7   Bossler, "Faithful Wives and Heroic Martyrs"; Ko, *Teachers of the Inner Chambers*; Widmer, "The Epistolary World"; Mann, *Precious Records*; Mann, *The Talented Women*.

GLOSSARY OF CHINESE CHARACTERS

For orthographic consistency, all characters in the glossary appear in "traditional" (*fan ti*) style.

ai jiao ming shi 愛交名士
an shan 埯扇

baihua 白話
bang jia zhi guang 邦家之光
Bao Xuan 鮑宣
Bao Zhihui 鮑之蕙
Beijing Zhongguofurenhui 北京中國婦
   人會
Benshe qishi 本社啓事
bian sheng 邊省
bin you 賓友
Bitao Hongxing ciren 碧桃紅杏詞人
bu gui ze fu 不貴則富
bu xi zhong pin 不惜重聘
Buluo Shanren 補蘿山人
Buluo Shanren shigao 補蘿山人詩稿

cainü 才女
caiyun 財運
Cao Zhuxiang 曹竹香
changhe 倡和
"Changhuai ci" 悵懷詞
Changli 昌黎
Changzhou 常州

Chen Gongman 陳公曼
Chen Hongbi 陳鴻璧 (1884–1966)
Chen Huan 陳奐
Chen Sanli 陳三立 (1853–1937)
Chen Wenshu 陳文述
Chen Yan 陳衍 (1856–1937)
Cheng Gui 成桂
Cheng Yili 程奕立 (Liqing 立卿)
chong'er 充耳
chuan chao shu pian 傳抄數篇
chuantong meide 傳統美德
ci 詞
cui zhuang 催粧
Cuimin nüxuexiao 粹敏女學校

da de xifu rou dao de mian 打的媳婦柔
   到的面
dahua 打花
dan 石
Danjuan nüshi 淡娟女史
daotai 道台
dazhangfu 大丈夫
de zhi tong hao zhen cang 得之同好珍藏
Deng Hongmei 鄧紅梅
Dianshizhaihuabao 點石齋畫報

die 叠

Ding Jing 丁敬

Dong'ou *nühaojie* 東歐女豪傑

Dongzhu *nüshi* 東珠女氏

Du Fu 杜甫 (712–70)

"Du *Honglou mengbu you gan er zuo*" 讀
紅樓夢補有感而作

Du Jinqing 杜晉卿

Du Qiukui 杜求煃

Duan Fang 端方 (1861–1911)

Duan Qirui 段祺瑞

Duanmu Ci 端木賜

duo zi er hao gu 多資而好古

Erya yishu 爾雅義疏

fakanci 發刊詞

fang wai 方外

Fanke shanqiao 飯顆山樵

"Fei hong xiang yuan yin" 飛鴻響遠音

Feijing 飛鯨

feng hua 風化

feng huang 鳳凰

fu dao 婦道

fu yi de wei zhu 婦以德為主

funü neng ding ban bian tian 婦女能頂
半邊天

funü shi ban bian tian 婦女是半邊天

Funü shibao 婦女時報

Funü zhoukan 婦女週刊

Fushan 福山

Fuzhou 福州

gai tuji wei hanmin 改土籍為漢民

gaitu guiliu 改土歸流

Gan Lirou 甘立媷

Gao Xiaoxian 高小賢

ge chaiguan ji nannü jiaren xingong dan
各差官暨男女家人薪工單

ge jiu suo zhi 各就所志

Ge Qilong 葛其龍

gexin 革心

Gongbu du shui si langzhong 工部都水
司郎中

gongdu 公牘

gongsheng 貢生

Gu Aying 顧阿英

gu en 孤恩

gu qiao 古峭

gu ren 賈人

Gu Tinglin 顧亭林 (1613–82)

"Guangfu shidai nüjie huodong shi" 光復
時代女界活動史

"Guangmu Zhongguo nüjie juanzhu zaiqu
liangshi gongqi" 廣募中國女界捐助
災區糧食公啟

"Guanguan jujiu" 關關雎鳩

guixiu 閨秀

Guomin yuekan 國民月刊

Guomindang 國民黨

guti 古體

Haichang 海昌

hainei nüshi 海內女師

Haining 海寧

Hankou 漢口

Hanyeping 漢冶萍

haohan 好漢

he 和

he li deng longmen 河鯉登龍門

He Tongyin 何通隱

Hengyang 衡陽

hong guo 紅果

hongdou 紅豆

Honglou meng 紅樓夢

Honglou mengbu 紅樓夢補

Hongxing ciren 紅杏詞人

Houqing xinlu 侯鯖新錄

Hu Wenkai 胡文楷

Hua Mulan 花木蘭 (ca. 500)

Huang Shiquan 黃式權

Huang Zongxi 黃宗羲 (1610–95)

Huangchao jingshi wenbian 皇朝經世文編

Huanyu suoji 寰宇瑣記

Huasheng 華盛

Huayunju shicun 花韻居詩存

Hunan zhu Ning Diyi nüxue 湖南駐寧第
一女學

ji 跡
ji yan jia lei 齏鹽家累
jian wen 見聞
Jiang Jiafang 蔣嘉芳
Jiang Shiquan 蔣士銓
Jiang Zuobin 蔣作賓 (1884–1941)
Jiangfu 江孚
Jiangwan xuzhi shiyan chang 江灣畜植
　　實驗場
jiangyan 講演
jianshang 鑒賞
jiao hua 教化
jiating huaxue 家庭化學
jiating zhiye 家庭職業
jie fu 節婦
jin 斤
Jin Song shu gu 晉宋書故
Jin Tianhe 金天翮
Jing Yuanshan 經元善
jingshi 經世
Jinhe guangrentang keshu 津河廣仁堂
　　刻書
jinhuabang 金花榜
"Jinlü qu, ti pianzhou misheng tu, wei
　　Haining Du Jinqing Maocai zuo" 金
　　縷曲, 題扁舟覓勝圖, 為海寧 杜晉卿
　　茂才作
jinshi 進士
jinti 近體
jishi 紀事
jiu xiao 九霄
Jiujiang 九江
juan 卷

kaifa qu 開發區
Kang Youwei 康有為
kaozheng 考證
kelian 可憐
Kezhong yiwen lu 客中異聞錄

Langao 蘭皋
lao nu 老奴
Lao Zunsan 勞尊三
li 裡 (inner)

li 力 (power)
Li Ciming 李慈銘
Li Hongzhang 李鴻章
Li Qingzhao 李清照
Li Yuanhong 黎元洪
"Li zhi" 勵志
li zu yi zhi zhi 力足以致之
Liang Hong 梁鴻
Liang Qichao 梁启超 (1873–1929)
Liao Yunjin 廖雲錦
Lidai funü zhuzuo kao 曆代婦女著作考
Lienü zhuan 列女傳
Liexian zhuan 列仙傳
Lin Daiyu 林黛玉
linsheng 廩生
Liu Fenglu 劉逢錄
Longqiu jiuyin 龍湫舊隱
Longyou *xian* 龍游縣
louzi 摟子
Lü Bicheng 呂碧城
lunzhu 論著

mantou 饅頭
meide 美德
Meng Guang 孟光
Meng shu 夢書
ming jiao 名教
mo 默 (silent)
mo 饃 (steamed bun)
Mou Moren 牟默人
mumian 木棉

nanren gandeliao, nüren ye gandeliao 男人
　　干得了女人也干得了
Nanshe 南社
nanting hua 難聽話
Nanyuan hangkong xuexiao 南苑航空
　　學校
nanzi 男子
Neize 內則
ni dao renjia wuli 你到人家屋裡
Ni Fengying 倪鳳瀛
Ni Zan 倪瓚
Ningbo 寧波

Nongxian 穠仙
Nongzheng quanshu 農政全書
nü dao 女道
nü jiaoshu 女校書
nüboshi 女博士
Nüjiao 女教
Nüjie 女誡
nüjie xianjin 女界先進
nüshi 女士 or 史
nüshi shiming 女氏失名
Nüxue 女學
Nüxuebao 女學報
"Nüxuetang neidongshi jie Guilin Wei
    Gongren shu" 女學堂內董事接桂林
    魏恭人書
"Nüxuetang zhongxi dahui ji" 女學堂中
    西大會記
Nüzi guomin yijuan hui 女子國民義捐會
nüzi shijie 女子世界

Ouyang Xun 歐陽詢

Pajing xiaoji 葩經小記
Pan Suchun 潘素春
Pan Yunfang 潘韻芳
Puren cishan hui 普仁慈善會
Puyuan 璞元

qi fa hou ren 啟發後人
qi yu 奇遇
Qiantang *guixiu* Wang Qingdi Nongxian
    錢塘閨秀王慶棣穠仙
Qiantang *nüshi* Wang Qingdi Nongxian
    錢塘女史王慶棣穠仙
qing 情
qing lou 青樓
qinying 親迎
qiqi chuchu 戚戚處處
Qiu Jin 秋瑾 (1875–1907)
"Qiushu dushu tu" 秋樹讀書圖
Qixia 棲霞
"Qu wen" 驅蚊
que shan 卻扇
Quxian 衢縣

Quxian zhi 衢縣志
Quzhou 衢州

Ruiyu 瑞玉

saiguo nanzi han 賽過男子漢
san tian buda shang fang jiewa 三天不打
    上房揭瓦
Sancai tuhui 三才圖會
sang hu peng shi liu 桑弧蓬矢六
sang hu peng shi yi she si fang 桑弧蓬矢
    以射四方
Sanma 三媽
Shao Yingduo 邵英多 (Nengneng 能能)
Shao Yuanchong 邵元冲 (1890–1936)
She 歙
Shen Chu 沈初
Shenbao 申報
Sheng Changyi 盛昌頤
"Sheng Dongshi juanzhu dongzhen qin-
    gyu jianfang zhe" 盛董氏捐助東賑請
    於建坊折
Sheng Peiyu 盛佩玉
Sheng Xiaoyi 盛筱頤
Sheng Xuanhuai 盛宣懷
Sheng Xuanhuai Dang'an 盛宣懷檔案
Sheng Zhihui 盛稚蕙
Shenzhou nübao 神州女報
Shenzhou nüjie xiejishe 神州女界協濟社
shi 士
shi 詩
shi gu you qi pi 嗜古有奇癖
shi ji 侍姬
Shi Shuyi 施淑儀 (1876–1945)
Shibao 時報
shidai butongle; nannü haishi buyiyang 時
    代不同了；男女還是不一樣
shihua 詩話
Shishuo xinyu 世說新語
shiye 師爺
shiyu 侍御
Shuangwang 雙王
Shujuan *nüshi* 淑娟女史
si wu xie 思無邪

Siming suoji 四溟瑣記
Song Jiaoren 宋教仁 (Dunchu 鈍初,
    1882–1913)
Songnan mengying lu 淞南夢影錄
Su Shi 蘇軾 (1037–1101)
Subao 蘇報
sui 歲
suizi 穗子
Sun Chendian 孫陳典
Sun Xingyan 孫星衍
suo ke 索刻
suo yu ke zhang ru pu 索余刻章入譜
Suzhou Da Han bao 蘇州大漢報

Taishun 泰順
Tan Sheying 談社英
Tan Yankai 譚延闓 (1880–1931)
"Tang duoling, ti dushu qiushugen tu" 唐
    多令，題讀書秋樹根圖
Tang Qunying 唐群英 (1871–1937)
Tang Shulian 湯淑蓮
Tao Yuanming 陶淵明 (Tao Jingjie 陶靖
    節, ca. 365–427)
Teng Chao 滕超
Tianjin 天津
Tianxiang nüshi 天香女氏
"Ting yu" 聽雨
Tong-Guang ti 同光体
tonghao 同好
Tongmeng hui 同盟會
tongren 同人
"Tongying an" 瞳影案
tongzhi 同志
Tongzhou 通州
tumin 土民
tusi 土司

wa ta ba 娃他爸
waishi 外史
waizhangfang 外賬房
Wang Baohua 王寶華
Wang Caipin 王采蘋 (d. 1893)
Wang Fuzhi 王夫之 (1619–92)
Wang Niansun 王念孫

Wang Nilan 汪妮蘭
Wang Qingdi 王慶棣
Wang Qishu 汪啟淑
Wang Ruixian 王蕊仙
Wang Shoumo 王守謨
Wang Wei 王維
Wang Wenzhi 王文治
Wang Xiqin 王西芹
Wang Yinzhi 王引之
Wang Yuying 王玉暎
Wanyan Yun Zhu 完顏惲珠
Wanyu 畹玉
Wei Lunxian 魏綸先
Weinan 渭南
wenming 文明
Wenzhou 溫州
Wu Men 吳門
wu ming 無名
Wu Pingxiang 吳蘋香
Wu Qiongxian 吳瓊仙
Wu Shanshan 吳珊珊
Wu Zao 吳藻
Wu Zhihui 吳稚暉
Wu Zhiying 吳芝瑛 (1868–1934)
Wuben nüxue 務本女學
Wuhu 蕪湖
Wuhu gongli nüxue 蕪湖公立女学
wuli 屋裡
wuqi wushi 無妻無室
"Wuti, sanshi jue" 無題，三十絕
Wuyi xiang 烏衣巷

xian gui 仙鬼
Xiangxiang 湘鄉
xianyuan 賢媛
xiao 孝
xiao gu 小姑
xiaohan ci 消寒詞
Xiaojing 孝經
Xiaoqin 小芹
(Xie) Junyu (謝) 君玉
Xie Tiao 謝朓 (Xie Xuanhui 謝玄輝,
    464–99)
xieqiao 斜橋

xifu 媳婦

xihuang taitai 牺惶太太

xinglue 行略

Xingshi tu 醒獅圖

"Xingsun gong xingshu" 杏蓀公行述

Xinwen bao 新聞報

Xinyu 新裕

Xiong Bingsan 熊秉三 (Xiong Xiling 熊
希齡)

Xu Guangqi 徐光啓

Xu Shouping 徐壽平

Xu Songjin 許誦金

Xu Songzhu 許誦珠

Xu Zihua 徐自华 (1873–1935)

Xue Shaohui 薛紹徽

xue si yan 雪斯言

Xun Chan 荀粲

Yang Jiwei 楊季威

Yang Tinggao 楊廷杲

Yangshupu 楊樹浦

Yaosheng *nüshi* 瑤生女史

"Yedu" 夜讀

Yichang 宜昌

yin pu 印譜

"Yin yu" 陰雨

Yinghuan suoji 瀛寰瑣記

yingxiong 英雄

Yishi 懿氏

Yixiaotang shiji 儀孝堂詩集

yiyao changshi 醫藥常識

"Yong ju" 詠菊

Yongxuelou gao 咏雪樓稿

youtong 郵筒

Yuan 元 (dynasty)

yuan 元 (origin)

Yuan Mei 袁枚

Yuan Shikai 袁世凱 (1859–1916)

yuan you 遠遊

yuan zhi 遠志

Yuelu shan 嶽麓山

yuhe 遇合

Yutai xinyong 玉臺新詠

zazhu 雜著

Zeng Guofan 曾國藩

Zeng Jifen 曾紀芬

Zhabei 閘北

Zhan Kai 詹塏

Zhan Lang 詹朗

Zhan Sizeng 詹嗣曾

Zhan Xi 詹熙

Zhang Hanying 張漢英 (1872–1915)

Zhang Mojun 張默君 (Zhaohan 昭漢,
1884–1965)

Zhang Qingsong 張慶松

Zhang Shujia 张淑嘉 (Zhang Chu 張楚,
fifth sister, ?–1938)

Zhang Tongdian 張通典 (Bochun 伯
純, Tianfang louzhu 天放楼主,
1859–1915)

Zhang Xiahun 張俠魂 (1895–1936)

Zhang Xunting 張遜亭

Zhang Yiting 張益廷

Zhang Yunyu 章韻玉

zhangfang 賬房

zhangfu 丈夫

zhangfu zhi zai sifang 丈夫志在四方

Zhao Tongyang 趙桐陽

Zhao Yi 趙翼

zhen nü 貞女

zheng 正

zheng er ba jing 正兒八經

Zheng Guanying 鄭觀應

Zheng Yongxi 鄭永禧

zhengwen 徵文

Zhenjiang 鎮江

Zhenzhou 真州

"Zhi qi Zhuangshijiashu" 致妻莊氏家書

Zhifang nüzhi 芝芳女史

Zhifu 芝罘

Zhinan bao 指南報

Zhiyun lou shi ji 織雲樓詩集

Zhiyun *nüshi* 織雲女史

zhong 忠

"Zhong feng" 終風

Zhongguo funü 中國婦女

Zhongguo jiaoyu gaijinshe 中國教育改
　　進社
Zhongguo pingmin jiaoyu yundong 中國
　　平民教育運動
Zhonghua nanguo 中華男國
Zhou Shici 周世慈
Zhou Xuanwu 周宣武
zhu 著
Zhu Dizhen 朱迪珍
Zhu Peiqiu 朱佩秋
Zhu Qihui 朱其慧
zhu xuan 屬選
Zhu Yigui 朱一貴
Zhu Zhang 朱璋
zhua hao de nanzi zou zhou xian, zhua
　　hao de nüzi guobian zhuan 抓好的男
　　子走州縣, 抓好的女子鍋邊轉
zhuan shu 篆書
Zhuang Cunyu 莊存與
Zhuang Dehua 莊德華
Zhuang Peiyin 莊培因
Zhuang Shuzu 莊述祖
zhuang yuan 狀元
Zhuang Yuying 莊毓瑩
zhushi 主事
Zou Hanfei 鄒翰飛
Zou Tao 鄒弢

BIBLIOGRAPHY

Barlow, Tani E. "Theorizing Woman: Funü, Guojia, Jiating." In *Body, Subject, and Power in China*, edited by Angela Zito and Tani E. Barlow, 253–89. Oxford: Oxford University Press, 1994.

"Benshe jishi" 本社記事 (Record of this association). *Shenzhou nübao* (Journal of Chinese women), *xunkan* 3 (December 1912).

Bernhardt, Kathryn. "A Ming-Qing Transition in Chinese Women's History? The Perspective from Law." In *Remapping China: Fissures in Historical Terrain*, edited by Gail Hershatter, Emily Honig, Jonathan N. Lipman, and Randall Stross, 42–58. Stanford, CA: Stanford University Press, 1996.

———. *Women and Property in China*. Stanford, CA: Stanford University Press, 1999.

"Bianji shi zhi tanhua" 編輯室之談話 (Conversation from the office of the editor). *Funü shibao* (Women's eastern times) 20 (November 1916): 112.

Birge, Bettine. "Chu Hsi and Women's Education." In *Neo-Confucian Education*, edited by William Theodore De Bary and John W. Chaffe, 325–67. Berkeley: University of California Press, 1985.

———. *Women, Property, and Confucian Reaction in Sung and Yüan China (960–1368)*. Cambridge: Cambridge University Press, 2002.

Bossler, Beverly. *Courtesans, Concubines, and the Cult of Female Fidelity: Gender and Social Change in China, 1000–1400*. Cambridge, MA: Harvard University Asia Center, 2013.

———. "Faithful Wives and Heroic Martyrs: State, Society and Discourse in the Song and Yuan." In *Chugoku no rekishi sekai: Togo no shisutemu to tagenteki hatten* (China's historical world: Unified system and diverse developments), edited by Chugokushi Gakkai, 507–56. Tokyo: Tokyo Metropolitan University Press, 2002.

———. "Gender and Entertainment at the Song Court." In *Servants of the Dynasty*, edited by Anne Walthall, 261–79. Berkeley: University of California Press, 2008.

Bray, Francesca. *Technology and Gender: Fabrics of Power in Late Imperial China*. Berkeley: University of California Press, 1997.

Cahill, Suzanne E. "Performers and Female Taoist Adepts: Hsi Wang Mu as Patron

Deity of Women in T'ang China." *Journal of the American Oriental Society* 106 (1986): 155–68.

———. *Transcendence and Divine Passion: The Queen Mother of the West in Medieval China*. Stanford, CA: Stanford University Press, 1993.

Carlitz, Katherine. "The Daughter, the Singing-Girl, and the Seduction of Suicide." *Nan Nü* 3, no. 1 (2001): 22–46.

———. "Desire, Danger, and the Body: Stories of Women's Virtue in Late Ming China." In *Engendering China*, edited by Christine Gilmartin et al., 101–24. Cambridge, MA: Harvard University Press, 1994.

———. "Shrines, Governing-Class Identity, and the Cult of Widow Fidelity in Mid-Ming Jiangnan." *Journal of Asian Studies* 56, no. 3 (August 1997): 612–40.

———. "The Social Uses of Female Virtue in Late Ming Editions of *Lienü zhuan*." *Late Imperial China* 12, no. 2 (December 1991): 117–48.

Carné, Gaston Louis Michel Marie. *Revue historique de l'ouest*. Nantes: Bureaux de la Revue, 1985.

Chaffee, John. "The Rise and Regency of Empress Liu (969–1033)." *Journal of Song-Yuan Studies* 31 (2001): 1–25.

Chang, Kang-i Sun. "A Guide to Ming-Ch'ing Anthologies of Female Poetry and Their Selection Strategies." *GEST Library Journal* 2 (1992): 119–60.

Chang, Kang-i Sun, Haun Saussy, and Charles Yim-tze Kwong. *Women Writers of Traditional China: An Anthology of Poetry and Criticism*. Stanford, CA: Stanford University Press, 1999.

Chen Dongyuan 陳東原. *Zhongguo funü shenghuoshi* 中國婦女生活史 (A history of the lives of Chinese women). Shanghai: Shangwu Shuju, 1937.

Chen Hongbi 陳鴻璧. "Guangfu shidai nüjie huodong shi, xu" 光復時代女界活動史，續 (A history of women's activities at the time [of the revolution], continued). *Shen-zhou nübao* (Journal of Chinese women), *xunkan* 2 (December 1912): 4–9.

Chen Huan 陳奐. *Sanbaitang wenji* 三百堂文集 (Collected works from the Sanbai Hall). Congshu jicheng xubian edition, vol. 134. Shanghai: Shanghai Shudian, 1994.

Chen Yulan 陳玉蘭. *Qingdai jiadao shiqi jiangnan hanshi shiqun yu guige shilü yanjiu* 清代嘉道時期江南寒士詩群與閨閣詩侶研究 (A study of humble poet groups and poetry couples of Jiangnan from the Jiaqing and Daoguang reigns of the Qing dynasty). Beijing: Renmin Wenxue Chubanshe, 2004.

Chen Zizhan 陳子展, annotator. *Shijing zhijie* 詩經直解 (A straightforward annotation of the *Book of Songs*). Shanghai: Fudan Daxue Chubanshe, 1983.

Chung, Priscilla Ching. *Palace Women in the Northern Song, 960–1126*. Leiden, Netherlands: Brill, 1981.

Classen, Albrecht. *The Medieval Chastity Belt: A Myth-Making Process*. New York: Palgrave Macmillan, 2009.

Clunas, Craig. *Chinese Export Watercolors*. London: Victoria and Albert Publications, 1984.

———. *Superfluous Things: Material Culture and Social Status in Early Modern China*. Urbana: University of Illinois Press, 1991.

Connerton, Paul. *How Societies Remember*. Cambridge: Cambridge University Press, 1989.

Croll, Elisabeth J. *The Women's Movement in China: A Selection of Readings, 1949–73.* Modern China Series. London: Anglo-Chinese Educational Institute, 1974.

Dangdai funü 當代婦女 (Contemporary women). Shanghai: Shanghai Shenxin Shudian, 1936.

Davis, Adrian. "Fraternity and Fratricide in Late Imperial China." *American Historical Review* 105, no. 5 (2000): 1630–40.

de Pee, Christian. *The Writing of Weddings in Middle-Period China: Text and Ritual Practice in the Eighth through Fourteenth Centuries.* Albany: State University of New York Press, 2007.

Deng Hongmei 鄧紅梅. *Nüxing cishi* 女性詞史 (The history of women's *ci* poetry). Jinan: Shandong Jiaoyu Chubanshe, 2000.

Deng Xiaonan 邓小南. " 'Neiwai' zhi ji yu 'zhixu' ge ju: Jian tan Song dai shidafu yu Zhou yi-Jiaren de chanfa" "內外" 之际与 "秩序" 格局: 兼谈宋代士大夫于《周易·家人》的阐发. In *Tang-Song nüxing yu shehui* 唐宋女性与社会, edited by Deng Xiaonan, 1:97–123. Shanghai: Shanghai Cishu Chubanshe, 2003.

Despeux, Catherine, and Livia Kohn. *Women in Daoism.* 1st ed. Cambridge, MA: Three Pines Press, 2003.

Di Ruqian 翟如潛. "Hao Yixing yu Wang Zhaoyuan" 郝懿行與王照圓 (Hao Yixing and Wang Zhaoyuan). *Yantai shifan xueyuan xuebao (zhe she ban)* (Social science journal of Yantai Normal College) 1 (1994): 18–24.

Ding Renchang 丁仁昌. "Houji" (Postface). In Lan, *Nüxue*, q.v.

Dongtai Xian Wenyituan Jiti 东台县文艺团集体文艺团集体. *Funü neng ding banbiantian (wudao)* 婦女能顶半边天舞蹈 (Women can hold up half the sky [dance]). Nanjing: Jiangsu Renmin Chubanshe, 1974.

Doolittle, Justus. *Social Life of the Chinese.* London: Samson Low, Son, and Marston, 1866.

du Halde, Jean Baptiste. *Ausführliche Beschreibung des chineseischen Reiche und der grossen Tartarey.* 1747. Reprint, Rostock, Germany: Johann Christian Koppe, 1749.

———. *Description geographique, historique, chronologique, politique, et physique de l'empire de la Chine et de la Tartarie chinois.* 4 vols. Paris: P. G. Le Mercier, 1735.

———. *Description of the empire of China and Chinese-Tartary, together with the kingdoms of Korea, and Tibet, containing the geography and history (natural as well as civil) of those countries. Enrich'd with general and particular maps, and adorned with a gread number of cuts. From the French of P. J. B. Du Halde, Jesuit: with Notes geographical, historical, and critical; and other improvements, particularly in the maps, by the translator.* London: printed by T. Gardner in Bartholomew-Close, for Edward Cave, at St. John's Gate, 1738.

———. *The General History of China, Containing a geographical, historical, chronological, political and physical description of the Empire of China, . . . adorn'd with curious maps, and . . . copper plates. Done from the French of P. du Halde.* London: printed by and for John Watts, 1736.

Du Jinqing 杜晉卿. "Huanhua guan shihua" 浣花館詩話 (Poetry talks of Huanhua studio). In *Houqing xinlu* 侯鯖新錄 (New delicacies), 5. 1876.

———. *Kezhong yiwen lu* 客中異聞錄 (Strange stories heard during travels). Shanghai: Shenbaoguan Congshu Ben, 1879.

Duan Jihong 段繼紅. "Xiu dao renjian ciazi fu, bu ci qingshuo si meihua" 修到人間才子婦，不辭清瘦似梅花—清代知識女性對理想婚姻的設想 ([If I could] become the wife of a talented man through strenuous cultivation [in a previous life], I would not care that I be as thin as a plum blossom—the ideal marriage envisioned by educated women of the Qing dynasty). *Xihua shifan daxue xuebao* (Zhexue shehui kexue ban) 3 (2007): 1–4.

Ebrey, Patricia Buckley. *Accumulating Culture: The Collections of Emperor Huizong.* Seattle: University of Washington Press, 2008.

———. "Concubines in Sung China." *Journal of Family History* 11, no. 2 (1986): 1–24.

———. "The Early Stages in the Development of Descent Group Organization." In *Kinship Organization in Late Imperial China, 1000–1940*, edited by Patricia Buckley Ebrey and James L. Watson, 16–61. Berkeley: University of California Press, 1986.

———. "Empress Xiang (1046–1101) and Biographical Sources beyond Formal Biographies." In *Beyond Exemplar Tales: Women's Biography in Chinese History*, edited by Joan Judge and Ying Hu, 193–211. Berkeley: University of California Press, 2011.

———. *Family and Property in Sung China: Yuan Ts'ai's Precepts for Social Life.* Translated by Patricia Buckley Ebrey. Princeton, NJ: Princeton University Press, 1984.

———. *The Inner Quarters: Marriage and the Lives of Chinese Women in the Sung Period.* Berkeley: University of California Press, 1993.

Edwards, Louise. *Gender, Politics, and Democracy: Women's Suffrage in China.* Stanford, CA: Stanford University Press, 2008.

———. "Zhang Mojun." In *Biographical Dictionary of Chinese Women: The Twentieth Century, 1912–2000*, edited by Lily Xiao Hong and A. D. Stefanowska, 685–88. Armonk, NY: M. E. Sharpe, 2003.

Egan, Ronald. *The Problem of Beauty: Aesthetic Thought and Pursuits in Northern Song Dynasty China.* Cambridge, MA: Harvard University Press, 2006.

Elliott, Mark. *The Manchu Way: The Eight Banners and Ethnic Identity in Late Imperial China.* Stanford, CA: Stanford University Press, 2001.

———. "Manchu Widows and Ethnicity in Qing China." *Comparative Studies in Society and History* 41, no. 1 (1999): 33–71.

Elman, Benjamin. *Classicism, Politics, and Kinship: The Chang-chou School of New Text Confucianism in Late Imperial China.* Berkeley: University of California Press, 1990.

———. *From Philosophy to Philology: Intellectual and Social Aspects of Change in Late Imperial China.* Cambridge, MA: Harvard University Press, 1984.

Elvin, Mark. "Female Virtue and the State in China." *Past and Present* 104 (August 1984): 111–52.

Epstein, Maram. *Competing Discourses: Orthodoxy, Authenticity, and Engendered Meanings in Late Imperial Chinese Fiction.* Cambridge, MA: Harvard University Press, 2001.

Evans, Harriet. " 'Comrade Sisters': Gendered Bodies and Spaces." In *Picturing Power in the People's Republic of China*, edited by Harriet Evans and Stephanie Donald, 63–78. New York: Rowman and Littlefield, 1999.

Fan Ye 范曄. *Hou Han shu* 後漢書 (Latter Han history). Beijing: Zhonghua Shuju, 1965.

Fanshu ouji 販書偶記 (Occasional records of the book trade). *Bieji lei, guixiu zhi shu* 別

集類 · 閨秀之屬 (Collected works: Gentrywomen). 1936. Reprint, Shanghai: Shanghai Guji Chubanshe, 1982.

Feuerwerker, Albert. *China's Early Industrialization: Sheng Hsuan-Huai (1844–1916) and Mandarin Enterprise*. Cambridge, MA: Harvard University Press, 1958.

Finnane, Antonia. *Changing Clothes in China: Fashion, History, Nation*. New York: Columbia University Press, 2008.

Fong, Grace. "Alternative Modernities, or a Classical Woman of Modern China: The Challenging Trajectory of Lu Bicheng's (1883–1943) Life and Song Lyrics." *Nan Nü* 6, no. 1 (2004): 12–59.

———. *Herself an Author: Gender, Agency and Writing in Late Imperial China*. Honolulu: University of Hawai'i Press, 2008.

Fong, Grace S., and Ellen Widmer. *The Inner Quarters and Beyond: Women Writers from Ming through Qing*. Women and Gender in China Studies. Leiden, Netherlands: Brill, 2010.

Foss, Theodore N. "A Jesuit Encyclopedia for China: A Guide to Jean-Baptiste Du Halde's *Description de la Chine* (1735)." PhD diss., University of Chicago, 1979.

Fraisse, Jean-Antoine. *Livre de desseins chinois: D'après des originaux de Perse, des Indes, de la Chine et du Japon: 1735*. Saint-Rémy-en-l'Eau, France: M. Hayot, 2011.

Funü zhoukan 婦女週刊 (Women's weekly). March 20, 1919.

Furth, Charlotte. *A Flourishing Yin: Gender in China's Medical History, 960–1665*. Berkeley: University of California Press, 1999.

———. Review of *The Talented Women of the Zhang Family*, by Susan Mann. *China Perspectives*, no. 4 (2008): 102–4, http://chinaperspectives.revues.org/4752.

Gao Mengbi 高夢弼. "Daningtang nianpu" 大凝堂年譜 (Chronological biography of Zhang Mojun [from the Hall of Great Concentration]). In *Zhang Mojun xiansheng wenji* 張默君先生文集 (Collected writings of Zhang Mojun), by Zhang Mojun 張默君. Edited by Zhongguo Guomindang Zhongyang Weiyuanhui Dangshi Weiyuanhui 中國國民黨中央委員會黨史委員會. Taipei: Zhongguo Guomindang Zhongyang Weiyuanhui Dangshi Weiyuanhui, 1983.

Geng Huamin 耿化敏. "Guanyu 'tieguniang zai sikao' yi wen jige shishi de tantao" 关于铁姑娘在思考一文几个事实的探讨 (A discussion of several points in the essay "Rethinking the iron girls"). *Dangdai Zhongguoshi yanjiu* 当代中国史研究 14, no. 4 (July 2007).

Han Yu 韓愈. *Han Yu quanji jiaozhu* 韓愈全集校註 (Complete works of Han Yu, annotated). Edited by Qu Shouyuan 屈守元 and Chang Sichun 常思春. Chengdu: Sichuan Daxue Chubanshe, 1996.

Handlin, Joanna. *Action in Late Ming Thought*. Berkeley: University of California Press, 1983.

Hansson, Anders. *Chinese Outcasts: Discrimination and Emancipation in Late Imperial China*. Leiden, Netherlands: Brill, 1996.

Hanyu da cidian 漢語大詞典. 12 vols. Shanghai: Hanyu Da Cidian Chubanshe, 1989.

Hao Juheng 郝巨恒. *Shenzhou diyi ren* 神州第一人 (Historic firsts in China). Beijing: Zhongguo Jingji Chubanshe, 1999.

Hao Peiyuan 郝培元. *Meisou xianping* 梅叟閑評 (Leisurely commentaries by Meisou). In *Haoshi Yishu* 郝氏遺書. Tongzhou, [1884?].

Hao Yixing 郝懿行. *Shaishutang ji* 曬書堂集. Xuxiu siku quanshu, vol. 1481. Shanghai: Shanghai Guji Chubanshe, 2002.

Hao Yixing 郝懿行 and Wang Zhaoyuan 王照圓. *Shi Wen* 詩問 (An inquiry into the Book of Songs). Xuxiu siku quanshu, vol. 65. Shanghai: Shanghai Guji Chubanshe, 2002.

Harrell, Stevan. *Cultural Encounters on China's Ethnic Frontiers.* Seattle: University of Washington Press, 1995.

He Chenghui 何承徽. "Fakanci" 發刊詞 (Inaugural essay). *Shenzhou nübao* (Journal of Chinese women), *xunkan* 1 (December 1912): 1–2.

Hershatter, Gail. *The Gender of Memory: Rural Women and China's Collective Past.* Berkeley: University of California Press, 2011.

———. *Women in China's Long Twentieth Century.* Berkeley: Global, Area, and International Archive / University of California Press, 2007.

Hinsch, Bret. *Passions of the Cut Sleeve: The Male Homosexual Tradition in China.* Berkeley: University of California Press, 1992.

Ho, Clara Wing-chung. "The Cultivation of Female Talent: Views on Women's Education in China during the Early and High Qing Periods." *Journal of the Economic and Social History of the Orient* 38, no. 2 (1995): 191–223.

Ho Pien. "Millions Go Swimming." *Women of China* 5 (1965): 20–21.

Ho Ping-ti. "The Salt Merchants of Yang-chou: A Study of Commercial Capitalism in Eighteenth-Century China." *Harvard Journal of Asiatic Studies* 17 (1954): 130–68.

Holmgren, Jennifer. "The Economic Foundations of Virtue: Widow-Remarriage in Early and Modern China." *Australian Journal of Chinese Affairs* 13 (January 1985): 1–27.

———. "Family, Marriage and Political Power in Sixth Century China: A Study of the Kao Family of Northern Ch'i, c. 520–550." *Journal of Asian History* 16, no. 1 (1982): 1–50.

———. "Imperial Marriage in the Native Chinese and Non-Han State, Han to Ming." In *Marriage and Inequality in Chinese Society*, edited by Rubie Watson and Patricia Buckley Ebrey, 58–96. Berkeley: University of California Press, 1991.

———. "Observations on Marriage and Inheritance Practices in Early Mongol and Yuan Society, with Particular Reference to the Levirate." *Journal of Asian History* 20, no. 2 (1986): 127–92.

Honig, Emily. "Iron Girls Revisited: Gender and the Politics of Work in the Cultural Revolution." In *Re-drawing Boundaries: Work, Households, and Gender in China*, edited by Barbara Entwisle and Gail E. Henderson, 97–110. Berkeley: University of California Press, 2000.

———. "Tiaoyue xingbie fenjie: Wenge shiqi de tieguniang xingxiang yu zhiqing" 跳躍性別分界文革时期的铁姑娘形象与知青 (Crossing the gender divide: Iron girl-ism and sent-down youth during the Cultural Revolution). In *Bainian Zhongguo nüquan sichao yanjiu* 百年中国女权思潮研究, edited by Wang Zheng 王政 and Chen Yan 陈雁, 245–58. Shanghai: Fudan University Press, 2005.

Hostetler, Laura. "Mapping Dutch Travels to and Translations of China: Jan Nieuhof's

Account of the First East India Company Embassy, 1655–57." *Horizons* (Seoul National University) 1, no. 2 (2010): 147–73.

Hou Zhongyi 侯忠義. *Zhongguo wenyan xiaoshuo shigao* 中國文言小說史稿 (Draft history of the Chinese classical tale). Beijing: Beijing Daxue Chubanshe, 1990–93.

Houqing xinlu 侯鯖新錄 (New Delicacies). 1876.

Hsia, Ronnie. "The Question of Who? Chinese in Europe." In *Europe Observed: The Reversed Gaze in Early Modern Encounters*, edited by Kum Kum Chatterjee and Clement Hawkes. Lewisburg, PA: Bucknell University Press, 2008.

Hu, Ying. *Burying Autumn: Death, Mourning, and Poetry*. Cambridge, MA: Harvard University Press, forthcoming.

———. "Naming the First 'New Woman.' " In *Rethinking the 1898 Reform Period: Political and Cultural Change in Late Qing China*, edited by Rebecca E. Karl and Peter Zarrow, 180–211. Cambridge, MA: Harvard University Asia Center, 2002.

———. *Tales of Translation: Composing the New Woman in China, 1899–1918*. Stanford, CA: Stanford University Press, 2000.

Hu Siao-chen. "The Construction of Gender and Genre in the 1910s New Media: Evidence from *The Ladies' Journal*." In *Different Worlds of Discourse Transformation of Gender and Genre in Late Qing and Early Republican China*, edited by Nanxiu Qian, Grace Fong, Richard Joseph Smith, 349–82. Leiden, Netherlands: Brill, 2008.

———. *Xin lixiang, jiu tilie yu bukesiyi zhi shehui: Qingmo Minchu Shanghai 'Chuantongpai' wenren yu guixiu zuojia de zhuanxing xianxiang* 新理想，酒提列與不可思議之社會：清末民初上海 '傳統派' 文人與閨秀作家的轉型現象 (The unfolding of a conflicted new world). Taipei: Zhongyang Yanjiu Yuan Zhongguo Wenzhe Yanjiusuo, 2010.

Hu Wenkai 胡文楷. *Lidai funü zhuzuo kao* 歷代婦女著作考 (A survey of women writers through the ages). Shanghai: Shangwu Yinshuguan, 1957.

———. *Lidai funü zhuzuo kao* 曆代婦女著作考 (A survey of women writers through the ages). Reedited and supplemented by Zhang Hongsheng 張宏生. Shanghai: Shanghai Guji Chubanshe, 2008.

Huang, Martin W. "Male Friendship and *Jiangxue* (Philosophical Debates) in Sixteenth-Century China." *Nan Nü* 9, no. 1 (2007): 146–78.

———. "Male Friendship in Ming China: An Introduction." *Nan Nü* 9, no. 1 (2007): 2–33.

———. "Male-Male Sexual Bonding and Male Friendship in Late Imperial China." *Journal of the History of Sexuality* 22, no. 2 (May 2013): 312–31.

———. *Negotiating Masculinities in Late Imperial China*. Honolulu: University of Hawai'i Press, 2006.

Huang Liuhong. *A Complete Book Concerning Happiness and Benevolence*. Translated by Djang Chu. Tucson: University of Arizona Press, 1984.

Huang Shiquan 黃式權. *Songnan mengyinglu* 淞南夢影錄 (Account of a dream journey to Shanghai). Shanghai: Shanghai Guji Chubanshe, 1989.

Huang Ye 黃晔. " 'Wenge' nüxing bu ai hongzhuang ai wuzhuang" '文革' 女性不爱红装爱武装 (Cultural revolution women prefer military uniforms to fashion). *Guangxi dangshi* 广西党史 3 (2006).

Huanyu suoji 寰宇瑣記 (Miscellaneous accounts of the world). 1876.

Hucker, Charles. *A Dictionary of Official Titles in Imperial China*. Stanford, CA: Stanford University Press, 1985.

Hummel, Arthur. *Eminent Chinese of the Ch'ing Period*. Washington, DC: U.S. Government Printing Office, 1943–44.

Hunt, Tamara L., and Micheline R. Lessard, eds. *Women and the Colonial Gaze*. New York: New York University Press, 2002.

Idema, W. L., and Beata Grant, eds. *The Red Brush: Writing Women of Imperial China*. Harvard East Asian monographs. Cambridge, MA: Harvard University Asia Center, 2004. Distributed by Harvard University Press.

Jabour, Anya. *Marriage in the Early Republic: Elizabeth and William Wirt and the Companionate Ideal*. Baltimore: Johns Hopkins University Press, 1998.

Jami, Catherine, et al. *Statecraft and Intellectual Renewal in Late Ming China: The Cross-Cultural Synthesis of Xu Guangqi, 1562–1633*. Leiden, Netherlands: Brill, 2001.

"Jiade furen zhi Zhang Mojun nüshi shu" 嘉德婦人致張默君女士書 (Letter from [head of international women's suffrage association Wanguo tongmeng canzheng hui 萬國參政同盟會] Mrs. C. C. Catt to Zhang Mojun). *Shenzhou nübao* (Journal of Chinese women), *xunkan* 5 (December 1912): 4–5.

Jiang Yi 蔣怡. "Xiang gangtie jinjun de nü zhanshi" 向钢铁进军的女战士 (Women soldiers in steel production). In *Tulupang de Chen Guiying* 土炉旁的程桂英, by Jiangsu Sheng Fulian. Nanjing: Jiangsu Renmin Chubanshe, 1958.

Jiang Zuobin 蔣作賓. "Jinzhu *Shenzhou nübao*" 謹祝神州女報 (Sincere congratulations on the publication of *Shenzhou nübao*). *Shenzhou nübao* (Journal of Chinese women), *xunkan* 2 (December 1912): 1–3.

Jiangsu Sheng Fulian 江苏省妇联. "Jiangsu sheng di'er jie nü daibiao dahui daibiao fayan" 江苏省第二届女代表大会代表发言 (Speech of the Jiangsu Province second tier of the meeting of women representatives). April 1958. Jiangsu Provincial Archives.

Jiangsu Sheng Funü Lianhehui 江苏省妇女联合会. "Nongcun funü laodong baohu de qingkuang he yijian" 农村妇女劳动保护的情况和意见 (Opinions on the condition of rural women's labor protection). February 16, 1962. Jiangsu Provincial Archives.

———. "Sheng fulian gongzuo baogao" 省妇联工作报告 (Report on the work of the provincial women's federation). April–August 1961. Jiangsu Provincial Archives.

Jiangsu Sheng Funü Lianhehui Bangongshi 江苏省妇女联合会办公室. "Jiangsu sheng funü lianhehui guanyu quanguo shengshi zizhiqu fulianhuiyi qingkuang shibao" 江苏省妇女联合会关于全国省市自治区妇联会议情况时报 (Report of the Jiangsu Women's Federation on the condition of women's federations in all of China's provinces and autonomous districts). February 16, 1962. Jiangsu Provincial Archives.

Jiangsu Sheng Zonggonghui Nügong Bu 江苏省总工会女工部. "Sheng zonggonghui guanyu zhaokai nügong jiawu gongzuo huiyi de wenjian" 省总工会关于召开女工家务工作会议的文件 (Document on the provincial labor bureau's meeting on work concerning women workers' housework). October 8, 1962. Jiangsu Provincial Archives.

"Jiji canjia jishu geming yundong nuli zheng zu jinnian nongye de fengshou" 积极参加

技术革命运动努力整组今年农业的丰收 (Actively participate in the technological revolution and seize the agricultural surplus of this year). *Zhongguo funü* 中国妇女 (April 1959): 1–2.

Jin Jiang. "Times Have Changed; Men and Women Are the Same." In *Some of Us: Chinese Women Growing Up in the Mao Era*, edited by Xueping Zhong, Wang Zheng, and Bai Di, 100–119. New Brunswick, NJ: Rutgers University Press, 2001.

Jin Yihong et al. "Rethinking the 'Iron Girls': Gender and Labour during the Chinese Cultural Revolution." *Gender and History* 18, no. 3 (2006): 613–34.

Jing Yuanshan 經元善. *Jing Yuanshan ji* (Jing Yuanshan's literary collection) 經元善集. Edited by Yu Heping 虞和平. Wuchang: Huazhong Shifan Daxue Chubanshe, 1988.

Johnson, Kay Ann. *Women, the Family, and Peasant Revolution in China*. Chicago: University of Chicago Press, 1985.

Judge, Joan. "Everydayness as a Critical Category of Gender Analysis: The Case of *Funü shibao* 婦女時報 (Women's eastern times)." *Jindai Zhongguo funü shi yanjiu* 近代中国婦女史研究 20 (December 2012): 1–28.

———. "Portraits of Republican Ladies: Materiality and Representation in Early Twentieth Century Chinese Photographs." In *Visualizing China*, edited by Christian Henriot and Yeh Wen-hsin, 131–70. Leiden, Netherlands: Brill, 2012.

———. *The Precious Raft of History: The Past, the West, and the Woman Question in China*. Stanford, CA: Stanford University Press, 2008.

———. "Reforming the Feminine: Female Literacy and the Legacy of 1898." In *Rethinking the 1898 Reform Period: Political and Cultural Change in Late Qing China*, edited by Rebecca Karl and Peter Zarrow, 158–79. Cambridge, MA: Harvard University Press, 2002.

Judge, Joan, and Hu Ying, eds. *Beyond Exemplar Tales: Women's Biography in Chinese History*. Berkeley: University of California Press, 2011.

Kennedy, Thomas L., translator. *Testimony of a Confucian Woman: The Autobiography of Mrs. Nie Zeng Jifen, 1852–1942*, by Chi-fen Tseng. Annotated by Thomas Kennedy. Athens: University of Georgia Press, 1993.

Ko, Dorothy. "The Body as Attire: The Shifting Meanings of Foot-Binding in Seventeenth Century China." *Journal of Women's History* 8, no. 4 (Winter 1997): 8–27.

———. *Cinderella's Sisters: A Revisionist History of Footbinding*. Berkeley: University of California Press, 2005.

———. *Teachers of the Inner Chambers: Women and Culture in Seventeenth-Century China*. Stanford, CA: Stanford University Press, 1994.

Kutcher, Norman. "The Fifth Relationship: Dangerous Friendships in the Confucian Context." *American Historical Review* 105, no. 5 (2000): 1615–29.

Lan Dingyuan 藍鼎元. *Luzhou chuji* 鹿洲初集. Siku quan shu edition, vol. 1327. Taipei: Shangwu yinshuguan, 1983.

———. *Luzhou zoushu* 鹿洲奏疏. *Jindai zhongguo shiliao congkan xuji* 近代中國史料叢刊續集, 41. Taipei: Wenhai Chubanshe, 1977.

———. *Nüxue* 女學. Taipei: Wenhai chubanshe, 1976.

Landry-Deron, Isabelle. *La Preuve par la Chine: La "Description" de J.-B. Du Halde, jésuite, 1735*. Paris: École des Hautes Études en Sciences Sociale, 2002.

Le Corbeiller, Clare. *China Trade Porcelain: Patterns of Exchange.* New York: Metropolitan Museum of Art, 1974.

Leath, Robert A. "After the Chinese Taste: Chinese Export Porcelain and Chinoiserie Design in Eighteenth-Century Charleston." *Historical Archaeology*, 33, no. 3 (1999): 48–61.

Lee, Haiyan. *Revolution of the Heart: A Genealogy of Love in China, 1900-1950.* Stanford, CA: Stanford University Press, 2007.

Lee, Hui-shu. *Empresses, Art, and Agency in Song Dynasty China.* Seattle: University of Washington Press, 2010.

Lee, Jen-der (Li Zhende). "Gender and Medicine in Tang China." *Asia Major* 16, no. 2 (2003): 1–32.

Levering, Miriam L. "The Dragon Girl and the Abbess of Mo-shan: Gender and Status in the Ch'an Buddhist Tradition." *Journal of the International Association of Buddhist Studies* 5, no. 1 (1982): 19–35.

Li Changli 李長莉. *Jindai Zhongguo shehui wenhua bianqian lu* 近代中國社會文化變遷錄 (Record of change in recent China's social culture). Hangzhou: Zhejiang Renmin Chubanshe, 1998.

Li Chi: Book of Rites: An Encyclopedia of Ancient Ceremonial Usages, Religious Creeds, and Social Institutions. Translated by James Legge. New Hyde Park, NY: University Books, 1967.

Li, Chu-Tsing, and James Watt, eds. *The Chinese Scholar's Studio: Artistic Life in the Late Ming Period: An Exhibition for the Shanghai Museum.* New York: Thames and Hudson, published in association with the Asian Society Galleries, 1987.

Li, Guotong. "Imagining History and the State: Fujian *Guixiu* (Genteel Ladies) at Home and on the Road." In *The Inner Quarters and Beyond: Women Writers from Ming through Qing*, edited by Grace Fong and Ellen Widmer, 315–38. Leiden, Netherlands: Brill, 2010.

———. "Reopening the Fujian Coast." PhD diss., University of California, Davis, 2007.

Li Liming 李立明. *Zhongguo xiandai liubai zuojia xiaozhuan* 中國現代六百作家小傳 (Short biographies of six hundred modern Chinese writers). Hong Kong: Bowen Shuju, 1978.

Li, Wai-yee. "The Collector, the Connoisseur, and Late Ming Sensibility." *T'oung Pao*, 2nd ser., 81 (1995): 269–302.

Li Xiaorong. "Fuchang fushui: Ming Qing guodu shiqi Li Yuanding he Zhu Zhongmei de shige changhe" 夫唱婦隨: 明清過渡時期李元鼎和朱中楣的詩歌唱和 (Wife echoing husband: The poetic exchange between Li Yuanding and Zhu Zhongmei during the Ming-Qing transition). *Qingdai wenxue yanjiu jikan* (Journal of Qing literature) 5 (2012): 144–60.

———. "Singing in Dis/harmony in Times of Chaos: Poetic Exchange of Xu Can and Chen Zhilin during the Ming-Qing transition." *Research on Women in Modern Chinese History* 19 (December 2011): 215–54.

Li Zhisui. *The Private Life of Chairman Mao.* New York: Random House, 1994.

Liang Qichao 梁啟超. "Bian fa tong yi lun nüxue" 變法通議: 論女學. In *Yinbingshi heji* 飲冰室合集, *wenji* 1. Beijing: Zhonghua Shuju, 1989.

Lingmu Zhifu (Suzuki Tomoo) 鈴木智夫. "Shanghai jiqi zhibuju de chuangshe guo-cheng" 上海機器織佈局的創設過程 (The establishment process of Machine Weaving Company in Shanghai), translated by Chi Buzhou 池步洲 and Ding Richu 丁日初. *Jindai Zhongguo* 近代中國 (Modern China) (1995): 248–99.

Liu Feng 刘峰. "Ou Mei jingxiang xia de *Shenzhou nübao* yanjiu" 欧美镜像下的《神州女报》研究 (Research on *Shenzhou nübao* as a mirror image of Europe and America). *Shantou daxue xuebao* 汕头大学学报 27, no. 5 (2011): 29–32.

———. "Shiji suidong li de nüxing weisuo: He Chenghui he ta de nüermen" 世纪隧洞里的女性微缩: 何承徽和她的女儿们 (A microcosm of women in the tunnel: He Chenghui and her daughters). *Gudai wenxue* 古代文學 8 (2010): 68–70.

———. "Wan Qing nüxing zuopinzhong de yingxiong qili yu huixing shuxie—yi nüjie Zhang Mojun shici wei gean yanjiu" 晚清女性作品中的英雄气力与慧心抒写—以女杰张默君诗词为个案研究 (Heroic talent and emotional intelligence in late Qing women's writings: A study of the case of the heroine Zhang Mojun's *shi* and *ci*). *Hunan keji daxue xuebao* (*Shehui kexue ban*) 湖南科技大学学报 (社会科学版) 13, no. 4 (2010): 98–100.

Liu Minzhi 劉敏智. "Zhongguo zhi nü feixingjia" 中國之女飛行家 (China's female flier). *Funü shibao* (Women's eastern times) 20 (November 1916): 81–83.

Liu Yongcong (Clara Ho). "Qingdai zhi fufu hegao" 清代之夫婦合稿 (Husband and wife coauthored manuscripts of the Qing dynasty). *Haide gongyuan ziyou yanlun* 8 (2002).

Longxi Shengshi zongpu 龍溪盛氏宗譜 (Longxi Sheng family genealogy). N.p., 1943.

Louie, Kam. *Theorising Chinese Masculinity: Society and Gender in China*. Cambridge: Cambridge University Press, 2002.

Lu, Weijing. *True to Her Word: The Faithful Maiden Cult in Late Imperial China*. Stanford, CA: Stanford University Press, 2008.

———. "Uxorilocal Marriage among Qing Literati." *Late Imperial China* 19, no. 2 (December 1998): 64–110.

Lui Hoi-ling 呂凱鈴. "Li Shangzhang, Qian Yunsu heji suojian zhi fufu qingyi: Qingdai youai hunyin yili" 李尚暲、錢韞素合集所見之夫婦情誼: 清代友愛婚姻一例 (Loving husband-wife relationship seen in the coauthored work of Li Shangzhang and Qian Yunsu: A case study of companionate marriage of the Qing period). *Zhongguo wenhua yanjiusuo xuebao* 50 (2010): 189–216.

Lystra, Karen. *Searching the Heart: Women, Men, and Romantic Love in Nineteenth-Century America*. New York: Oxford University Press, 1989.

Mann, Susan. "Biographical Sources and Silences." In *Beyond Exemplar Tales: Women's Biography in Chinese History*, edited by Joan Judge and Hu Ying, 17–35. Berkeley: Global, Area, and International Archive / University of California Press, 2011.

———. "Dowry Wealth and Wifely Virtue in Mid-Qing Gentry Households." *Late Imperial China*, supplement, 29, no. 1 (2008): 64–76.

———. "The Education of Daughters in the Mid-Ch'ing period." In *Education and Society in Late Imperial China, 1600–1900*, edited by Benjamin A. Elman and Alexander Woodside, 12–49. Berkeley: University of California Press, 1994.

———. "Grooming a Daughter for Marriage: Brides and Wives in the Mid-Qing

Period." In *Marriage and Inequality in Chinese Society*, edited by Rubie Watson and Patricia Ebrey, 204–30. Berkeley: University of California Press, 1991.

———. "The Lady and the State: Women's Writings in Times of Trouble during the Nineteenth Century." In *The Inner Quarters and Beyond: Women Writers from Ming through Qing*, edited by Grace Fong and Ellen Widmer, 283–314. Leiden, Netherlands: Brill, 2010.

———. "Learned Women in the Eighteenth Century." In *Engendering China: Women, Culture, and the State*, edited by Christina K. Gilmartin, Gail Hershatter, Lisa Rofel, and Tyrene White, 27–46. Cambridge, MA: Harvard University Press, 1994.

———. "The Male Bond in Chinese History and Culture." *American Historical Review* 105, no. 5 (2000): 1600–1614.

———. *Precious Records: Women in China's Long Eighteenth Century*. Stanford, CA: Stanford University Press, 1997.

———. *The Talented Women of the Zhang Family*. Berkeley: University of California Press, 2007.

———. "The Virtue of Travel for Women in the Late Empire." In *Gender in Motion: Divisions of Labor and Cultural Change in Late Imperial and Modern China*, edited by Bryna Goodman and Wendy Larson, 55–74. Lanham, MD: Rowman and Littlefield, 2005.

———. "Widows in the Kinship, Class, and Community Structures of Qing Dynasty China." *Journal of Asian Studies* 47, no. 1 (1987): 37–56.

———. "Women's History, Men's Studies: New Directions in Research on Gender in Late Imperial China." In *Papers from the Third International Conference on Sinology, History Section: Gender and Medical History*, edited by Ko-Wu Huang, 73–103. Taipei: Institute of Modern History, Academia Sinica, 2002.

———. "Work and Household in Chinese Culture: Historical Perspectives." In *Redrawing Boundaries: Work, Household, and Gender in China*, edited by Barbara Entwisle and Gail Henderson, 15–32. Berkeley: University of California Press, 2000.

Manning, Kimberley Ens. "The Gendered Politics of Woman-Work: Rethinking Radicalism in the Great Leap Forward." *Modern China*, 32 no. 3 (July 2006): 349–84.

Mao Liping 毛立平. *Qingdai jiazhuang yanjiu* 清代嫁妆研究 (Research on dowry in the Qing dynasty). Beijing: Beijing Renmin Daxue Chubanshe, 2007.

Mao Zedong. *Mao Zhuxi shici* 毛主席诗词 (Poems by Chairman Mao). Beijing: Renmin Wenxue Chubanshe, 1963.

Marcus, Sharon. *Between Women: Friendship, Desire and Marriage in Victorian England*. Princeton, NJ: Princeton University Press, 2007.

Maynes, Mary Jo, and Ann Waltner. "Women's Life-Cycle Transitions in a World-Historical Perspective: Comparing Marriage in China and Europe." *Journal of Women's History* 12, no. 4 (2001): 11–21.

McDermott, Joseph P. "The Chinese Domestic Bursar." Special issue, *Ajia bunka kenku*, no. 2 (November 1990): 15–32.

Metcalf, Barbara. "Islam and Power in Colonial India: The Making and Unmaking of a Muslim Princess." *American Historical Review* 116, no. 1 (2011): 1–30.

Meyer-Fong, Tobie. "Packaging the Men of Our Times: Literary Anthologies, Friendship Networks, and Political Accommodation in the Early Qing." *Harvard Journal of Asiatic Studies* 64, no. 1 (June 2004): 5–56.

Miller, Susan. "Jean-Antoine Fraisse at Chantilly: French Images of Asia." *East Asian Library Journal* 9, no. 1 (2001): 78–222.

Min Erchang 閔爾昌. *Bei zhuan ji bu* 碑傳集補. Taipei: Mingwen Shuju, 1985.

Mittler, Barbara. *A Newspaper for China?: Power, Identity, and Change in Shanghai's News Media, 1872–1912.* Cambridge, MA: Harvard University Asia Center, 2004.

Mungello, David. *The Great Encounter of China and the West.* Lanham, MD: Rowman and Littlefield, 2012.

Nanjingshi Fulian 南京市妇联, ed. *Yuejin zhong de Nanjing funü* 跃进中的南京妇女 (Nanjing women in the Great Leap Forward). Nanjing: Nanjing Renmin Chuban-she, 1958.

"The Nanyang Exhibition: China's First Great National Show." *Far Eastern Review* 6, no. 4 (April 1910): 503–7.

Nieuhoff, Johan. *Der Gesandschaft der Ost-Indischer Geselshaft in den Vereingten Nie-derlanden an der Tartarsichen Cham und nunmehr auch sinischen Jaiser.* Amster-dam: n.p., 1666.

Odell, Dawn. "Porcelain, Print Culture, and Mercantile Aesthetics." In *The Cultural Aesthetics of Eighteenth-Century Porcelain*, edited by Aidan Cavanaugh et al. Burl-ington, VT: Ashgate, 2010.

———. " 'The Soul of Transactions': Illustration and Johan Neuhoff's Travels in China." In *'Tweeingger eener dragt' Woord en beeld in den Nederlanden 1500–1750*, edited by Karen Bostoen et al. Hilversum, Netherlands: Verloren, 2001.

Ōki, Yasushi. "Mao Xiang and Yu Huai: Early Qing Romantic *yimin*." In *Trauma and Transcendence in Early Qing Literature*, edited by Wilt Idema, Wai-yee Li, and Ellen Widmer, 231–48. Cambridge, MA: Harvard University Asia Center, 2006.

Pan Jintang. "Shidai butongle, nan nü haishi bu yiyang" (The times have changed; men and women are still not the same) 时代不同了，男女还是不一样. *Zhongguo renli ziyuan kaifa* 中国人力资源开发 (February 1993).

Piling Zhuangshi zupu 毗陵莊氏族譜 (Piling Zhuang family genealogy). N.p., 1887.

Qian, Nanxiu. "The Mother *Nü xuebao* versus the Daughter *Nü xuebao*: Generational Differences between 1898 and 1902 Women Reformers." In *Different Worlds of Discourse: Transformations of Gender and Genre in Late Qing and Early Republican China*, edited by Nanxiu Qian, Grace Fong, and Richard Joseph Smith, 257–91. Leiden, Netherlands: Brill, 2008.

———. "Revitalizing the *Xianyuan* (Worthy Ladies) Tradition: Women in the 1898 Reform." *Modern China* 29, no. 4 (2003): 399–454.

Qian Wanwei 錢琬薇. "Shiluo yu mianhuai: Zoutao yu qi 'Haishang chentianying'yanjiu" 失落與緬懷：鄒弢及其《海上塵天影》研究 (Loss and remembrance: Research on Zou Tao's "Shadows of Heaven and Earth in Shanghai"). Master's thesis, Zhengzhi University Chinese Department, Taipei, 2006.

Qin Zuyong 秦祖永. *Qi jia yin ba* 七家印跋. Reprinted in *Mei shu cong shu* 美術叢書, edited by Huang Binhong 黃賓虹 and Deng Shi 鄧實. Second collection, vol. 3. Taipei: Yiwen Yinshuguan, 1962.

Qing dai guanyuan lüli dang' an quan bian 清代官員履歷檔案全編. Edited by Qin Guo-
jing 秦國經. Shanghai: Huadong Shifan Daxue Chubanshe, 1997.

Quxian Zhi Bianzuan Weiyuan Hui 衢縣志編纂委員會. *Quxian zhi* 衢縣志 (Gazetteer
of Qu County). Hangzhou: Zhejiang Renmin Chubanshe, 1992.

Rankin, Mary. *Elite Activism and Political Transformation in China: Zhejiang Province,
1865–1911*. Stanford, CA: Stanford University Press, 1986.

Raphals, Lisa. *Sharing the Light: Representations of Women and Virtue in Early China*.
SUNY Series in Chinese Philosophy and Culture. New York: SUNY Press, 1998.

Rawski, Evelyn. *Education and Popular Literacy in Ch'ing China*. Ann Arbor: University
of Michigan Press, 1979.

Reed, Marcia, and Paola Demattè. *China on Paper: European and Chinese Works from
the Late Sixteenth to the Early Nineteenth Century*. Los Angeles: Getty Research
Institute, 2011.

Renmin ribao 人民日报 (People's Daily).

Ropp, Paul S. "Love, Literacy, and Laments: Themes of Women Writers in Late Imperial
China." In *Women's Historical Review* 2, no. 1 (1993): 107–41.

Rouzer, Paul. *Articulated Ladies: Gender and the Male Community in Early Chinese
Texts*. Cambridge, MA: Harvard University Press, 2001.

Rowe, William T. *Saving the World: Chen Hongmou and Elite Consciousness in Eighteenth-Century China*. Stanford, CA: Stanford University Press, 2001.

———. "Women and the Family in Mid-Qing Social Thought: The Case of Ch'en
Hung-mou." *Late Imperial China* 13, no. 2 (1992): 1–41.

Schoenhals, Michael. *Doing Things with Words in Chinese Politics: Five Studies*.
Research Monograph No. 41. Berkeley: Center for Chinese Studies, University of
California, Berkeley, 1992.

Schram, Stuart. *Chairman Mao Talks to the People: Talks and Letters, 1956–1971*. New
York: Pantheon, 1975.

———. *Mao's Road to Power: Revolutionary Writings, 1912–194*. 10 vols. Armonk, NY:
M. E. Sharpe, 1992.

Shaanxi Sheng Funü Lianhehui 陕西省妇女联合会. *Shaanxi funü yundong 40 nian da
shiji, 1949–1989* 陕西妇女运动 40 年大史记 (Chronology of 40 years of the Shaanxi
women's movement). Xi'an: Shaanxi Sheng Funü Lianhe Hui, 1994.

Shanghai Shehui Kexueyuan 上海社会科学院. *Shanghai laodong zhi* 上海劳动志
(Shanghai labor gazetteer). Shanghai: n.p., 1998.

Shanghai Tushuguan 上海圖書館. *Zhongguo jindai qikan pianmu huilu* 中國近代期
刊篇目匯錄 (Collected tables of contents of modern Chinese periodicals). 3 vols.
Shanghai: Shanghai Renmin Chubanshe, 1965–84.

Shanghaishi Laodongju, Laodong Baohuchu 上海市劳动局劳动保护处. "Nongchang
nüzhishi qingnian tizhi pubian xiajiang de qingkuang yao yinqi zhongshi" 农场
女知识青年体质谱偏下降的情况要引起重视 (It is crucial to pay attention to the
declining condition of bodies among female sent-down youth on state farms). In
Tuan de qingkuang 团的情况, No. 82, edited by Gongqingtuan Shanghaishi Weiyuanhui Bangongshi 共青团上海市委员会办公. May 28, 1974. Shanghai Municipal
Archives.

Shao, Yuanchong 邵元冲 (Chong 冲). "Nüquan yu guojia zhi guanxi" (The relation-ship between women's rights and the nation). *Shenzhou nübao* (Journal of Chinese women), *yuekan* 1 (April 1, 1913): 5–13.

———. *Shao Yuanchong riji* 邵元冲日記 (Diary of Shao Yuanchong). Annotated by Wang Yangqing 王仰清 and Xu Yinghu 許映湖. Shanghai: Shanghai Renmin Chu-banshe, 1990.

Shen Jikai *zhiyan* 沈姬鎧直言 (Forthright words of Shen Jikai). "Tianlai" 天籟 (Sounds of nature). *Shenzhou nübao* (Journal of Chinese women), *xunkan* 3 (December 1912): 1–2.

Shen Qiyuan 沈啓元. "Tiao chen Taiwan shi yi zhuang" 條陳台灣事宜狀 (A memorial on Taiwan affairs). In *Huangchao jingshi wenbian* 皇朝經世文編, 84.51–54. 1826. Reprint, Taipei: Guofeng, 1963.

Shenbao 申報 (Shanghai News). 1872–1949.

Sheng Peiyu 盛佩玉. *Shengshi jiazu: Shao Xunmei yu wo* 盛氏家族. 邵洵美與我 (The Sheng family: Shao Xunmei and I). Beijing: Renmin Wenxue Chubanshe, 2004.

Sheng Xuanhuai 盛宣懷. *Sheng Xuanhuai weikan xingao* 盛宣懷未刊信稿 (Unpub-lished letter manuscripts of Sheng Xuanhuai). Beijing: Zhonghua Shuju, 1960.

———. *Yuzhai cungao* 愚齋存稿 (The extant manuscripts of Sheng Xuanhuai). Xuxiu siku quanshu, vol. 1571. Shanghai: Shanghai Guji Chubanshe, 2002.

"Shenzhou nüjie xiejishe zhangcheng" 神州女界協濟社章程 (The Shenzhou United Women's Assistance Society regulations). *Shenzhou nübao* (Journal of Chinese women), *xunkan* 4 (December 1912): 1–6.

Shepherd, John Robert. *Statecraft and Political Economy on the Taiwan Frontier, 1600–1800*. Stanford, CA: Stanford University Press, 1993.

Shi Changyu 石昌渝. *Zhongguo gudai xiaoshuo zongmu* 中國古代小說總目 (General catalogue of traditional Chinese fiction). Taiyuan: Shanxi Jiaoyu Chubanshe, 2004.

Siming suoji 四溟瑣記 (Miscellaneous accounts of the world). 1875–76.

Skinner, G. William. *The City in Late Imperial China*. Stanford, CA: Stanford University Press, 1977.

Sommer, Matthew H. "Dangerous Males, Vulnerable Males, and Polluted Males: The Regulation of Masculinity in Qing Dynasty Law." In *Chinese Femininities, Chinese Masculinities: A Reader*, edited by Susan Brownell and Jeffrey N. Wasserstrom, 67–88. Berkeley: University of California Press, 2002.

———. "The Penetrated Male in Late Imperial China." *Modern China* 23, no. 2 (April 1997): 140–80.

———. *Sex, Law, and Society in Late Imperial China*. Law, Society, and Culture in China. Stanford, CA: Stanford University Press, 2000.

———. "The Uses of Chastity: Sex, Law, and the Property of Widows in Qing China." *Late Imperial China* 17, no. 2 (December 1996): 77–130.

———. "Was China Part of a Global Eighteenth-Century Homosexuality?" *Historical Reflections/Réflexions Historiques* 33, no. 1 (Spring 2007): 117–33.

Song Cen 松岑. "Zhengji zhengrenxin shuo" 正己正人心說 (Rectifying the self, rectify-ing others). *Shenzhou nübao* (Journal of Chinese women), *xunkan* 4 (December 1912): 10.

Song, Geng. *The Fragile Scholar: Power and Masculinity in Chinese Culture.* Hong Kong: University of Hong Kong Press, 2004.

Song Jun 宋軍. *Shenbao de xingshuai* 申報的興衰 (*Shenbao*'s rise and decline). Shanghai: Shanghai Shehui Kexue Chubanshe, 1996.

Song Qingxiu 宋清秀. "Qingdai cainü wenhua de diyuxing tedian: Yi Wang Zhaoyuan, Li Wanfang wei li" 清代才女文化的地域特點：以王照圓、李晚芳為例 (The geographic characteristics of the culture of talented women in the Qing dynasty: A case study of Wang Zhaoyuan and Li Wanfang). *Journal of Zhejiang Normal University (Social Sciences)* 4 (2005): 35–38.

Standaert, Nicolas. *The Interweaving of Rituals: Funerals in the Cultural Exchange between China and Europe.* Seattle: University of Washington Press, 2008.

———. *Yang Tingyun, Confucian and Christian in Late Ming China: His Life and Thought.* Leiden, Netherlands: Brill, 1988.

Strand, David. *An Unfinished Republic: Leading by Word and Deed in Modern China.* Berkeley: University of California Press, 2011.

Sung, Doris. "Redefining Female Talents: *Funü shibao, Funü zazhi*, and the Development of 'Women's Art' in China." Unpublished paper, 2012.

Szonyi, Michael. "The Cult of Hu Tianbao and the Eighteenth Century Discourse of Homosexuality." *Late Imperial China* 19, no. 1 (1998): 1–25.

Tan Yankai 譚延闓. "Xu" 序 (Preface). In Zhang He Chenghui 張何承徽, *Yixiao tang shiji: 2 juan* 儀孝堂詩集: 2 卷 (Poetry anthology from the Hall of Rites and Filiality: 2 *juan*). N.p., 1917.

Tang Jicang 湯濟滄. "Nüzi shi ci jiangxi she zhiqu shuye jianzhang" 女子詩詞講習社旨趣書並簡章 (Objectives and regulations of Women's Poetry [*shi* and *ci*] Lecture Society) *Shenzhou nübao* (Journal of Chinese women), *xunkan* 7 (January 1912): 2–4.

Tang Yan. "Qixiannü chayang shensu rufei" 七仙女插秧神速如飞 (The seven fairy maidens speedily transplant rice seedlings). *Zhongguo funü* 中国妇女 (April 7, 1959): 3–4.

Teng, Emma Jinhua. *Taiwan's Imagined Geography: Chinese Colonial Travel Writing and Pictures, 1683–1895.* Cambridge, MA: Harvard University Press, 2004.

Terrill, Ross. *Madame Mao: The White-Boned Demon.* Stanford, CA: Stanford University Press, 2000.

Theiss, Janet M. *Disgraceful Matters: The Politics of Chastity in Eighteenth-Century China.* Berkeley: University of California Press, 2004.

———. "Love in a Confucian Climate: The Perils of Intimacy in Eighteenth-Century China." *Nan Nü: Man, Women and Gender in China* 11, no. 2 (2009): 197–233.

T'ien Ju-K'ang. *Male Anxiety and Female Chastity: A Comparative Study of Chinese Ethical Values in Ming-Ch'ing Times.* Monographies du T'oung Pao, vol. 14. Leiden, Netherlands: Brill, 1988.

Volker, T. *The Japanese Porcelain Trade of the Dutch East India Company after 1683.* Leiden, Netherlands: Brill: 1959.

Volpp, Sophie. "Drinking Wine and Reading "Encountering Sorrow": A Reflection in Disguise by Wu Zhao (1799–1862)." In *Under Confucian Eyes: Writing on Gender in Chinese History*, edited by Susan Mann and Yu-yin Cheng, 239–50. Berkeley: University of California Press, 2001.

———. "The Literary Circulation of Actors in Seventeenth-Century China." *Journal of Asian Studies*, 61, no. 3 (August 2002): 949–84.

Wagner, Rudolph. "China's First Literary Journals." Unpublished manuscript, 1998.

———. "Joining the Global Imaginaire: The Shanghai Illustrated Newspaper *Dian-shizhai huabao*." In *Joining the Global Public: Word, Image, and City in Early Chinese Newspapers, 1870–1910*, edited by Rudolph G. Wagner, 105–74. Albany: State University of New York Press, 2007.

———. "Women in *Shenbaoguan* Publications, 1872–90." In *Different World of Discourse: Transformations of Gender and Genre in Late Qing and Early Republican China*, edited by Nanxiu Qian, Grace S. Fong, and Richard J. Smith, 227–56. Leiden: Brill, 2008.

Waley, Arthur, trans. *The Book of Songs: The Ancient Chinese Classic of Poetry*. New York: Grove Press, 1996.

Waltner, Ann. "Breaking the Law: Family Violence, Gender, and Hierarchy in the Legal Code of the Ming Dynasty." *Ming Studies* 36 (1996): 29–43.

———. "Infanticide and Dowry in Ming China." In *Chinese Views of Childhood*, edited by Anne Behnke Kinney. Honolulu: University of Hawai'i Press, 1995.

Wang, David Der-wei. *Fin-de-Siècle Splendor: Repressed Modernities of Late Qing Fiction, 1848–1911*. Stanford, CA: Stanford University Press, 1997.

Wang Jiading 王家鼎 and Wang Qishu. *Fei hong yi ji* 飛鴻遺蹟 (Traces of the Flying Swan Studio). Fengtian: Cui Wen Zhai Shu Dian, [1937?].

Wang Jingyue 王靜悅. *Zhongguo gudai minsu* 中國古代民俗 (China's customs of the past). Harbin: Heilongjiang Renmin Chubanshe, 2004.

Wang Nilan. Personal interview by Gao Xiaoxian and Gail Hershatter. August 31, 2006.

Wang Qingdi 王慶棣. *Zhiyun lou shici* 織雲樓詩詞 (Poems from Weaving Cloud Tower). Quzhou City, Zhejiang: Shici Xuehui, 2010.

———. *Zhiyun lou shici ji* 織雲樓詩詞集 (Collected poems from Weaving Cloud Tower). Ms. hand-copied by descendant. 1984. Held in Quzhou Museum.

———. *Zhiyunlou shicao* 織雲樓詩草 (Transcribed poems of Weaving Cloud Tower). Printed text of 1857. Held in Quzhou Museum.

Wang Qishu 汪啟淑. *Chun hui tang yin shi* 春暉堂印始 (The seal impressions of Chun Hui Studio). 1749.

———. *Fei hong tang chu gao* 飛鴻堂初稿 (First anthology of the Flying Swan Studio). Xuxiu siku quanshu, vol. 1446. Shanghai: Shanghai guji chubanshe, 2002.

———. *Fei hong tang mo pu* 飛鴻堂墨譜 (Ink stick illustrations from the Flying Swan Studio). Qianlong version. Xuxiu siku quanshu, vol. 1113. Shanghai: Shanghai Guji Chubanshe, 2002.

———. *Fei hong tang yin pu* 飛鴻堂印譜 (Seal impressions from the Flying Swan Studio). Qianlong version. Reprint, n.p.: Ling Shi Shan Fang, 1912–30.

———. *Fei hong tang yin ren zhuan* 飛鴻堂印人傳 (Collection of biographies of the seal carvers of Flying Swan Studio). Reprinted as *Xu yinren zhuan* 續印人傳, in *Ming Qing yin ren zhuan* 明清印人傳, by Zhou Liyuan et al. Jiulong: Boyazhai, 1977.

———. *Han tong yin cong* 漢銅印叢 (Bronze seal impressions of the Han dynasty). 1752.

———. *Ji gu yin cun* 集古印存 (Collection of ancient seal impressions; reprint of *Ren'an ji gu yin cun*), edited by Wang Shaozeng 汪紹增. 1804.

———. *Ren'an ji gu yin cun* 訒庵集古印存 (Ren'an's collection of ancient seal impressions). 1760.

———. *Shui cao qing xia lu* 水漕清暇錄 (Records of leisure from a water transportation official). Collated by Yang Huijun 楊輝君. Reprint, Beijing: Beijing Guji Chubanshe, 1998.

———, comp. *Xie fang ji* 擷芳集 (Collected fragrances). 1785.

Wang Shi 王石. "Shidai butongle, nan nü dou yiyang ma?" 时代不同了，男女都一样吗？(The times have changed; are men and women the same?). *Zhongguo qiyejia* 中国企业家 (March 11, 2010).

Wang, Shuo. "Qing Imperial Women: Empresses, Concubines, and Aisin Gioro Daughters." In *Servants of the Dynasty*, edited by Anne Walthall. Berkeley: University of California Press, 2008.

Wang Xiqin. Personal interview by Gao Xiaoxian and Gail Hershatter. August 6, 1966, and August 30–31, 2006.

Wang, Yan. "Idle Consumers or Productive Workers: Leisured Ladies in the Urban Commercial Culture and the Discourses of Modernity in Late Qing China (1860–1911)." PhD diss., University of California, Davis, 2010.

Wang Yingzhi 王英志, comp. *Qingdai guixiu shihua congkan* 清代閨秀詩話叢刊 (A series of commentary texts on female poets and their poems from the Qing dynasty). Vol. 1. Nanjing: Fenghuang Chubanshe, 2010.

Wang Zhaoyuan 王照圓. *Lienü zhuan buzhu* 列女傳補注 (Supplementary commentary on the *Biographies of Exemplary Women*). Xuxiu siku quanshu, vol. 515. Shanghai: Shanghai Guji Chubanshe, 2002.

———. *Shaishutang gui zhong wencun* 曬書堂閨中文存 (Extant prose from the boudoir of the Hall of Sunning Books). Haoshi yishu edition.

Wang Zhaoyuan 王照圓 and Hao Yixing 郝懿行. *Heming ji* 和鳴集 (Singing in harmony). Qingdai shiwenji huibian, vol. 449. Shanghai: Shanghai Guji Chubanshe, 2010.

Wang, Zheng. "Call Me 'Qingnian' but Not 'Funü': A Maoist Youth in Retrospect." In *Some of Us: Chinese Women Growing Up in the Mao Era*, edited by Xueping Zhong, Zheng Wang, and Di Bai, 27–52. New Brunswick, NJ: Rutgers University Press, 2001.

———. "Dilemmas of Inside Agitators: Chinese State Feminists in 1957." *China Quarterly* 188, no. 1 (2006): 913–32.

———. " 'State Feminism?' Gender and Socialist State Formation in Maoist China." *Feminist Studies* 31, no. 3 (Fall 2005): 519–51.

———. *Women in the Chinese Enlightenment: Oral and Textual Histories*. Berkeley: University of California Press, 1999.

Weidner, Marsha Smith. *Flowering in the Shadows: Women in the History of Chinese and Japanese Painting*. Honolulu: University of Hawai'i Press, 1990.

Widmer, Ellen. "The Epistolary World of Female Talent in Seventeenth-Century China." *Late Imperial China* 10, no. 2 (December 1989): 1–43.

Widmer, Ellen, and Kang-i Sun Chang. *Writing Women in Late Imperial China*. Stanford, CA: Stanford University Press, 1997.

Wolf, Margery. *Women and the Family in Rural Taiwan*. Stanford, CA: Stanford University Press, 1972.

Wolf, Margery, and Roxanne Witke, eds. *Women in Chinese Society*. Stanford, CA: Stanford University Press, 1975.

Woo, Margaret Y. K. "Chinese Women Workers: The Delicate Balance between Protection and Equality." In *Engendering China: Women, Culture, and the State*, edited by Christina K. Gilmartin et al., 279–95. Cambridge, MA: Harvard University Press, 1994.

Wu Bonian 吳伯年. "Yanjiu tuhua yijian" 研究圖畫意見 (Opinions on painting research). In *Nanyang quanyehui yanjiuhui baogaoshu* (Reports by the research committee of Nanyang Industrial Exposition). 1913. Reprinted in *Nanyang quanyehui baogaoshu* 南洋勸業会报告书 (Reports of the Nanyang Industrial Exposition), edited by Bao Yong'an 鲍永安 et al., 173–74. Shanghai: Shanghai Jiaotong Daxue Chubanshe, 2010.

Wu Hung. *The Wuliang Shrine: The Ideology of Early Chinese Pictorial Art*. Stanford, CA: Stanford University Press, 1989.

Wu Renshu 巫仁恕. *Pin wei she hua: Wan ming de xiaofei shehui yu shidaifu* 品味奢華：晚明的消費社會與士大夫 (Luxurious tastes: Late Ming consumer society and the gentry). Beijing: Zhonghua Shuju, 2008.

Wu, Yi-Li. *Reproducing Women: Medicine, Metaphor, and Childbirth in Late Imperial China*. Berkeley: University of California Press, 2010.

Xia Dongyuan 夏東元. *Sheng Xuanhuai nianpu changbian* 盛宣懷年譜長編 (Long chronology of Sheng Xuanhuai). Shanghai: Shanghai Jiaotong Daxue Chubanshe, 2004.

———. *Sheng Xuanhuai zhuan* 盛宣懷傳 (Sheng Xuanhuai biography). Shanghai: Shanghai Jiaotong Daxue Chubanshe, 2007.

Xia Xiaohong 夏曉虹. *Wanqing nüxing yu jindai shenghuo* 晚清女性與近代生活 (Women in late Qing China and the modern life). Beijing: Beijing Daxue Chubanshe, 2004.

"Xinhai geming shihua: Zhang Mojun xianxian" 辛亥革命史画张默君先贤 (Portrait of the 1911 Revolution: The late sage Zhang Mojun), www.ntdtv.com/xtr/gb/2013/09/28/a460635.html.

Xinwen Bao 新聞報 (News journal).

Xiong Yuezhi 熊月之. *Shanghai tong shi* 上海通史 (General history of Shanghai). 15 vols. Shanghai: Shanghai Renmin Chubanshe, 1999.

Xu Chengyao 許承堯. *She shi xian tan* 歙事閒談. 1936. Reprint, Hefei: Huang Shan Shu She, 2001.

Xu Ke 徐珂. *Qing bai lei chao* 清稗類鈔. Reprint, Zhonghua Shuju, 1984.

Xu Leiwu 徐累武. "Nanren neng gan funü yiyang neng gan" 男人能干妇女一样能干 (Whatever men can do, women can do too). In *Xin funü xin fengge* 新妇女新风格,

edited by Jiangsu Sheng Funü Lianhehui 江苏省妇女联合会, 9–11. Nanjing: Jiangsu Renmin Chubanshe, 1958.

Xu, Sufeng. "Domesticating Romantic Love during the High Qing Classical Revival: The Poetic Exchanges between Wang Zhaoyuan (1763–1851) and Hao Yixing (1757–1829)." *Nan Nü* 15, no. 2 (2013): 219–64.

Xu Weiyu 許維遹. *Hao Langao (Yixing) fufu nianpu* 郝蘭皋（懿行）夫婦年譜 (Yearly records of Hao Yixing and Wang Zhaoyuan). Reprint, Hong Kong: Chongwen Shudian, 1975.

Xu Xingwu 徐興無. "Qingdai Wang Zhaoyuan Lienü zhuan buzhu yu Liang Duan Lienü zhuan jiaodu ben" 清代王照圓《列女傳補注》與梁端《列女傳校讀本》(Wang Zhaoyuan's *Lienü zhuan buzhu* and Liang Duan's *Lienü zhuan jiaodu ben* of the Qing dynasty). In *Ming Qing wenxue yu xingbie yanjiu*, edited by Zhang Hong-sheng, 916–31. Nanjing: Jiangsu Guji Chubanshe, 2002.

Yan Jiaqi and Gao Gao. *Turbulent Decade: A History of the Cultural Revolution*. Honolulu: University of Hawai'i Press, 1996.

Yang Jiwei 楊季威. "Shiping" 時評 (Short commentary). *Shenzhou nübao* (Journal of Chinese women), *xunkan* 2 (December 1912): 1–2.

Ye Weili with Ma Xiaodong. *Growing Up in the People's Republic*. New York: Palgrave Macmillan, 2005.

Young, Marilyn B., ed. *Women in China: Studies in Social Change and Feminism*. Ann Arbor: Center for Chinese Studies, University of Michigan, 1973.

Yu Yingshi 余英時. *Zhongguo jinshi zongjiao lunli yu shangren jingshen* 中國近世宗教倫理與商人精神. Hefei: Anhui Jiaoyu Chubanshe, 2001.

Yuan Mei 袁枚. *Sui yuan shi hua bu yi* 隨園詩話補遺. In *Sui yuan shi hua* 隨園詩話. Collated by Gu Xuejie 顧學頡. Beijing: Renmin Wenxue Chubanshe, 1982.

———. *Yuan Mei quanji* 袁枚全集. 8 vols. Nanjing: Nanjing guji chubanshe, 1993.

Zang Yong 臧庸 et al. *Lienü zhuan buzhu jiaozheng* 列女傳補注校正 (Annotation and correction to the *Supplementary Commentary on the Biographies of Exemplary Women*. Xuxiu siku quanshu, vol. 515. Shanghai: Shanghai Guji Chubanshe, 2002.

Zarrow, Peter. *China in War and Revolution, 1895–1949*. London: Routledge, 2005.

Zeng Jifen 曾紀芬. *Chongde laoren ziding nianpu* 崇德老人自訂年譜 (Self-compiled chronology of the old lady Chongde). In *Zeng Baosun huiyilu* 曾寶蓀回憶錄 (Memoir of Zeng Baosun). Changsha: Yuelu Shushe, 1986.

Zhan Kai 詹塏. Rouxiang yunshi 柔鄉韻史. Shanghai: Wen Yi Xiao Qian Suo, 1914.

Zhandou zai nonglin zhanxianshang de funü 战斗在农林战线上的妇女 (Women who are at the forefront of struggle in agriculture). Beijing: Nongye Chubanshe, 1974.

Zhang Haipeng 張海鵬 and Wang Tingyuan 王廷元, eds. *Ming Qing hui shang zi liao xuan bian* 明清徽商資料選編 (Selected sources on Huizhou merchants in the Ming and Qing dynasties). Hefei: Huangshan Shushe, 1985.

Zhang He Chenghui 張何承徽. *Yixiao tang shiji* 儀孝堂詩集 (Poetry anthology from the Hall of Rites and Filiality). 2 *juan*. N.p., 1917.

Zhang Mojun 張默君 (Zhang Zhaohan 張昭漢). "Ai Song Dunchu xiansheng lei" 哀宋遯初先生誄 (Eulogy for Song Jiaoren). *Guomin yuekan* 國民月刊 (Citizens' monthly) 1, no. 1 (1913): 2–3.

———. "Ding si chun Jiangwan guan Shi Tiansun nü shi hang kong" 丁巳春江灣觀史天孫女士航空 (Watching Ms. Shi Tiansun flying [an airplane] at Jiangwan in the spring of 1917). *Funü shibao* (Women's eastern times) 21 (April 1917): 101.

———. "Ku Song Dunchu xiansheng wen" 哭宋鈍初先生文 (Weeping for Song Dunchu [Jiaoren]). *Shenzhou nübao* (Journal of Chinese women), *yuekan* 2 (May 1913): 125–26.

———. "Shenzhou nüjie xiejishe zhuidao Song Dunchu xiansheng ge" 神州女界協濟社追悼宋遯初先生歌 (A song by the Shenzhou Women's Assistance Society in mourning for Song Dunchu [Jiaoren]). *Shenzhou nübao* (Journal of Chinese women), *yuekan* 2 (May 1913): 128.

———. "Xiandai Zhongguo funü zhi daren" 現代中國婦女之大任 (The great responsibility of Chinese women today). In *Dangdai funü* 當代婦女 (Contemporary women), 1–5. Shanghai: Shanghai Shenxin Shudian 上海申新書店, 1936.

———. *Xiankao Bochungong xinglüe* 先考伯純公行略 (Record of deeds of my deceased father, the honorable Bochun). N.p., n.d.

———. *Xichui yinhen* 西陲吟痕 (To chant the traces of the Western frontier). Nanjing: Guomin Yinwuju, 1935.

———. *Zhang Mojun xiansheng wenji* 張默君先生文集 (Collected writings of Zhang Mojun). Edited by Zhongguo Guomindang Zhongyang Weiyuanhui Dangshi Weiyuanhui 中國國民黨中央委員會黨史委員會. Taipei: Zhongguo Guomindang Zhongyang Weiyuanhui Dangshi Weiyuanhui, 1983.

———. *Zhanhou zhi Ou Mei nüzi jiaoyu, Wo zhi jiashi jiaoyu guan, hekan* 戰後歐美女子教育，我之家事教育觀 (Combined edition: Postwar women's education in Europe and America; my view of household education). 3rd ed. Nanjing: Jiangsu Shengli Diyi Nüzi Shifan Xuexiao, 1926.

———. *Zhongguo zhengzhi yu minsheng zhexue* 中國政治與民生哲學 (Chinese politics and the philosophy of the people's livelihood). Nanjing: Yishe, 1946.

———. "Ziti 'meiren yima kanjian tu' " 自題美人倚馬看劍圖 (是圖為油畫作於四年九月五日) (Colophon for my own painting *A Beauty Inspecting a Sword While Leaning on a Horse*). *Funü shibao* (Women's eastern times) 21 (April 1917): 102. The painting was done on September 5, 1915.

Zhang Naihua. "In a World Together Yet Apart." In *Some of Us: Chinese Women Growing Up in the Mao Era*, edited by Xueping Zhong, Wang Zheng, and Bai Di, 1–26. New Brunswick, NJ: Rutgers University Press, 2001.

Zhang Xiahun 張俠魂. "Shenzhou nüxuesheng Zhang Xiahun (Tiexue)" 神州女學生張俠魂 (鐵血), 'Nüzi canzheng lun.' " *Shenzhou nübao* (Journal of Chinese women), *xunkan* 6 (January 1913): 1–3.

———. "Song xiansheng bei ci zhi yuanyin" 宋先生被刺之原因 (The reason Mr. Song was assassinated). *Shenzhou nübao* (Journal of Chinese women), *yuekan* 2 (May 1913): 119–20.

———. "Zongjiao zhi youlie guanyu guoshi zhi qiangruo" 宗教之優劣關于國勢之強弱 (The relationship between the merits and demerits of religion and national strength). *Nüzi zazhi* 女子雜誌 1 (1915): 10–12.

"Zhang Xiahun feixing yuxian jinxun" 張俠魂飛行遇險近訊 (Recent news of Zhang

Xiahun's dangerous flight). Benbu xinwen 本埠新聞 (City news). *Shenbao* 11, no. 15678 (October 4, 1916).

Zhang Xuecheng 章學誠. *Bingchen zhaji* 丙辰札記 (Notes from the year of Bingchen). Beijing: Zhonghua Shuju, 1986.

Zhao Erxun 趙爾巽 et al. *Qingshi gao* 清史稿 (Draft history of the Qing dynasty). Beijing: Zhonghua Shuju, 1977.

Zhejiang Sheng Zhengxie Wenshi Ziliao Yanjiu Weiyuan Hui 浙江省政协文史资料研究委员会. "Yidai zongshi Zhu Kezhen" 一代宗师竺可桢 (A great scholar of his generation, Zhu Kezhen). In *Zhejiang wenshi ziliao xuanji, di* 40 *ji* 浙江文史资料选辑 第 40 辑 (Selections from literary and historical materials from Zhejiang, vol. 40). Hangzhou: Zhejiang Sheng Zhengxie Wenshi Ziliao Yanjiu Weiyuan Hui, 1990.

Zheng Guanying 鄭觀應. "Nüjiao" 女教. In *Sheng shi wei yan* 盛世危言. Taipei: Taiwan Xuesheng Shuju, 1965.

Zheng Yongxi 鄭永禧. *Quxian zhi* 衢縣志. Reprinted in *Quxian zhi: Zhejiang sheng* 衢縣志：浙江省. Taipei: Cheng Wen Chubanshe, 1984.

Zhijia quanshu, shang 治家全書, 上 (Comprehensive volume on regulating the household, volume 1). [Shanghai?]: Jiaotong tushuguan, 1919.

Zhonggong Shanghaishi Nongyeju Weiyuanhui 中共上海市农业局委员会. Report of June 15, 1974. Shanghai Municipal Archives.

Zhongguo funü 中国妇女 (Women of China).

Zhou Shici 周世滋. *Danyong shanchuang shiji* 淡永山窗詩集 (Collected poems of Danyong Mountain Study). Hangzhou: n.p., 1862. Held in National Library of China.

Zhu Kezhen 竺可桢. *Zhu Kezhen quanji* 竺可桢全集 (Collected works of Zhu Kezhen). 12 vols. Shanghai: Shanghai Keji Jiaoyu Chubanshe, 2004.

Zhu Xiaoping 朱小平. *Xiandai Hunan nüxing wenxue shi* 现代湖南女性文学史 (History of modern Hunan women writers). Changsha: Hunan Shifan Daxue Chubanshe, 2005.

Zurndorfer, Harriet T. "The 'Constant World' of Wang Chao-yuan: Women, Education, and Orthodoxy in 18th Century China—a Preliminary Investigation." In *Family Process and Political Process in Modern Chinese History*, comp. Institute of Modern History, Academia Sinica, 1:581–619. Taipei: Academia Sinica, 1992.

———. "The *Lienü zhuan* Tradition and Wang Zhaoyuan's (1763–1851) Production of the *Lienü zhuan buzhu* (1812)." In *Beyond Exemplar Tales: Women's Biography in Chinese History*, edited by Joan Judge and Hu Ying, 55–69. Berkeley: University of California Press, 2011.

———. "Wang Zhaoyuan (1763–1851) and the Erasure of 'Talented Women' by Liang Qichao." In *Different Worlds of Discourse: Transformations of Gender and Genre in Late Qing and Early Republican China*, edited by Grace Fong, Nanxiu Qian, and Richard Smith, 29–56. Leiden, Netherlands: Brill, 2008.

Contributors

BEVERLY BOSSLER is professor of history at the University of California, Davis. Her research focuses on gender and social history in the Song and Yuan dynasties. Her most recent book is *Courtesans, Concubines, and the Cult of Female Fidelity: Gender and Social Change in China, 1000–1400.*

GAIL HERSHATTER is distinguished professor of history at the University of California, Santa Cruz. She is a past president of the Association for Asian Studies. Her most recent book is *The Gender of Memory: Rural Women and China's Collective Past.*

EMILY HONIG is the author of *Sisters and Strangers: Women in the Shanghai Cotton Mills, 1919–1949* and *Creating Chinese Ethnicity: Subei People in Shanghai, 1850–1980,* and the coauthor (with Gail Hershatter) of *Personal Voices: Chinese Women in the 1980s.* She has also written about issues of gender during the Cultural Revolution.

JOAN JUDGE is a professor in the Department of History at York University in Toronto, Canada. She is the author of *The Precious Raft of History: The Past, the West, and the Woman Question in China* (2008) and *Print and Politics: "Shibao" and the Culture of Reform in Late Qing China* (1996), and the coeditor of *Beyond Exemplar Tales: Women's Biography in Chinese History* (2011). She is involved in an ongoing international collaborative project on the Chinese women's periodical press, which includes the creation of a periodicals database. Her book related to this project is *Republican Lens: Gender, Visuality, and Experience in the Early Chinese Periodical Press* (2015). She is also beginning a new project that involves both periodicals and encyclopedias, titled *Quotidian Concerns: Everyday Knowledge and the Rise of the Common Reader in China, 1850–1950.*

GUOTONG LI is associate professor of Chinese history at California State University, Long Beach. She is the author of *In Quest of Immortality: Women's Education in Late Imperial China, 1368–1911* (Nüzi zhi buxiu: Ming Qing shi qi de nü jiao guan nian) (2014).

WEIJING LU is associate professor of history at the University of California, San Diego. She is the author of *True to Her Word: The Faithful Maiden Cult in Late Imperial China* (2008) and guest editor of a special issue on China for the *Journal of the History of Sexuality* (May 2013). Her current research focuses on family and marital practices in China from the seventeenth century through the nineteenth.

ANN WALTNER teaches Chinese and world history at the University of Minnesota. She was founding director of the Institute for Advanced Study (2005–14) and served as the editor of the *Journal of Asian Studies* (2000–2005). She has published extensively on gender, kinship, and religion in late imperial China. Recent publications include *Family: A World History* (with Mary Jo Maynes, 2012). Most recently, she has written for and performed in multimedia performances with the early-music group Sacabuche, including *Matteo Ricci: His Map and Music* and *Venetia 1500.*

YAN WANG is assistant professor of history at East China Normal University in Shanghai. Her interests include Chinese women's and gender history, cross-cultural women's and gender history, and China studies overseas. She is the author of "Converge to the Mainstream: Chinese Women's History in the U.S." (*Chinese Social Sciences Report*, May 2013 [in Chinese]). Her current project, titled *Genteel Ladies and Commerce in the Shanghai Concessions,* examines Chinese women and consumption in late Qing Shanghai.

ELLEN WIDMER is the Mayling Soong Professor of Chinese Studies at Wellesley College. Her research fields include Chinese women's literature of the Ming and Qing dynasties, history of the book, missionary history, and traditional Chinese fiction and drama. She is the author of two monographs, *The Margins of Utopia: Shui-hu hou-chuan and the Literature of Ming Loyal-*

ism (1987), and *The Beauty and the Book: Women and Fiction in Nineteenth Century China* (2006). Her edited volumes include *Writing Women in Late Imperial China* (with Kang-i Sun Chang, 1997), *Trauma and Transcendence in Early Qing Literature* (with Wilt Idema and Wai-yee Li, 2006), *China's Christian Colleges: Cross-Cultural Connections* (with Daniel Bays, 2008), and *The Inner Chambers and Beyond: Women Writers from Ming to Qing* (with Grace Fong, 2010).

YULIAN WU is an assistant professor in the history department at the University of South Carolina. Her interests are material culture and gender relations in late imperial China. She is currently completing a book manuscript titled *Tasteful Consumption: Huizhou Salt Merchants and Material Culture in Eighteenth-Century China*. Her next project concerns the production and consumption of jade objects in high Qing China (1760–99).

INDEX

J

Jesuits, 21, 22, 30, 35, 36
Jiang Jiafang, 177
Jiang Jin, 185, 186
Jiang Qing, 197–98, 203
Jiang Shiquan, 69
Jiang Zuobin, 141, 156–57
Jin Yihong, 194
Jing Yuanshan, 168, 172, 175–76
journals, 113–15, 116, 123, 125–26, 128–29, 133, 143; photographs in, 145–48. *See also* media, new
Judge, Joan, 9, 11, 14, 48

K

Kaempfer, Engelbert, 24
Kang Youwei, 162
kaozheng. See philological study
Kircher, Athanasius, 25
Ko, Dorothy, 6, 84, 224

L

labor. *See* work
Lan Dingyuan, 12–13, 41; biography of, 43; and the "civilizing mission," 49–51, 53–54; and colonization policy, 59–53; and women's education, 43–47; *Women's Learning,* 43–47; and women's work, 50–51, 53, 54–55
Lan Tingzhen, 48
land reform, 210, 213
Landry-Deron, Isabelle, 25
Lao Zunsan, 43
late imperial, vs. early modern, 12
"leisured lady of means," 162–65
Li, Guotong, 11, 12
Li Bai, 96
Li Ciming, 88
Li Hongzhang, 167
Li Qingzhao, 88
Li Yuanhong, 141
Liang Hong, 96
Liang Qichao, 43, 54, 175–76
Lin, Lady (mother of Wang Zhaoyuan), 85–86, 89

literacy, womens', 6, 11, 46–47, 84, 103, 149–50, 172, 210
Liu Shaoqi, 187, 203
Louie, Kam, 61
Lu, Weijing, 8, 13
Lü Kun, 47
Lystra, Karen, 104

M

Ma Xiaodong, 186
Manchu, 26, 28, 30, 36, 42, 55
Mann, Susan, 6, 8, 31, 42, 47, 48, 59–60, 157, 224
Mao, Liping, 31
Mao Yuanxin, 189
Mao Zedong, 185, 187–89, 203
marriage, 13, 28, 210; companionate, 84, 103–4, 140; Confucian images of, 96–97; costs of, 166–67; customs, 28–30, 31–35, 49; emotional expression in, 97–98, 102; interethnic, 52–53; liminality in, 32, 33–34; love in, 91–93, 104; poetry in, 84; and women's activism, 155
masculinity, 10, 13; definitions of, 60–61; and male networks, 65–68, 69–70; men as audience for, 61; and merchants, 60, 61–62; and patronage, 68; and status negotiation, 62; study of, 59–60; and travel, 70–72; and wealth, 72–76
May Fourth Movement, 140
media, new, 164, 170, 172–74, 175–76. *See also* journals
memory, 15, 210, 212, 216; historical, 153
Meng Guang, 96
merchants, 13; Huizhou, 60; and masculinity, 72–74, 76–77
Merchants' Steam Navigation Company, 163, 167–68, 174
Meyer-Fong, Tobie, 117
microhistory, 150
modernization, 12, 13, 54, 104, 121, 150; socialist, 223; women's use of, 162–64, 167–69, 170–74
Montanus, Arnoldus, 24